Post-Qualitative Research and Innovative Methodologies

Social Theory and Methodology in Education Research series
Edited by Mark Murphy

The Bloomsbury *Social Theory and Methodology in Education Research* series brings together books exploring various applications of social theory in educational research design. Each book provides a detailed account of how theory and method influence each other in specific educational research settings, such as schools, early childhood education, community education, further education colleges and universities. Books in the series represent the richness of topics explored in theory-driven education research, including leadership and governance, equity, teacher education, assessment, curriculum and policy studies. This innovative series provides a timely platform for highlighting the wealth of international work carried out in the field of social theory and education research, a field that has grown considerably in recent years and has made the likes of Pierre Bourdieu and Michel Foucault familiar names in educational discourse. Books in the *Social Theory and Methodology in Education Research* series offer an excellent resource for those who wish to use theoretical concepts in their research but are not sure how to do so, and who want to better understand how theory can be effectively applied in research contexts, in practically realisable ways.

Also available in the series

Foucault and School Leadership Research, Denise Mifsud
Education Governance and Social Theory, edited by
Andrew Wilkins and Antonio Olmedo
International Perspectives on Theorizing Aspirations, edited by Garth Stahl,
Derron Wallace, Ciaran Burke and Steve Threadgold
Education Research with Bourdieu, Julie Rowlands and Shaun Rawolle
Norbert Elias and the Sociology of Education, Eric Lybeck
Poststructuralist Theory and Educational Research, Tim Jay
Social Theory for Teacher Education Research, edited by Kathleen Nolan and
Jennifer Tupper
Social Theory and the Politics of Higher Education, edited by Mark Murphey,
Ciaran Burke, Cristina Costa and Rille Raaper

Forthcoming in the series

Subjectivity and Social Change in Higher Education, Liezl Dick and
Marguerite Müller
Poststructuralist Theory and Educational Research, Tim Jay

Post-Qualitative Research and Innovative Methodologies

Edited by Matthew Krehl Edward Thomas
and Robin Bellingham

BLOOMSBURY ACADEMIC
LONDON • NEW YORK • OXFORD • NEW DELHI • SYDNEY

BLOOMSBURY ACADEMIC
An imprint of Bloomsbury Publishing Plc
1385 Broadway, New York, NY 10018, USA
50 Bedford Square, London, WC1B 3DP, UK
29 Earlsfort Terrace, Dublin 2, Ireland

BLOOMSBURY, BLOOMSBURY ACADEMIC and the Diana logo are trademarks of
Bloomsbury Publishing Plc

First published 2020
This paperback edition published in 2021

Matthew Thomas and Robin Bellingham have asserted their right under the Copyright,
Designs and Patents Act, 1988, to be identified as Editors of this work.

Series design by Louise Dugdale
Cover image © Nanette Hoogslag

A catalogue record for this book is available from the British Library.

A catalog record for this book is available from the Library of Congress.

ISBN: HB: 978-1-3500-6204-7
PB: 978-1-3502-1514-6
ePDF: 978-1-3500-6205-4
ePub: 978-1-3500-6206-1

Typeset by Deanta Global Publishing Services, Chennai, India

To find out more about our authors and books visit www.bloomsbury.com
and sign up for our newsletters.

Contents

Series editor's foreword

Mark Murphy

Education research has a long history of adapting ideas from social theory. While this has always been the case when it comes to educational foundations, in recent years there has been an enormous growth in the adoption of social theory in the field of educational research. The names of theorists such as Pierre Bourdieu, Jürgen Habermas, Judith Butler and Michel Foucault have become commonplace in the field, making social theory evermore familiar to those who both conduct education research and utilize it in their teaching.

As its familiarity increases, so too does the desire to engage with social theory in more thoughtful and effective ways. There is currently a pressing desire to apply social theory in educational research contexts, which makes sense, as without theory, much education research can be overly descriptive and/ or restricted by narrow definitions of professional practice. Social theory can assist in efforts to transcend the everyday taken-for-granted understandings of education, while also reflecting erstwhile concerns around power, control, social justice and transformation.

The issue then becomes one of applying theory to method, with the focus shifting to a growing interest in the art of application itself. This interest comes with a set of key questions attached:

- How best to apply concepts such as habitus, subjectivation and performativity in educational research contexts?
- What are the ways in which methodological concerns meet theoretical ones?
- In what ways does social theory shape the quality of research outcomes?

These questions require thoughtful responses and the purpose of this book series is to help provide solutions to these issues, while also helping to develop the capacity, in particular of postgraduate and early career researchers, to successfully put social theory to work in research. This is especially important as theory application in method is a challenging and daunting enterprise. The set of theories developed by the likes of Foucault, Jacques Derrida, Bourdieu et al., could never be described as 'simple' or easy to navigate. On top of that there are a variety of issues faced when applying such ideas in research contexts, a field of complex interwoven imperatives and practices in its own right. These challenges – epistemological, operational, analytical – inevitably impact on researchers and our attempts to make sense of research questions, whether these be questions of governance and political regulation, social reproduction, power, cultural or professional identities (among others). So care needs to be taken when applying a challenging set of ideas onto a challenging set of practices, incorporating a consideration for both intellectual arguments alongside the concerns of the professional researcher.

The series should hold a strong appeal to the growing numbers of researchers who are keen to apply social theory in their research, as evidenced by the growing audience for the editor's own website *www.socialtheoryapplied.com*. It will offer an excellent resource for those who wish to begin using theoretical concepts in their research, and will also appeal to readers who have an interest in better understanding how theory can be effectively applied in research contexts, in practically realizable ways.

In terms of output, this series is designed to provide a collection of books exploring various applications of social theory in educational research design. Each book provides a detailed account of how theory and method influence each other in specific educational research settings, such as schools, early years, community education, further education colleges and universities. The series represents the richness of topics explored in theory-driven education research, including leadership and governance, equity, teacher education, assessment, curriculum and policy studies. It also provides a timely platform for highlighting the wealth of work done in the field of social theory and education research – a field that has grown considerably in recent years and has made the likes of Pierre Bourdieu and Michel Foucault familiar names in educational discourse.

Embedded in the design of the series is an explicit pedagogical component, with a focus on the 'how' of applying theory in research methodology and an emphasis on operationalizing theory in research. This pedagogical remit is addressed explicitly in the texts in different ways – the responsibility of addressing this falls to the authors and editors, but can take the form of case studies, learning activities, 'focus' sections and glossaries detailing the key theoretical concepts utilized in the research.

This book, *Post-Qualitative Research and Innovative Methodologies*, edited by Matthew K. E. Thomas and Robin Bellingham, is a strong addition to this growing series. The collection as a whole delivers a wonderful set of theory-oriented case studies of education research. Theorists such as Karen Barad, Lauren Berlant, Gilles Deleuze, Michel Foucault, Donna Haraway, Bruno Latour and Anna Tsing are represented, which makes for some unique and challenging takes on educational research methodology. This is joined by interplay between social theory, fiction and popular culture throughout the text, which provides the collection with an impressive cross-disciplinary orientation.

The book has been produced very much in the spirit of its parent book series *Social Theory and Methodology in Education Research*. This is obvious from the offset when the editors in the introduction state that 'theory has a generative role that cannot be overstated in conversations about making a difference through research in and through the future'. For the book editors, the 'vitality of theory' revolves around 'the making of new knowledge'. This generative role in the production of knowledge and the deployment of this knowledge to disrupt and innovate, represent a core rationale for the series more generally. As series editor I see this rationale as a form of counter-narrative to prevailing trends in education research methodology, a field that is in real danger of reducing itself to what Berger called 'methodological fetishism' (Berger 2002). The a-historical and a-theoretical stance of much educational research, not helped by an over-reliance on methods training as a proxy for research quality, needs to be confronted, interrogated and where possible, held to account for its contribution to academic rigour and conceptual development of the discipline. For me, collections such as this constitute a form of confrontation and counter-narrative and at the very least offers alternative ways of engaging with methodological issues in education.

There is, then, a political aspect to connecting theory and methodology, which certainly reflects the broad thrust of much social theory, and which is also a running theme in the current collection. This politics reflects both the theorists engaged with in the book and the focus on post-qualitative forms of education research. (Post)qualitative approaches often have to justify themselves when juxtaposed with supposedly more 'scientific' and reliable quantitative research methodologies. This suspicion around quality is acknowledged in the book, and the contributions provide a suitable and convincing riposte to those who doubt the relevance of this form of research. The rigour is especially evident in the way in which different authors have explored the theory-methodology relation: there are detailed descriptions of how innovative methodologies have been deployed in education research – the text is rich with methodological detail on how concepts such as diffraction, disturbance, heterotypology, assemblage, poetics and refrains have been operationalized as part of the research design. The connections between theory and method are made in such a way that readers can grasp how the researchers have 'captured' the evidence of theoretical concepts under investigation (Costa et al. 2018) and how these concepts wove their way into the actual design of the research. Examples of this include the deployment of experimental critical qualitative inquiry to study biraciality, guided by Barad's concept of agential realism (Travis Marn and Jennifer Wolgemuth, Chapter 3), and the use of collective biographical method, shaped by Foucault's notion of heterotopia, to study spaces of crisis and deviance (Marguerite Jones and Jennifer Charteris, Chapter 9).

The collection illustrates that post-qualitative approaches are to be taken seriously in the politics of education research methodologies. It is an outstanding collection, and the editors have done a superb job of bringing the contributors together. It is evident that all authors have grasped what the book series is attempting to do – many thanks to Matthew, Robin and all the contributors for delivering such a strong addition to the series, Mark.

References

Berger, P. (2002). Whatever happened to sociology? *First things* (online) https://www.fir
    stthings.com/article/2002/10/whatever-happened-to-sociology
Costa, C., Burke, C. and M. Murphy (2018). 'Capturing habitus: Theory, method and
    reflexivity', *International Journal of Research & Method in Education*, 42 (1): 19–32.

Foreword

Julianne Moss

This book sets out an ambitious agenda. The focus is on theory and methods and the exploration of co-constituting elements of research in the social sciences. As indicated in the title of the book, *Post-Qualitative Research and Innovative Methodologies* presents a welcome interruption to thinking *through* research practices. The authors identify as early career and/or innovative researchers. Markers however are often misleading and can form rigid binaries that are not helpful.

Reading across the three parts of the book, 'Disruption, Subjectivity and Agency'; 'Frontiers: Possibility, Timespace and Materiality' and 'Entanglements and Innovations: Method and Theory', indicates that some things are clearly unfolding in post-qualitative research. This book is thinking about the future/s of post-qualitative research. Scholars in the social sciences and particularly in a field such as education where many of the authors who have created this book identify, bring deep understandings from practice-related fields.

The provocations from the titles of the parts of the book lead me to ask – why this book – and now? The Anthropocene has made it very clear that our planet is not thriving. In Australia, where I reside, the Great Barrier Reef in Queensland, Australia is dying, as are the numbers of birds declining in our wetlands. Globally, humans have managed to halve the number of trees since the dawn of human civilization. Education in Australia and elsewhere remains potently unjust. In itself the interrelationships across the twelve chapters of the book work at destabilizing categories in research that traverses studies of youth, participatory approaches, doctoral pedagogy, ethico-political issues, black-white biracial identity, environmental education, teachers' work and lives, researching education and research writing. The conception of the book is a generative set of practices that turn and return us to the tensions that occupy our existential sense of hope, wondering and belonging about the world.

Over the last decade social theorists such as Barad (2007, 2014), Braidotti (2011; Braidotti et al. 2018), Deleuze and Guttari (1987) and St Pierre, Jackson and Mazeii (2016) have detailed our changing moods and thought lines about the planet and our social world that put to work previously unnamed concepts in post-qualitative and quantitative research. The intellectual traditions that the authors draw upon range from scholars who are geographically very widely dispersed and encompass places of living and working from the 'north' to the 'south'. The authors work in Western intellectual traditions, and there are more so-called 'early career' researchers than established scholars. Being considered expert or an early career researcher defies how and why groups self-organize and deliberate. However what is evident is that there are collaboration and learnings from recent doctoral studies which are embraced and refined through both co-constructed and single-authored chapters. This is a both a good thing to notice and to celebrate in the publication. In this book where researchers have come together to work with two concepts 'new empiricisms' and 'new materialisms' (St. Pierre, Jackson and Mazzei 2016) that have emerged in the humanities and social sciences over the past two decades, it is expected that innovation is coupled with experimentation and emergent methods.

Overall the contributors embody social theory as 'nomadic' (Metcalfe 2017), and as the cracks and fissures of intellectual and applied endeavours through practice unfold, we are reminded that there are few published examples gathered together in a single volume that simultaneously acknowledge that this is 'an impossible task because they are in process and they are not one thing' (St. Pierre et al. 2016). The work of agential realism, diffraction and entanglement and how relational ontologies might (re)turn the enduring and never-ending struggles for the social sciences are opened up in an edited collection that shares nuance with clear articulations of how research practices are explicating the affordances of methods. Supported by glossaries and pedagogical aids, practical connections between theory and method, examples for adopting or adapting methods should these features be of interest of the reader are included.

As an edited collection, the volume works at doing more than showcasing recent research and scholarship that is innovative or anew. The editorial curation shows a determination to think differently through methodological orientations that are both agential and animated. Many of the very foundations of post-qualitative inquiry are brought into sharp focus and matters of matter and new materialism are introduced and put to work. We are working and researching in times that despite decades of thought and the substantive body of work and the significant contribution by scholars internationally which are unsettling to the notions of an individual subject; discourses in the social sciences and education here and elsewhere hang tight to normed, singular and self-contained subjects and an 'order of things' (Foucault 1970).

The mood in education, for example, has an ambivalent relationship to a number of things. The global tsunami of the two decades of policy-driven accountability has resulted in disquiet among teachers, principals, but probably not our politicians. Such practices are counter to what our past has told us and what are social theorists telling us about the 'flows and energies, affects, desires and imaginings' (Metcalfe 2017) that broadly animate the work of the humanities and social science and educational researchers are unfolding.

The affordances of differing understandings of data (Moss 2016) prompt us to ask how these contradictory developments of the Anthropocene are staging the ambiguous consequences that today signify 'the mood of the world' (Bude 2018). In every generation somethings stay and somethings go. Openness to a world of post-qualitative research marked out by innovation has to be affirming for the future/s of the social sciences.

References

Barad, K. (2007), *Meeting the Universe Halfway: Quantum Physics and the Entanglement of Matter and Meaning*, Durham: Duke University Press.

Barad, K. (2014), 'Diffracting diffraction: Cutting together-apart', *Parallax* 20 (3): 168–87.

Braidotti, R. (2011), *Nomadic Subjects: Embodiment and Sexual Difference in Contemporary Feminist Theory*, 2nd edn, New York: Columbia University Press.

Braidotti, R., Bozalek, V., Shefer, T. and Zembylas, M. (2018). *Socially Just Pedagogies: Posthumanist, Feminist and Materialist Perspectives in Higher Education*, London: Bloomsbury.

Bude, H. (2018), *The Mood of the World*, Medford, MA: USA Polity Press.

Deleuze, G. and Guattari, F. (1987), *A Thousand Plateaus: Capitalism and Schizophrenia*, London: Athlone Press.

Foucault, M. (1970), *The Order of Things*, Andover Hants: Tavistock.

Metcalfe, A. S. (2017), 'Nomadic political ontology and transnational academic mobility', *Critical Studies in Education*, 58 (2): 131–49.

Moss, J. (2016), '2014 Australian Association for Research in Education presidential address: educational research and the tree of knowledge in a post human digital age', *Australian Educational Researcher*, 43 (5): 505–25. doi:10.1007/s13384-016-0215-6

St. Pierre, E. A., Jackson, A. Y. and Mazzei, L. M. (2016), 'New empiricisms and new materialisms: Conditions for new enquiry', *Cultural Studies* ↔ *Critical Methodologies* 16 (2): 99–110.

Contributors

Chessa Adsit-Morris is a doctoral candidate at the University of California, Santa Cruz. She is a curriculum theorist, environmental educator and arts-based activist. She is Assistant Director of the Center for Creative Ecologies. She is the author of the book: *Restorying Environmental Education: Figurations, Fictions, Feral Subjectivities* (2017). Her interests include educational theory, feminist science studies, SF, ecological thought, art activism and environmental justice.

Jesse Bazzul is Associate Professor of Science and Environmental Education at the University of Regina. He believes imagination is needed more than ever to find new collective ways of living together. Jesse recently published a co-edited volume with Dr Christina Siry entitled *Critical Voices in Science Education Research: Narratives of Hope and Struggle* (2019).

Robin Bellingham is Senior Lecturer in Pedagogy and Curriculum at Deakin University, Melbourne. Her research explores how stories and narratives help to bring worlds into being. Damaging and problematic conditions of modernity are co-constituted with the stories we tell about what the world is and what it means. Drawing on encounters and diffractions with cultural, material, experiential, fictional, historic and scientific stories, Robin considers their ethical, political and ontic possibilities and limitations, and how we might recover and reimagine stories that help to constitute the world differently.

Jennifer Charteris is Senior Lecturer in School Pedagogy in the School of Education, University of New England, Australia. She conducts research in the area of the politics of teacher and student learning, identity and subject formation. Critical, poststructural and posthuman theories influence much of her published work. Her most recent article is 'The Nuances of Posthumanism' (2018).

Mary Dixon is Associate Professor in Curriculum and Pedagogy at Deakin University, Melbourne Australia. Her research interests focus on posthumanist readings of pedagogy. Her recent works move between the classroom and the public. She is co-founder of the Public Pedagogies Institute.

Rachel Fendler is Assistant Professor at Florida State University in the Department of Art Education. Her research looks at how visual and audiovisual arts-based methods can be activated in participation with youth, to explore and examine life in urban space. This work draws on poststructuralist and new materialist theory. She has published in journals including *Qualitative Inquiry, Studies in Art Education, International Journal of Education through Art* and *Learning Landscapes.*

Annette Gough is a Professor in the School of Education and the School of Global, Urban and Social Studies at RMIT University, Australia. She has been an adjunct/visiting professor at universities in Canada, South Africa and Hong Kong, and worked with UNESCO, UNEP and UNESCO-UNEVOC on research and development projects. Her research interests span environmental, sustainability and science education, research methodologies, posthuman and gender studies. She has over 130 publications (books, chapters and articles as well as curriculum materials) and is currently co-editing Green Schools Movements around the World: Stories of impact on Education for Sustainable Development (forthcoming).

Noel Gough is Professor Emeritus in the School of Education at La Trobe University, Melbourne, Australia, following his retirement as Foundation Professor of Outdoor and Environmental Education (2006–14). He co-edited and contributed to *Curriculum Visions* (2002) and *Internationalisation and Globalisation in Mathematics and Science Education* (2007) and is founding editor of *Transnational Curriculum Inquiry.* In 1997, he received the inaugural Australian Museum Eureka Prize for environmental education research. He is a past president (2008) and honorary life member of the Australian Association for Research in Education.

Catherine Hart teaches in the Faculty of Kinesiology and Health Studies and the Faculty of Education at the University of Regina, Canada. Her research interests include environmental subjectivity and discourses, intersections between environment and human health, and gender issues in environmental education. She is also interested in post-qualitative approaches to research at onto-epistemic, theoretical and (non)methodological levels. She is currently engaged in publishing from her doctoral thesis and as a co-author in the 50th Anniversary Edition of the *The Journal of Environmental Education.*

Marguerite Jones has recently retired from her position as Lecturer in School Pedagogy in the School of Education, University of New England, Australia. Her research areas include innovations to pre-service teacher professional experience, teacher mentoring and the politics of casual teaching. Her most recent article is 'Posthuman Ethical Practice: Agential Cuts in the Pedagogic Assemblage'(2019).

Travis M. Marn (PhD, University of South Florida) is an assistant professor in the Curriculum & Learning Department at Southern Connecticut State University where he teaches child development, educational psychology and research methods. His scholarship focuses on philosophically informed empirical accounts of performative identities, employing new materialism and posthumanism in psychological research, and contributing to the development of qualitative and post-qualitative methods and methodologies.

Eve Mayes is a senior lecturer in Pedagogy and Curriculum at Deakin University. Her research is concerned with exploring and problematizing 'experiences' of educational institutions, through creative and philosophical experimentation with issues of 'voice'/participation, affect, space and materiality, and ethnographic, participatory and arts-based research approaches. She utilizes conceptual resources from poststructural and posthumanist/materialist thinking to enquire into the (re)production and potential interruption of intersecting inequalities in and through education.

Julianne Moss is Alfred Deakin Professor at Deakin University. She is Director of Deakin University's strategic research centre in Education – REDI (Research for Educational Impact. Her research interests are in innovative post qualitative approaches and pedagogical and curriculum change.

Mark Murphy is a Reader in Education and Public Policy at the University of Glasgow. He previously worked as an academic at King's College, London, University of Chester, University of Stirling, National University of Ireland, Maynooth, University College Dublin and Northern Illinois University. Mark is an active researcher in the fields of education and public policy. His research interests include educational sociology, critical theory, accountability in higher education, and public sector reform.

Matthew Krehl Edward Thomas is a senior lecturer in Pedagogy and Curriculum at Deakin University in Melbourne, Australia. He is a former schoolteacher with a background in leadership, strategy and negotiation. His research interests focus on time, power, artificial intelligence and surveillance.

His most recent publications explore the implications of time and artificial intelligence on human rights and relationships.

Laura Trafí-Prats is Senior Lecturer at the School of Childhood, Youth and Education Studies at Manchester Metropolitan University (MMU), and former Associate Professor at the University of Wisconsin-Milwaukee. She is a member of the Children and Childhood Research Group at MMU's Education and Social Research Institute. Her research connects visual arts, childhood studies, place-based pedagogies and video as method. Her interests include poststructuralist, new materialist and decolonizing philosophies and methodologies. Her work has been published in journals like *Studies in Art Education, Qualitative Inquiry, Cultural Studies ↔ Critical Methodologies* and *Discourse: Studies in the Cultural Politics of Education*.

Jennifer R. Wolgemuth is Associate Professor in Research and Measurement at the University of South Florida where she directs the graduate certificate in qualitative research. Her qualitative and post-qualitative research focuses on the ethics and politics of education and social science research, addressing material, discursive, and affective questions about the (un)intended consequences of conducting and reporting research. She has published in journals such as *Educational Researcher, Qualitative Inquiry, Qualitative Research* and *Cultural Studies ↔ Critical Methodologies*.

The vitality of theory in research innovation

Matthew Krehl Edward Thomas and Robin Bellingham

The vitality of theory

We (the editors) use the opportunity of producing this text to provide a place for early career authors to conduct theoretically rich experimental work that contributes to conversations about the generativity and possibilities of post-qualitative research. Because '[m]aking knowledge is not simply about making facts but about making worlds, or rather, it is about making specific worldly configurations' (Barad 2007, p. 91), theorizing has a generative role that cannot be overstated in conversations about making a difference through research inquiries and outcomes. We use an acknowledgement of the role of theory in research to place at the forefront of our minds, the unfixed nature of knowledge and the fact that theorizing is a boundary-making practice that is both limiting and productive of knowledge categories and processes. The vitality of theory in the making of new knowledge is a movement sustained across this text. Theory is vital, that is, it is both alive and essentially entangled with life. In this volume, theoretical premises and methodological designs are given life in real-world applications in schools, offices, ecologies, the margins of texts and the flutters of birds in a playground. This theory 'has to be aware of the state of things in order to acknowledge current challenges and be open to possibilities' (Ferrando 2012, p. 11). It is a premise of this text that its uses of theory should be capable of both directing nuanced attention to people, contexts, conditions, and relations and problematizing or transforming them, bringing 'an energising, catalytic role' (Lather 2018a, p. 74), and meaningful new opportunities for disturbance and/or coherence in life. Attention to the possibilities of theory means asking, how does theory provoke ethical onto-epistemological shifts (Barad 2010) that enable methodology, methods and data to be seen and enacted anew?

The authors of this volume are, in the main, Early Career Researchers (ECRs): those who are within four to five years of finishing a PhD. They come from Australia, Canada, the United Kingdom and the United States. Some are more experienced academics who work closely with ECRs in reciprocal and theoretically generative relationships. Their choice to do this tentative and provocative work indicates something about their interest in what they might contribute to shaping the shifting and uncertain social, academic and chronopolitical times in which they are already entangled. This work creates an assemblage of the research of ECRs and those who stand with them in their projects, as a way of vitalizing the generativity of these early career works and their dispersive connections, outward and onward through the future. As ECRs, editors and contributors, Matthew and Robin came to the creation of this book via a strong pull towards the testing of new thinking and imaginaries and what they might offer to larger projects for better education, democracy and wider notions of planetary ethics. Equally, we came to this project through experiences as secondary teachers and then as tertiary educators with shared responsibility for the curriculum and direction of postgraduate Initial Teacher Education programmes. This has meant that while attracted to what have been sometimes termed 'the posts', as we negotiate these roles and feel the creeping influence of reductive, competitive and economically driven education, academic and research agendas, we are concerned at the magnitude of the task of reimagining these differently in ways that might not only provoke spectres of democratic hope but also manifest as forces for change. We are mindful that communicating not just why but also how this might be done is important (Apple 2013; Barad 2007; Bauman 2005; Bellingham et al. 2019; Lather 2018b).

The authors of this volume differentially and iteratively demonstrate a forward tilt – a future orientation. In brief and overt terms this is signalled in the authors' desire for an 'interrogation of the normative status quo' (Vargova 2007, p. 417), in particular to present challenges to humanism and humanistic notions of identity, power, agency and education in research, but also in broader interrogations of normative notions of environment, place, space, time, history, technologies and materiality and the relations between these. Future orientation is also seen in the willingness of the authors to turn the interrogations on themselves; to consider the ethics of the ways in which we participate in life, relations, learning and research; and to channel this into the temerity to take meaningful risks and to experiment in order to seek new horizons. As St. Pierre, Jackson and Mazzei (2016, p. 100) state, 'an ethical imperative to rethink the nature of being' and 'a heightened curiosity and accompanying experimentation' are two of the enabling conditions of experimental projects that might help us consider ways of living different existences. Additional forms of future orientation offered in this book include a chief aim of the text, which is to engage others in the spirit of hopeful connection and democratic participation. Authors have aimed to use chapters as open invitations to readers to share in their theorizing, questioning, vocabulary and pedagogical tools and as encouragements to 'leave sight of shore' as Jennifer Charteris and Marguerite Jones (2020, p. 188) advocate; to suggest readers engage in their own research with courage, compassion and originality.

If you have found yourself thumbing this particular text, hoping to glean a neat summation of trends in the history, present and future of post-qualitative research practices, we are sorry to disappoint. Many fine authors have attempted to delineate such trends and should this be your need, you might see Lather (2013), McKenzie (2005), Preissle (2011), Rosiek (2013), Somerville (2016) or St. Pierre (2013). This book is for those unsettled by the discourses and agendas of these testing times and by unpredictable environments and their implications for democratic research, education, society, and the globe; and who want to explore theory as a transformative force in these contexts. If this volume is itself considered a particular kind of becoming space (Kristeva 2002) creating particular kinds of possibilities, a question raised in this rubble is: What is provoked or generated by this assemblage of theorizing and practice and how might we understand the potential for theory to make a difference in research and the future?

Post-Qualitative Research and Innovative Methodologies is structured around three distinct but interwoven concerns:

1. subjectivity, agency and identity;
2. time, space and materiality;
3. entanglements of innovation and methodology.

Our first concern centres around disruptions to notions of subjectivity, agency and identity. Agency and identity politics are well-established areas of concern in post-qualitative research. But where are research innovators and ECRs using theory to differently tackle these discussions and to transpose them into new applications of social theory and method? Such transposition creates new possibilities for established theoretical designs and for emergent ones. Differently theorized, the reconfiguration of the borders of subjects and identities, and of the nature of subjectivity, agency and identity vitalize new concerns and implications. These include bringing new life to understandings of what 'participation' in education, in research, and in life does or could mean to the multiple parties involved, and what might be productive in thinking about participation differently in this and coming eras.

Our second concern turns to material and spatial frontiers and thresholds of research possibility. On the broad but shared premise that humanism has provided certain problematic limits to our capacity to engage seriously, vitally and ethically with the range of ontic phenomena and the processes with which they manifest, the collection of chapters in this section explore time, space and materiality, through alternative space-times, digital worlds and ruptured metaphors. Notions of matter, corporeality, temporality, context, embodiment and virtuality blur and adumbrate. The material/immaterial nature of the landscape of which schools and schooling, teachers and teaching, society and environment are a part is troubled. Considerations of how these things come to matter, in all senses of the word, are opened up to new possibilities.

Our final concern is to explore the embodied and entangled nature of theory, methodology, method and practice. A diverse set of case studies of how authors have drawn on entanglements of theory and experimentation and discovered how innovative research methods then co-emerge are offered. These discussions of negotiations in uncharted terrains illustrate how theory can vitalize in unlikely directions and with new sensibilities and subtle changes in emphasis, opening other doors to understanding how difference and repetition work in the (re)making of the world.

The disruption of categories and thematic imaginings is a manifest pattern in the theorizations which follow, and has been argued for explicitly and enacted performatively as one of the ways in which theory is alive and may be given life. To begin with, conventional categories of disciplinary research work are eschewed. This book embraces theory from the fields of anthropology, youth studies, communication, pedagogy, education, literature, science, ecology, cultural studies, feminism and psychology. As Barad argues, the 'cordoning off of concerns into separate domains' makes it almost impossible to notice generativity. Patterns of resonance and dissonance are 'elided' (Barad, in Dolphijn and van der Tuin 2012, p. 50) and the possibilities of entanglements are obscured. Intra-disciplinary research is research that is co-emergent, in which disciplines, theories and methods are not fixed constructs or practices, but are continuously co-emerging in relations together with research and the world. Consequently, dualisms and hierarchies of valued knowledge are also challenged, in particular the separation of the rational and the imaginative. Speculation and imagination are marked by many of the researchers in this volume as integral to the research thinking that needs to be undertaken. In addition to these common disturbance patterns, the authors' work with theory as a vital force imprints certain other patterns of resonance in this volume, discussed as follows.

Glows of vitality in open-ended research practices

In the chapter assemblage in this volume are patterns highlighting particular glows of vitality enabled by new theorizing or new applications of theory. These enable insights about theory and research methods as 'open-ended practices involving specific intra-actions of humans and nonhumans' (Barad 2007, p. 171). In these open-ended practices, the acknowledgement of the entangled and relational nature of theory, methods, and data (Barad 2007; St Pierre 2013) means that what counts as 'data' and why and how data are attended to are matters of interest and importance. The 'glow of data' (MacLure 2010; MacLure 2013) describes the sense of frisson and possibility emitted as connections and details emerge in the research. MacLure suggests that 'we are obliged to acknowledge that data have their ways of making themselves intelligible to us ... On those occasions, agency feels distributed and undecidable, as we have chosen something that has chosen us' (MacLure 2013, pp. 660–61). '(S)ome detail – a fieldnote fragment or video image – starts to glimmer, gathering our attention' (MacLure 2010, p. 282). In her chapter in this text, Eve Mayes reports: 'I do not view data as separated from the field, nor the researcher, nor texts written about data' (2020, p. 67). Data are the phenomena and their qualities which emerge with our theorizing and research and to which we direct our attention in order to understand the world. In this volume, patterns highlighting particular glows of vitality include the vitality of the entangled, embodied researcher; of entangled technoscientific practices; and of entangled ontic possibilities of space, time and materiality. The patterns do not suggest that the ontic, the researcher and technoscientific practices are distinct entities in the research apparatus, but offer considerations of how these phenomena emerge with and as part of the research.

(Re)considering embodiment and reciprocity: The glow of experiential human/knowledge/world relations

Theorization in this volume enables attention to researchers' own embodiment as part of research apparatuses and across the volume these patterns enable the emergence of insights about the nature of reciprocity as an ontological and a research phenomenon. As in other post-qualitative research problematizations of researcher involvement in the act of research, considerations of researcher involvement here move beyond the notion of reflexivity as a recognition of the researcher's standpoint, towards consideration of the confusion and entanglement of embodied researchers with embodied research apparatuses. These uses of theory are experiments in working through the nature and workings of reciprocity among humans, knowledge and the world. Barad's interpretation of the philosopher-physicist Bohr holds that 'We are part of the nature we seek to understand . . . our ability to understand the world hinges on our taking account of the fact that our knowledge making practices are social-material enactments that contribute to, and are part of the phenomena we describe' (Barad 2007, p. 26).

The vitality of theory is drawn on in attracting attention to some of the particular and veiled ways in which our corporeality and identity co-construct limitations and boundaries, potential and possibility. Travis Marn and Jennifer Wolgemuth (2020) discuss the difference made by Marn's own embodied presence and the materiality of the psychological measuring instruments he brought to the interview room. Drawing on Barad's agential realism (Barad 2007) they work to 'decenter the human subject as the sole agent and promote the role of material in the analyses of the social world' (Marn and Wolgemuth 2020, p. 36). In doing so they explore how the physicalization of racial identity of researcher and participants emerges and coalesces with the research, rather than being brought to it. In Mayes's (2020) research about agency and voice for young people in schools, she describes how her attention was drawn to her own researcher stuttering as a corporeal manifestation in the communicative act of 'ungovernable' (p. 71), 'ambivalent' (p. 74) and irreconcilable feelings about her own role and positioning and the implications of this for the young people and for the project. She draws on Deleuze and Guattari's (1994/2009) theorizations of shame, not to interpret what the stuttering meant but to notice how interest, shame, connection and participation emerge in differentiated forms in and of research, and the difference this makes to what the research can do. Our good intentions about participation, empowerment and voice are entangled with and limited by the inevitable presence of our human conditions and being in the research apparatus. Research itself is then one of the many shameful compromises we must make with life and time and shame leaves its mark in the research, its affects and its potentialities. In their chapter, Catherine Hart and Annette Gough's (2020) use of ecofeminism theory illuminates how gendered understandings emerge and are entangled with disciplinary knowledge such as that of environmental education, co-constructing particular gendered limits and views of the environment, that are often taken for granted.

In a Baradian analysis these patterns point to the need for an understanding of embodiment as emerging as a condition of relations, including research, and as providing an opportunity to experience ethical relations. That is, embodiment is not involved in a cause and effect relationship with research and knowledge, but is a means by which we can attune our attention in an experience, to ethics (Barad 2007). Race, identity, human roles and gender are parts of this embodied opportunity for ethical experience. Attention to embodiment in research and to the boundaries drawn by forms of embodiment means that the ways they both limit and create possibilities for agency for a range of human and non-human bodies can be examined. The need to attend more to boundary-drawing practices and to 'alternative publics and sites of relation' (Trafí-Prats and Fendler 2020, p. 7), in both human and non-human forms is indicated across this volume. The editors endorse Chessa Adsit-Morris and Noel Gough's (2020) identification of Indigenous knowledges as vital sites of such attention. Understandings that many Indigenous societies already hold about human/knowledge/world embodiment and reciprocity are essential to the future capacity of academic research to better equip itself to expand into transformed ethical, epistemological and ontological forms in research.

(Re)considering technoscientific practices: The glow of practices enabling ontological hesitation

Technoscientific practices are another foci of attention across this volume. Theory is drawn on to attend to the glow of vitality that presents itself in playing with technoscientific practices as performative and productive in making the boundaries of bodies and knowledge (Barad 2007). These practices include SF (inclusive of Science Fiction, Speculative Fiction and Fantasy) and other narrative genres, digital images, social media, diagrams and text. Innovations with these practices are highlighted for their alternative contributions to knowledge, life, relations and agency.

One of the co-constitutions of these experiments is the production of minor literatures (Deleuze and Guattari 1986); literatures that deterritorialize normative and authoritative narratives and instead produce rich, incomplete stories that lead to further stories. Adsit-Morris and Gough (2020) draw on theories of diffraction (Barad 2014; Haraway 1994) and Gough's own 'rhizosemiotic play' (Gough 2010, p. 43) to engage in diffractive play with SF and texts. This work with theory enables them to 'un-name' things, instead moving towards multiple naming practices that do not erase the complexities of worlds or sort them into pure categories of good or bad, cause or effect, primitive or advanced. This assists in their aim not to reify and fix the concept of the Anthropocene in their writing but to open the future to multiple possibilities. Mary Dixon's (2020) use of fabulation – a story in the style of magical realism – makes present the bodies of Dewey, Butler and Bourdieu in the supervisor's office and writes new narratives of timescales and space in ideas of what learning is. Jesse Bazzul comments that diagrammatic play (Deleuze and Parnet 2007) helps him to disturb thought and 'avoid myopic moral questions' (2020, p. 126). Among other imaginings, he diagrams disturbance in ways that enable the circulation and transformation of 'culture-positive' (p. 127) stories of history, place and Indigenous experience. Laura Trafí-Prats and Rachel Fendler (2020) are drawn to consider the co-emergence of digital content in research, as means to attend to everyday constraints, rhythms and activities, and the differences and repetitions that are produced therein, including the often unnoticed and underestimated in children's lives. The 'poor images' (Steyerl 2012) produced by youth in their study, using free software, copied images and borrowed devices, mimicked existing content, were disjointed or unfinished, or otherwise limited by the lives of the young people or the technology they had access to. Trafí-Prats and Fendler note the 'flat affect' (Berlant 2015) of both the digital content and their research, and theorize this seemingly motionless, direction-less characteristic as illuminating entangled, dull, repetitive everyday relations and the inventive, provisional and improvised practices which people use to engage with these relations. They argue that these are significant functions of research and of education, especially for youth, in times of pervasive precarity, wherein we must negotiate how to live in conditions of transition, or as they put it with 'broken parts and failing infrastructure' (Trafí-Prats and Fendler 2020, p. 20) and make connections in new ways.

These researchers utilize the potency of these practices to leave a story or a thesis unfinished, or to produce multiplicities in stories and meaning. These technoscientific practices emit a glow of latent or unnamed possibilities, suggestive of Barthes's description of the pleasure of the text:

> … the text: it produces, in me, the best pleasure if it manages to make itself heard indirectly; if, reading it, I am led to look up often, to listen to something else. I am not necessarily captivated by the text of pleasure; it can be an act that is slight, complex, tenuous, almost scatterbrained: a sudden movement of the head like a bird who understands nothing of what we hear, who hears what we do not understand. (Barthes 1974, pp. 24–5)

The irony inherent to these particular technoscientific practices enables an ontological hesitation (Todorov 1975); an indirect, tenuous, unnamable shift in our focus on and certainty of the world. The non-traditional logics and genres of these alternative practices work to suspend distinctions between reality, fantasy, metaphor, objective, subjective, known and unknown. Deleuze and Guattari (1994/2009) describe practices such as these, which draw lines from the known to the unknown by drawing on the virtual intensities or forces that connect and flow in events, as diagrammatic. Bellingham (2020) draws further on Deleuze (1989) to argue for the significance of these practices to combat the potentially dangerous banality of normative constructs and discourses of standardization in education. Dixon, Adsit-Morris and Gough, Bazzul, Bellingham and Trafí-Prats and Fendler leverage these lines from known to unknown, to free space to theorize anew, to bring a quality of wildness to theory, to un-name and to bring forth new metaphors, concepts and plural explanations of ecology, pedagogy, place, education, youth, culture, history and future.

(Re)considering time, space and materiality: The glow of figurations for living with precarity and with possibility

Ontic phenomena such as time, space, place and materiality yield a significant glow for many authors in this volume. Theory is used to attend to and reconsider our worldly context, including the natural, the material, the cultural, the political and the structural/systemic, in various new interpretations of ecologies, networks, relations and concepts. In many of these chapters a particular figuration is deployed in the reconceptualizing of time and space. Braidotti argues that in contrast to the representational function of 'metaphors', figurations are 'vehicles to imaginatively ground our powers of understanding within the shifting landscapes of the present' (Braidotti 2013, p. 75). New figurations provide concepts with a new image or form that holds new spatial, material and affective qualities and relations. They allow us to defamiliarize concepts and methods and see them anew, enabling relations, processes and meaning to remain malleable, transformative and subject to imaginative agency.

In this volume figurations help us interrogate the ways we materialize central concepts in research apparatuses, for example, time, space, methodology and pedagogy. The figuration of the pedagogical encounter as black hole (Deleuze and Guattari 1987) enables a way of analysing learning as event (Dixon 2020), its vibrations, thickness and uneven movement, and its existence beyond the individual subject. Pedagogy as black hole enables new kinds of contrast with the blunt instruments of measurement of teacher actions and learner outcomes, dependent on well-defined boundaries and outcomes and empirical or visible understandings of learning. As we enter the black hole, visual clues about the borders of bodies are misleading. In the black hole, time and space are collapsed and matter and light can only pass inward and nothing can escape, and therefore little can be observed about what happened in the pedagogical encounter: 'learning' cannot be seen. The black hole figuration enables insight into the way that inside the pedagogical event, everything resonates alongside everything else, and the implication that it therefore holds great promise and great danger. Swarms and murmurations are figurations put to use by Thomas (2020) to theorize methodology and behaviour materially and spatially. Swarms and murmurations illuminate how schools, culture and consumption create a dynamic system in which educators and students are politically and socially constrained parts of a self-organizing whole, and how collective agency and the production of order and professional identities emerge. Charteris and Jones's (2020) use of the figuration of the Deleuzian refrain (Deleuze and Guattari 1987) enables 'researchers to attune to features beyond the human voice, the "voices" of things that enter the research assemblage' (Charteris and Jones 2020, p. 189). In the morning routine of the classroom the refrain draws attention to the way that past rituals are linked to present functions but always also constitute difference in the relational affects within the space of the school. Refrains are manifestations and ways of tracing how we are immersed in the material conditions and rhythms of the world and the everyday, and yet participate in the differentiation of these, every day.

A number of authors in this volume use figurations to assist them in the struggle with the challenge to think capitalism through nature and nature through capitalism at the same time (Moore 2015). That is, authors draw on figurations to help them to resist the narrative that humans and capitalism are the cause of conditions and to instead consider humans and capitalism as neither cause nor effect but part of the world's becoming (Barad 2007), engaged in the continuous opening up and constraining of boundaries and possibilities. These figurations enable reconsiderations of how to live with precarity, how to make sense of a world that feels overwhelming, and how to understand co-responsibility for these conditions. Theorizing with the use of diffraction (Barad 2014) and an SF novel by Marge Piercy (2016/1976) enables Adsit-Morris and Gough to draw on the figuration of 'women on the edge of time'. They argue that to accept the Anthropocene thesis is to return to the concretization of the human–nature separation. They use this figuration of women on the edge of time to develop an argument for multiplicity in the image of the world, not in the sense 'that there are many possible worlds' and one actual one but in the sense that 'worlds are intrinsically manifold' (Adsit-Morris and Gough 2020, p. 182). Bazzul (2020), and Jones and Charteris (2020), draw on anthropological and poststructural traditions which explicitly theorize disruption and disturbance, applying this to space and time in 'disturbance-based ecologies' (Tsing 2015) and 'heterotopias' (Foucault 1984) respectively. They view the concepts of disruption and disturbance as important means for reconceptualizing normative relations in the unfixed ecological-social or spatial terms necessary for understanding how to live in changing realities. These theorizations and figurations recognize disturbance as a natural, ongoing phenomenon inherent to being, and integral to vitality and dynamism of both life and theory. Their approach conceptualizes research as investigations of disturbance in layered and relational knowledge, history, politics, economy, culture, nature, humans and place.

Research figurations such as these bring a 'decidedly embodied aspect' (MacLure 2013, p. 661) to the glow of data. Such nebulous but agentic embodiment is characterized in the postmodern fiction writer Fowles's notion of the maggot:

> A maggot is the larval stage of a winged creature; as is the written text, at least in the writer's hope. But an older though now obsolete sense of the word is that of a whim or quirk … This fictional maggot was written for very much the same reason as those old musical ones of the period in which it is set; out of obsession with a theme. For some years before its writing a small group of travellers, faceless, without apparent motive, went in my mind towards an event. Evidently in some past, since they rode horses, and in a deserted landscape; but beyond this very primitive image, nothing. I do not know where it came from, or why it

kept obstinately rising from my unconscious. The riders never progressed to any
destination. They simply rode along a skyline, like a sequence of looped film in
a movie projector; or like a single line of verse, the last remnant of a lost myth.
(Fowles 2010, p. 5)

The figurations in this volume hold a similar potency. The maggot is not a
beginning, but is an entanglement of phenomena that is already there. The
figurative maggot has agency: a nebulous but embodied form, a glow of potential,
an aesthetic and affective loop of resonance and hope. Collectively the maggot-
like figurations in this volume lend an agency to theory that is affective, material
and spatial, enabling new readings of entangled humans, nature and ways to live
in uncertain times.

Opening at the close: What matters in future-oriented research?

This chapter has considered what is manifest from the collective vitality of theory
within this volume, and the kinds of further research possibilities this collective
vitality suggests. The volume showcases a range of innovations in uses of theory,
including the leveraging of new or non-normative theoretical premises and
spaces; the repurposing and reinventing of practices, methods and tools; and
the re-examining of alternative or unseen life in the assumed, the supposedly
obvious, the mundane and the everyday. We argue in this chapter that across
these innovative uses of theory, the volume highlights certain patterns that are
important features in an epistemological and ethical analysis of the research
landscape in contemporary and coming times. Theory drawn on in considerations
of human and researcher embodiment frames this embodiment as emergent
opportunity to reconsider ethics in research and knowledge constructions from
experiential positions; to feel and notice how bodies are generated and involved
in affects in research and relations. The reconsideration of theory and methods
as technoscientific practices shows how particular genres, practices and media
may be used to facilitate momentary suspension of certainties and ontological
shifts or hesitations, which make new lines from known to unknown, space for
the new and possibilities of the multiple. New research figurations developed
from theory manifest across this volume, highlight the agency of material-spatial
figurations for reconceiving of ways of relating in worldly contexts that are often
experienced as chaotic, precarious and overwhelming.

While many would acknowledge that research should be 'made up of networked communities of scholarly practice' (Preissle 2011, p. 692) of the past and present, the implications of this project looking forward ask us to rethink co-responsibility alongside wider networks of phenomena. If participation is inescapable and is always already part of a relational understanding that is neither a choice nor an exercise of autonomy (Springgay 2016), then the implications for academic collaborations are that we conceive of these as more-than-human assemblages. This volume suggests that collaborative research involves non-human, multispecies and interspecies attention and relation, in finding and making connections with our world and ways to genially cohabit. We hope this text serves as a stepping off point for those who wish to pursue some of these, and other, kinds of possibilities.

References

Adsit-Morris, C. and Gough, N. (2020), 'Post-Anthropocene imaginings: Speculative thought, diffractive play and women on the edge of time', in M. K. E. Thomas and R. Bellingham (eds), *Post-Qualitative Research and Innovative Methodologies*, 172–86, London, UK: Bloomsbury Academic.

Apple, M. W. (2013), *Can Education Change Society?*, New York, NY: Routledge.

Barad, K. (2007), *Meeting the Universe Halfway: Quantum Physics and the Entanglement of Matter and Meaning*, Durham, NC: Duke University Press.

Barad, K. (2010), 'Re (con) figuring the ethico-onto-epistemologi-cal question of matter', *Interdisciplinarity: Methodological Aproaches*, 7 (1): 83.

Barad, K. (2014), 'Diffracting diffraction: Cutting together-apart', *Parallax*, 20 (3): 168–87.

Barthes, R. (1974), *The Pleasure of the Text*, New York, NY: Hill and Wang.

Bauman, Z. (2005), 'Education in liquid modernity', *Review of Education, Pedagogy, and Cultural Studies*, 27 (4): 303–17.

Bazzul, J. (2020), 'Disturbance and intensive methodology in capitalist ruins', in M. K. E. Thomas and R. Bellingham (eds), *Post-Qualitative Research and Innovative Methodologies*, 117–33, London, UK: Bloomsbury Academic.

Bellingham, R. (2020), 'Posthumanist poetics and the transcorporeal, hypercorporeal chronotope', in M. K. E. Thomas and R. Bellingham (eds), *Post-Qualitative Research and Innovative Methodologies*, 85–101, London, UK: Bloomsbury Academic.

Bellingham, R., Thomas, M. K. E., Charman, K., Dixon, M. and Cooper, J. (2019), 'What is valued knowledge and where does it live? Educational consciousness and the democratisation of education', in S. Riddle and M. W. Apple (eds), *Re-imagining Education for Democracy*, 77–91, London: Routledge.

Berlant, L. (2015), 'Structures of unfeeling: Mysterious Skin', *International Journal of Politics, Culture and Society*, 28: 191–213.

Braidotti, R. (2013), *The Posthuman*, Cambridge: Polity Press.

Charteris, J. and Jones, M. (2020), 'Replete sensations of the refrain: Sound, action and materiality in agentic posthuman assemblages', in M. K. E. Thomas and R. Bellingham (eds), *Post-Qualitative Research and Innovative Methodologies*, 187–202, London, UK: Bloomsbury Academic.

Deleuze, G. (1989), *Cinema II*, Minneapolis, MN: University of Minnesota Press (Orig, pub. 1985).

Deleuze, G. and Guattari, F. (1986), *Kafka: Toward a Minor Literature*, Literary and cultural studies. Minneapolis, MN: University of Minnesota Press.

Deleuze, G. and Guattari, F. (1987), *A Thousand Plateaus: Capitalism and Schizophrenia*, Minneapolis, MN: University of Minnesota Press.

Deleuze, G. and Guattari, F. (1994/2009), *What Is Philosophy?*, London and New York, NY: Verso.

Deleuze, G. and Parnet, C. (2007), *Dialogues II*, New York, NY: Columbia University Press.

Dixon, M. (2020), 'Who is in my office and which century/ies are we in? A pedagogical encounter', in M. K. E. Thomas and R. Bellingham (eds), *Post-Qualitative Research and Innovative Methodologies*, 102–16, London, UK: Bloomsbury Academic.

Dolphijn, R. and van der Tuin, I. (2012). *New Materialism: Interviews & Cartographies*. Ann Arbor: Open Humanities Press.

Ferrando, F. (2012), 'Towards a posthumanist methodology. A statement', *Frame Journal For Literary Studies*, 25 (1): 9–18.

Foucault, M. (1984), '"Des espaces autres" [Of other spaces]', *Architecture, Mouvement, Continuité*, no. 5: 46–9.

Fowles, J. (2010), *A Maggot*, London: Vintage Digital.

Gough, N. (2010), 'Performing imaginative inquiry: Narrative experiments and rhizosemiotic play', in M. Fettes, R. Fitzgerald and T. W. Nielsen (eds), *Imagination in Educational Theory and Practice: A Many-Sided Vision*, 42–60, Newcastle upon Tyne: Cambridge Scholars Publishing.

Haraway, D. J. (1994), 'A game of cat's cradle: Science studies, feminist theory, cultural studies', *Configurations: A Journal of Literature, Science, and Technology*, 2 (1): 59–71.

Hart, C. and Gough, A. (2020), 'Troubling binaries: Gendering research in environmental education', in M. K. E. Thomas and R. Bellingham (eds), *Post-Qualitative Research and Innovative Methodologies*, 51–65, London, UK: Bloomsbury Academic.

Jones, M. and Charteris, J. (2020), 'Transversalities in Education research: Using heterotopias to theorize spaces of crises and deviation', in M. K. E. Thomas and R. Bellingham (eds), *Post-Qualitative Research and Innovative Methodologies*, 134–50, London, UK: Bloomsbury Academic.

Kristeva, J. (2002). *The Portable Kristeva*, ed. K. Oliver, New York, NY: Columbia University Press.

Lather, P. (2013), 'Methodology-2.1: What do we do in the afterward?', *International Journal of Qualitative Studies in Education*, 26: 634–45.

Lather, P. (2018a), 'Thirty years after: Praxis in the ruins', in H. Malone, S. Roincon-Gallardo and K. Kew (eds), *Future Directions of Educational Change*, 71–85, New York, NY: Routledge.

Lather, P. (2018b), 'What new sensibility, configuration or "dominant" logic now for educational theory?' *Educational Philosophy and Theory*, 50 (14): 1602–3.

MacLure, M. (2010), 'The offence of theory', *Journal of Education Policy*, 25 (2): 277–86.

MacLure, M. (2013), 'Researching without representation? Language and materiality in post-qualitative methodology', *International Journal of Qualitative Studies in Education*, 26 (6): 658–67.

Marn, T. M. and Wolgemuth, J. R. (2020), 'Experimental critical qualitative inquiry: Disrupting methodologies, resisting subjects', in M. K. E. Thomas and R. Bellingham (eds), *Post-Qualitative Research and Innovative Methodologies*, 35–50, London, UK: Bloomsbury Academic.

Mayes, E. (2020), 'The shame of participation: rethinking the ontology of participation with a stutter', in M. K. E. Thomas and R. Bellingham (eds), *Post-Qualitative Research and Innovative Methodologies*, 66–82, London, UK: Bloomsbury Academic.

Mazzei, L. A. (2016), 'Voice without a subject', *Cultural Studies ↔ Critical Methodologies*, 16 (2): 151–61.

McKenzie, M. (2005), 'The "post-post period" and environmental education research', *Environmental Education Research*, 11 (4): 401–12.

Moore, J. (2015), *Capitalism in the Web of Life: Ecology and the Accumulation of Capital*, New York, NY: Verso.

Piercy, M. (2016/1976), *Woman on the Edge of Time*, New York, NY: Ballantine Books.

Preissle, J. (2011), 'Qualitative futures: Where we might go from where we've been', in N. K. Denzin and Y. S. Lincoln (eds), *The Sage Handbook of Qualitative Research*, 4th edn, 685–98, Los Angeles: Sage.

Rosiek, J. L. (2013), 'Pragmatism and post-qualitative futures', *International Journal of Qualitative Studies in Education*, 26: 692–705.

Somerville, M. (2016), 'The post-human I: Encountering "data" in new materialism', *International Journal of Qualitative Studies in Education*, 29 (9): 1161–72. doi: 10.1080/09518398.2016.1201611.

Springgay, S. (2016), 'Towards a rhythmic account of working together and taking part', *Research in Education*, 96 (1): 71–7.

St Pierre, E. (2013), 'The appearance of data', *Cultural Studies—Critical Methodologies*, 13 (4): 223–7.

St. Pierre, E. A. (2013), 'The posts continue: Becoming', *International Journal of Qualitative Studies in Education*, 26 (6): 646–57.

Steyerl, H. (2012), *The Wretched of the Screen*, Berlin: Stenberg Press.

Thomas, M. K. E. (2020), 'Swarms and murmurations', in M. K. E. Thomas and R. Bellingham (eds), *Post-Qualitative Research and Innovative Methodologies*, 153–71, London, UK: Bloomsbury Academic.

Todorov, T. (1975), *The Fantastic: A Structural Approach To A Literary Genre*, New York, NY: Cornell University Press.

Trafí-Prats, L. and Fendler, R. (2020), 'Postproductive methods: Researching modes of relationality and affect worlds through participatory video with youth', in M. K. E. Thomas and R. Bellingham (eds), *Post-Qualitative Research and Innovative Methodologies*, 19–34, London, UK: Bloomsbury Academic.

Tsing, A. L. (2015), *The Mushroom at the End of the World*, Princeton, NJ: Princeton University Press.

Vargova, M. (2007), 'Dialogue, pluralism, and change: The intertextual constitution of Bakhtin, Kristeva, and Derrida', *Res Publica,* 13 (4), 415–40. doi:10.1007/s11158-007-9042-y.

Part One

Disruption, subjectivity and agency

2

Postproductive methods: Researching modes of relationality and affect worlds through participatory video with youth

Laura Trafí-Prats and Rachel Fendler

Poor images and postproduction as participation

In an essay titled 'In Defense of the Poor Image', art critic Hito Steyerl (2012) describes as characteristic of contemporary times an economy of poor images circulating in the form of compressed video files that are uploaded, downloaded, modified, uploaded again, and that create alternative publics and sites of relation. These images are called poor for various reasons. They are produced by popular and amateur authors, with a do-it-yourself experimental aesthetic, around everyday experiences and with an interest for merging art with life. They are poor because they are imperfect, produced with technologies available to regular folk. They lack the high-end quality of corporative production design. Their role is not to be original or high-res but to circulate, move, flow intensively in the circuit of many other images in the pool of capitalistic semioticization, where everything/everyone is made visible, documented, surveilled. In their circulation across the World Wide Web poor images may provoke alienation and submission, but they also can incite transgression, contestation and fun. Steyerl (2012, p. 41) writes:

> Altogether, poor images present a snapshot of the affective condition of the crowd, its neurosis, paranoia, and fear, as well as its craving for intensity, fun, and distraction. The condition of the images speaks not only of countless transfers and reformattings, but also of the countless people who cared enough about them to convert them over and over again, to add subtitles, reedit, or upload them.

Steyerl sees the political and imaginative role of poor images not coming from representation or contemplation but from a permanent dematerialization and deterritorialization, which enables their recombination and integration in new sequences and relations. The role of the poor image is not to deliver a fetishist visibility but to create visual bonds between dispersed audiences that do not necessarily share any form of solidarity but link via images in 'a physical sense by mutual excitement, affective attunement, anxiety' (Steyerl 2012, p. 43).

Laura and Rachel are interested in how the theory of the poor image and its emphasis on collective affect seems to resonate with emerging views of participation in research with youth inspired by the new materialisms (Grosz 2010; Barad 2007) and new empiricisms (Manning 2016; Manning and Massumi 2014; Massumi 2011), that demand to do research from the middle, a way of joining in activity that is already going on (Springgay and Truman 2018; Springgay 2016; Rotas 2016) with existing practices of consuming, creating, sharing, living with images. Considering this, Laura and Rachel propose to redefine participation in video-making as *postproduction* (Bourriaud 2005), a cultural practice not based on creating new and original objects but on reusing existing forms to produce new relational modes and zones of activity. Bourriaud (2005, p. 17) offers an example of postproduction practice through the figure of the DJ and her use of the sampler:

> [A] machine that reprocesses musical products, also implies constant activity; to listen to records becomes work in itself, which diminishes the dividing line between reception and practice … This recycling of sounds, images, and forms implies incessant navigation within the meanderings of cultural history, navigation which itself becomes the subject of artistic practice. Isn't art, as Duchamp once said, 'a game among all men of all eras'? Postproduction is the contemporary form of this game.

Therefore, the aim of postproduction is not outputting results but developing *practice*, through active, intense, relational inhabitation of existing forms, so to create new circuits of movement through culture. Laura and Rachel are interested in working with this understanding of participation as an immanent relationality of emergent zones of activity to consider the affect worlds organizing video-making with youth in contexts of precarity. Precarity refers to the material and affective *conditions of transition* that individuals collectively improvise and negotiate to live with broken parts and failing infrastructures (Berlant 2016). Since the financial crisis of 2008, when many Western countries implemented programmes of austerity and cuts in youth provision (Bradford and Cullen 2012), precarity is something intrinsic to youth services with special impact in the arts education sector (Parsad et al. 2011). Within these conditions, Laura and Rachel develop video projects with small groups of urban youth from economically disadvantaged backgrounds. They have become accustomed to operating with meagre conditions, broken parts and missing pieces. Their projects reside in schools and youth centres, which partially cede their spaces and share resources such as teacher support, classrooms, outdated computers, snacks. They use free or trial software, combined with donated used phones and cameras borrowed from campus libraries and resource centres. Laura and Rachel and the youth they work with develop practices of poor making and postproduction, in the sense that they make do with what is available. In inventing provisional arrangements, they improvise technological, material and affective relations (Bourriaud 2005), as the cases presented later on in the chapter discuss in detail.

This parallels with contemporary perspectives in social theory, which interrogate the exhaustion of capitalism and suggest that life originates not only in conditions of growth and progress but also in situations of precarity that provoke unpredictable encounters and collaboration between unlikely gatherings of actors (Tsing 2015). Laura and Rachel have found in the work of Lauren Berlant (2016, 2015, 2011) important concepts to further think precarity both as a latent and pervasive condition and as a site from which to engage in experiments of living through new aesthetic, sensorial, affective forms.

Affect, slow research and postproductive genres

Berlant proposes the concept of *cruel optimism* (2011) to argue that individuals organize their ways of belonging to the world through attachments to fantasies of good life that do not hold up. These fantasies revolve around desires for upward mobility, political representation, romantic love and others. Good life fantasies are attached to different objects that organize such desires. These could be an education degree, a technological device, a new drug or many others. Berlant argues that attachments are optimistic. Optimism is what gets subjects to bind with worlds, and the attachment to an object of desire is a way to feel closer to a good life fantasy. However, Berlant sees optimism as having a double bind. On the one hand, fantasies of good life are built around the continuity of the networks of resource supply that organized the welfare state of the post-war societies. However, in current times this network (quality jobs, public education, public health, expansion of university access, etc.) is affected by disruption and systemic failures. Consequently, the distribution of resources is not ensured, thus putting in danger our sense of good life. On the other hand, the abandonment of such fantasies of good life feels unbearable. Without them subjects lose their attachment to lifeworlds and their sense of belonging.

Participation in education could be thought in terms of the double bind of cruel optimism. Participation is something that is deemed as good, and that helps subjects to belong to the collective world of the school, youth centre or other institutions. At the same time, participation is predetermined to exist in normative parameters of school behaviour and affect worlds. Other existing forms of relational activity will not be seen as participative. Thus, rather than binding subjects to the world this other activity can contribute to their exclusion from it. Springgay (2016, p. 72) writes:

> Participation is commonly understood as either voluntary or as a way of being successful. As voluntary it is assumed that one chooses to participate. That participation is something we do, rather than something immanent to the event itself. Moreover, in a neo-liberal space, such as a school, participation is rewarded and deemed valuable. To choose not to participate, to say no, is to exclude oneself.

Berlant (2016) calls for not saturating the field of sociality with normative emotions and interrogates the prerogative that the affects of collective worlds ought to only be thought in terms of belonging. She suggests the concept of *proximity* to think in modes of being together in ambivalent and difficult-to-discern situations that do not necessarily correspond with the prerogative of having something in common. She writes:

> This project looks to nonsovereign[1] relationality as the foundational quality of being in common, seeing, for example, individuality as a genre carved from within dynamics of relation rather than a state prior to it or distinct from it. As a result, this project works against the pervasive critical theory discourse of 'belonging' insofar as 'belonging' operates as a synonym for being in social

[1] The nonsovereign is a concept that Berlant (2016) proposes to think a form of life in common that does not begin with the idea of sovereignty. She proposes a politics of nonsovereignty that cultivate understandings of subjectivity as made of incoherences, tensions and contradictions. The concept of the nonsovereign addresses forms of being in proximity with others which neither presume that belonging is something that unites nor presuppose that subjects are in proximity because they have something in common. The nonsovereign subjectivity involves modes of a relationality detached from the object and fantasies of good life. It is a subjectivity open to experiment with modes of living that go beyond the common genres in which life in common is explained and understood (e.g. romance, friendship, family). It interrogates how intimacy, proximity, and communal infrastructure feels and what it does to other collective modes of being like being a mentor, a co-worker, a collaborator in a project.

worlds ... The crowded but disjointed propinquity of the social calls for a proxemics, the study of sociality as proximity quite distinct from the positive attachment languages of belonging. (Berlant 2016, pp. 394–5)

Another important question that Berlant (2016, 2015, 2011) addresses is how these nonsovereign modes of being together feel. In this respect, Berlant (2011) differs from contributions in social theory that have concentrated on the concept of trauma to explain how individuals manage sensing a world that is overwhelming. She suggests that the event of living in ordinary crisis can have 'other inexpressive but life-extending actions throughout the ordinary and its situations of living' (p. 81). These do not necessarily need to be expressed as trauma but in the form of other genres like the happening, the joke, the conversation – perhaps the poor image – that speak of 'other forms of sensual activity toward and beyond survival' (p. 9). In this context, Berlant (2015, 2011) pays attention to what she calls the *impasse of the present*. The impasse corresponds with a time that is open and not saturated yet by normative feelings. It is the time of what comes up, the time where one can be changed by the encounter. Rather than being filled with a sense of eventuality where some action takes place, it is typical of the impasse to have a *flat affect*. In the time of the impasse connections between subjects, and subjects, things and places are neither defined by communication nor articulated through distinctive feelings. Flat affect is carried by an atmospheric sense of quietness, banality and slow time in which life is presented as a mundane activity of hanging up.

Laura and Rachel have found the concepts of the impasse and flat affect quite useful to consider other affects of participation in moments of low eventuality, where the research did not seem to move anywhere and where the activity of participants did not build in any clear direction, remaining in a state of indeterminacy. The impasse seems to remark the importance of slow forms of research that stick to ambivalent practices and atmospheres, and that go along with incidents, situations, anecdotes that unfold. Slow research moves with the ways young people see, make, share, relate with images. The impasse calls for a speculative use of methods, in which research is not so much a procedure for extracting data from the world, but the ways we become entangled in relations and the movement of thinking propelled by navigating the circuits of poor imaging and postproduction (Springgay and Truman 2018).

More recently, Berlant (2016) has proposed the concept of the *glitch*, which she defines as a broken or failing infrastructure, an interruption inside the bonds and systems that sustain ordinary life. More than a space where activity stops, Berlant sees the glitch as an infrastructure where creative forms of repair and provisional maintenance emerge that carry the potential for experimenting with transformational forms of togetherness not foreclosed by optimism. The glitch is a concept that merges well with the ideas of the poor image and postproduction, in the sense that a glitchstructure is an infrastructure in a constant state of transition constituted by loss and practices of reusing, recombining and adjusting to what is available and what is left in situations of failure. Glitchstructures 'can provide a pedagogy of unlearning while living with the malfunctioning world, vulnerable confidence, and the rolling ordinary' (Berlant 2016, p. 396). Such pedagogy is based on processes of experimentation that retrain the sensorium and become proximate to collective modes of life that are fraying, queer, speculative, ongoing, incoherent without the desire to straighten them (see also Sellar and Zipin 2018).

Berlant (2011) proposes the concept of *genre* to explain how world-shifting events, their intensities and heterogeneous sense become organized in ways that can be collectively sensed. Genre is a placeholder of conventions that permits both acting on and interpreting feelings and consequently building a public sense of shared reciprocity. These conventions can produce processes not only based on ideology and normativity but also on adjustment and improvisation. Consequently, the carving of the event into some aesthetic form or genre is a key process to understand the management of ambivalence as a public feeling. Berlant (2015, 2011) has discussed the waning of the genres of historical realism and melodrama (sentimentality), and the emergence of alternative genres that address the subjective processes of adjustment to the erosion of the welfare state, the growth of alternative urban and sexual cultures, and the rise of the neoliberal economy. Connected with the concept of infrastructures of transition and the glitch, Berlant (2016) calls for new genres that address life in the space of broken forms and speculates on how precarious infrastructures can multiply conditions of possibility. Berlant also argues for the cultivation of genres of the common that are 'carved out from within dynamics of relation rather than a state prior to it or distinct from it' (2016, p. 394). Aligning with this idea, Rachel and Laura propose three postproductive genres: the meme, reformatting and montage. They utilize these three postproductive genres to think with three research situations in their respective video-research projects with youth. While the three postproductive genres allude to processes of digital image-making, hardware care and film, Rachel and Laura's interest is not limited to their resulting objects (e.g. an image, a series of composed images or a repurposed technology). Following Berlant (2016) their focus is on the dynamics of relations and how using these genres as methods of analysis allows for more complicated understandings of participation and being in common in video-research with youth. We end this section with a brief introduction of how these postproductive genres function to then proceed to the discussion of their associated case studies.

1. Formally the concept of the meme refers to a mode of cultural production built around the practice of distributing repackaged forms of digital material, where modified content is passed 'person to person by means of copying or imitation' (Shifman 2011, p. 188). As a postproductive genre the meme alludes to collective processes of image-making that grow out from inhabiting, borrowing and appropriating images and artistic practices that are already in circulation.
2. Reformatting is a practice commonly performed when digital devices are affected by data corruption. As a postproductive genre reformatting enacts processes in which image-making is used as a practice of adjustment and improvisation in response to unexpected life shifts and ordinary crises.
3. In Deleuze's (1989; see also Rodowick 1997) film theory montage refers to the arrangement of images in relation and the potential of transformation that such relationality introduces in the film narrative as whole. As a postproductive genre, the montage refers to the possibility of representing the research as a differential process of emergent and ongoing relations between bodies, technologies, images and places in space and time.

The mimetic chain: Linking up through YouTube production

In the summer of 2016 Rachel initiated a weekly video workshop at a teen centre in Tallahassee, Florida. Publicly funded, the drop-in centre provides afterschool and summer programmes for local teens. From the outset, Rachel followed the teens' lead as they explored their interest in developing a presence on YouTube. For three teens – Ice, Sage and Thunder – this process drew on a series of YouTube styles the youth were fluent in and relied on a set of free editing apps that could be used on the teens' borrowed smartphones and the centre's PCs. These teens developed videos with one-shot takes and single song audio tracks, engaging a mode of production that reflects the intensity and fast pace of poor image circuits (Steyerl 2012). The group was able to film, edit and upload videos in the span of just one or two project sessions (two to four hours).

The videos the teens produced were predictable. Replicability is a key characteristic of how amateur content circulates in YouTube across a loosely organized public (Burgess 2014; Steyerl 2012; Shifman 2011). The output focused on generating memetic videos where the authors responded to existing content by mimicking its visual style. As a postproductive genre, *the meme* is a form of cultural participation. Methodologically, this leads to the observation that these videos are 'the mediating mechanisms via which cultural practices are originated, adopted and (sometimes) retained within social networks' (Burgess 2014, p. 87). The teens' interaction with YouTube was built through processes of assembling tools, bodies and scenarios. Their practice was one where 'notions of originality (being at the origin of) and even of creation (making something from nothing) are slowly blurred in this new cultural landscape' (Bourriaud 2005, p. 7).

The video production, upload and visualization created spaces of shared activity. As Berlant (2016) would argue, this shared activity did not imply a sense of belonging, but occurred through what Steyerl (2012) calls visual bonds which are more ephemeral, erratic and physical in the sense that they connected bodies through excitement, intensification but also boredom and surfing. The teens opened a shared YouTube channel.[22] This platform prompted the teens to place advertisements on their videos, which they saw as an opportunity. The teens wondered if they could monetize their channel and began tracking their view count. One day a disagreement arose regarding the proprietorship of *Black Superman*;[33] the person who acted as Superman wanted to upload the video on his personal channel, to capture its traffic, but the collective prevailed.

The teens' memetic production could be interpreted to situate youth as depoliticized agents in a system of communicative capitalism (Dean 2005). Indeed, Steyerl (2012, p. 32) suggests the poor image 'mocks the promises of digital technology'. However such promises do not come into contact with the teens' lifeworlds. Rather, researching alongside these teens revealed modes of relationality, or 'scenes of genuine ambivalence [that] better disclose some matters of managing being in proximity' (Berlant 2016, p. 395). The teens' non-sentimental and constrained engagement with poor video equipment, the material environment of the centre and ongoing YouTube viewing oriented research towards young people's proximity with and within the ambivalent circuits of poor images and afterschool spaces marked by precariety.

---

[2]   This channel can be accessed via the following link: https://www.youtube.com/channel/UC4KtfSO hCELDJnxNQ8iL3zg.
[3]   The video in question can be viewed online: https://www.youtube.com/watch?v=ET7PgQ7ec6c.

Reformatting: Destiny not-making the video self-portrait of her favourite place in the city

During the months of January to June 2008 Laura worked with a group of fifteen third graders in a public school in Milwaukee, Wisconsin, in the development of video self-portraits of place. The project sought to collaborate with a classroom teacher, children and their families to capture and edit footage of places in the city that children frequented, liked and developed activity. Among the fifteen children in the class only eleven were able to get parental permission to borrow a camera for the weekend and be supported by an adult with the time to take them to the place they wanted, and spend time with them in that place. A number of children became aware of such limitations fairly early in the development of the project and decided to excuse themselves from its activities. It soon became obvious that the spaces that children were allowed to navigate, and when and how they were allowed to navigate them, were highly dependent on their guardians' time and availability to help (Zeiher 2003).

Destiny was one of the girls in the group whose family did not support the borrowing of the camera so she could videotape the place of her choice, the neighbourhood library. Destiny had told Laura that she would go to the library daily for a couple of hours to do her homework with her grandfather, who meanwhile would read the newspapers and use the computer. The classroom teacher explained to Laura that Destiny was not living with her mother and father, and that her legal guardians were her grandparents. After having a phone conversation with the aim of explaining further the project to the grandparents, the teacher described their mood as feeling disappointed because Destiny had lost other school materials that they had to replace. She explained that the situation at home was 'tight'. The grandparents feared that Destiny would lose or damage the camera and that they would have to pay for it. The teacher shared with the grandparents how much interest Destiny had showed for this project. Destiny had written detailed descriptions of the library and had made several drawings with different views of the place in order to plan her camera framings and movements. She had also prepared a script and participated in tutorials on how to compose different styles of frames with a Flip™ video camera.

Despite being aware of the antagonism of her grandparents towards the project, Destiny committed to it by intensifying her productivity in ways not seen in other participant children. Thinking Destiny's activity from a perspective of cruel optimism (Berlant 2011), one can see that the making of the video was an object of desire that Destiny could not easily give up. As Berlant (2011, p. 3) affirms, in contexts of overwhelming impediments 'adjustment seems as a big accomplishment'. The teacher and Laura decided to ask Destiny if she would like to do her self-portrait of place in the school library rather than her local library. In this way, Destiny could adjust rather than drop the object of desire. Destiny agreed. This is how the postproductive genre of *reformatting* came into place.

Reformatting refers to agentive modes that involve adjustment and improvisation towards a situation of disturbance (Berlant 2011). The participative process between adult, child, place and things was reformatted so Destiny's video self-portrait could be made in a different place and time. In the school library Destiny could not record herself doing her homework, commenting on her favourite book collections, or playing video games. She could not capture the librarian, the locals and her grandfather reading the newspaper, as included in her planning script. Additionally, Laura was left to be the adult with whom Destiny could rely on to enact her project. As Azoulay (2016) explains, in image-making collaboration does not aim or imply a given form. It takes its shape in response to specific circumstances. In the case of Destiny, her project required solidarity and someone who listened and recognized Destiny's presence and desire to produce a movie.

The resulting video self-portrait that Destiny co-filmed and co-edited with Laura is a disjoined visual-collage of dispersed mundane gestures that at first sight do not seem atypical in a school context. Destiny shows her classroom, reads a book about Rosa Parks, talks about the assignment connected to the book, searches the shelves of the library for more books on Rosa Parks, interviews the librarian, uses the library computer, shows other favourite books, and reads a personally authored composition (see Figure 2.1).

From a postproductive perspective, Destiny's performance, its video recording and editing can be conceived as an assemblage of embodiments, things, spaces that portray ambivalence or a dynamic of affirmation and constraint that is characteristic of flat affect. As mentioned earlier, Berlant (2015, 2011) describes flat affect as manifested through ordinary activities that more than showing growth or progress present pure maintenance. On the one hand, we see the affirmation of Destiny being a competent reader, someone capable of eloquently arguing why Rosa Parks changed the world, someone who defines herself as a poem writer, someone who reads a nicely crafted composition with a personal and evocative atmosphere that fills the viewer with curiosity. On the other hand, Destiny's statement that if she was Rosa Parks she would not give up her seat when she reads the book, along with the sense of freedom and joy summoned in her composition, highly contrast with the flat and controlled environment where

Figure 2.1 Stills and quotes from Destiny's video self-portrait.

these actions took place. Such optimistic feelings also seem anomalous when considering the limitations that Destiny experienced to develop her project.

Postproductive methods conceive of participation as a process of going along with young people lives, as these lives are lived. As Horton and Kraftl (2006) have pointed out, this going along may involve a reformatting of research plans and habituated methods so to invent alongside the dull, repetitive rhythms of young people's routines. As it happened with Destiny's video, its making process opened up a way of seeing the 'unnoticed, often unsaid, often unsayable, often unacknowledged and often underestimated' (Horton and Kraftl 2006, p. 259) in children's everyday lives.

Montage: Navigating disturbances in the contested present of JT's ongoing video project

The final case study returns to the weekly video workshop Rachel hosted in the summer of 2016 at a local teen centre. It considers how the postproductive genre of *montage* acts as both film technique and a relational mode of participation. Early in the project teen participant JT filmed a walk home from the centre using his mobile phone. In this fourteen-minute continuous shot, JT and his friend documented litter, crooked street signs and parking lots, while maintaining a colourful conversation about how everything they came across was 'disgusting' and 'trashed'. The following week JT captured his route to the centre in the morning. There is no voiceover in the day scenes where JT quietly filmed a landscape bathed in sunlight, documenting trees and fluttering leaves, zooming in on flowing water and growing tadpoles, and panning across a wooded area and a field.

JT sought to continue his engagement with this material through postproduction and envisioned bringing the day and night scenes together in a back-and-forth montage. Deleuze (1989, p. 179) observes that montage, which does not blend images into a coherent whole, operates as a mechanism of 'differentiation'. Colman (2011, p. 21) further suggests that montage consists of 'affective intervals created between movement and within time, dialectic movements productive of mutations of form'. For JT's video project, and arguably for his participation in the project, the work of montage consisted in such a mutation of form. In postproduction JT encountered an obstacle; using a free video editing software program, the long video clips exceeded the programme's capacity, making the process of editing unbearably slow. Undeterred, this stilted process seemed acceptable to JT who drifted into workshop sessions sporadically, happy to comment on his vision for the project in lieu of dedicating blocks of time to editing.

The postproductive genre of montage acted as a 'glitch' which introduced 'hiccups in the relations among structural forces that alter a class's *sense* of things' (Berlant 2011, p. 198). At impasse, over the course of the project JT consistently tinkered with his compilation but never exported it. For Berlant (2011, p. 199), an impasse is a 'formal term for encountering the duration of the present'. In other words, the montage-as-glitch replaced a directional, finite task of editing with an open and ongoing engagement that altered JT's relationship to the video and the workshop. In this glitched system, montage loses its narrative quality of meaning making. Following Deleuze (1989, p. 155), montage is seen as capable, paradoxically, of 'introduc[ing] an enduring interval in the moment itself'. This interval, as a 'stretch of time that is being sensed and shaped—an impasse' (Berlant 2011, p. 199), emphasizes the atemporal quality of JT's ongoing montage. Within JT's project the unresolved relationship between day and night scenes turn into a topology comprised of 'the simultaneity of incompossible presents' (Deleuze 1989, p. 131), which situates JT's neighbourhood in an ambivalent now.

The glitched process guiding JT's postproductive engagement with his landscape allowed montage to manifest as a 'contested present', one that 'emerges through activities of disturbance' (Berlant 2015, p. 194). Within this disturbance the postproductive genre of montage gains value as a research orientation. Tsing signals how, in 'disturbance-based ecologies' (2015, p. 5), new forms of world making emerge specifically in assemblage: 'assemblages don't gather lifeways; they make them' (2015, p. 23). In a context that does not (or cannot) aspire to a linear vision of progress, 'assemblages are open-ended gatherings. They allow us to ask about communal effects without assuming them. They show us potential histories in the making' (2015, pp. 22–23). In this workshop, the poor quality of the montage shifted the project's focus from product, or the 'real thing', to its 'conditions of existence' (Steyerl 2012, p. 8). Forced into an open-ended register, ultimately JT's manipulation of time-space rehearsed possibilities for togetherness, speculating on unrealized modes of engagement, in collaboration and with the city.

Glossary

Affect Affect is a pervasive concept in contemporary theory, especially in the context of the new materialisms, the new empiricisms and non-representational theories. For Berlant (2013), affect is a way of talking about the impact of the world in subjects. It focuses on how subjects form and sustain attachments with the world and how these attachments feel. Most particularly, Berlant is interested in affects connected to ordinary practices of ongoingness and adjustment characteristic of a time when the post-war infrastructures that ensured the continuity of life are failing. Berlant suggests that practices of learning to live with broken parts and transitional infrastructures constitute transformative experiments of living and sensing. This is relevant to participative research with youth, because many places and spaces where youth meet with educators are precarious, underfunded and require inventive practices of infrastructuration.

Genre For Berlant (2011) genres are placeholders of conventions that permit the collective feeling of complex events. Berlant (2015) suggests that contemporary genres presented in the novel, cinema, visual art and popular music offer forms to sense the times, moods and atmospheres of ordinary crises. In this chapter, we have thought with postproductive genres like the meme, reformatting and the montage, which emerged from video practices of/with different groups of young people. This has allowed us to approach the affects, moods, sensations that make research events while grappling with their difficulty, ambivalence and ongoingness.

Participation Thinking with Springgay (2016) and Berlant (2011), we have suggested that educational research should anticipate neither the format nor the affect of participation. Participation is not a thing, but *a doing* that is immanent to events constituted by situations of being together, proximate or in relation to others. Influenced by these theorists, we have suggested an approach to participation as a *joining with* the activity that is already ongoing related to consuming, creating and sharing images. The aim of this research is to pay attention and intensify modes of connection, relation and affectivity within ecologies of poor imaging and postproduction.

Poor image It is a concept developed by art critic Hito Steyerl (2012). Poor images are images circulating over the World Wide Web that are produced, shared, manipulated, downloaded and uploaded again and again utilizing everyday technologies such as mobile phones and desktop computers. The role of the poor image is not to be a high-quality image to be contemplated but one to circulate, move, become intense and eventually dematerialize. Our projects worked with the assumption that young people are already active and implicated in the circuits of the poor image. The poor image situates the concept of participation in the territory of deterritorialized activity and affect.

Postproduction It is a term proposed by art critic Nicolas Bourriaud (2005) to describe contemporary cultural practices consisting in reusing existing forms, not to produce new objects but to explore practice, create new relational modes and produce (even if it is only ephemerally) new sites of collective existence. We propose that the poor image is a case of postproductive practice that, as Steyerl (2012) notes, creates visual bonds between people living in different places. These visual bonds do not correspond to traditional ideas of participation based on commonality or solidarity. Instead the social form of the poor image is the production of collective affect through its flows and movements through the World Wide Web.

References

Azoulay, A. (2016), 'Photography consists of collaboration: Susan Meiselas, Wendy Ewald, and Ariella Azoulay', *Camera Obscura*, 91 (31): 187–201.

Barad, K. (2007), *Meeting the Universe Halfway: Quantum Physics and the Entanglement of Matter and Meaning*, Durham, NC: Duke University Press.

Berlant, L. (2011), *Cruel Optimism*, Durham, NC: Duke University Press.

Berlant, L. (2015), 'Structures of unfeeling: Mysterious Skin', *International Journal of Politics, Culture and Society*, 28: 191–213.

Berlant, L. (2016), 'The commons: Infrastructures for troubling times', *Environment and Planning D: Society and Space*, 34 (3): 393–419.

Bourriaud, N. (2005), *Postproduction. Culture as Screenplay, How Art Reprograms the World*, Berlin: Stenberg Press.

Bradford, S. and Cullen, F. (2012), *Research and Research Methods for Youth Practitioners*, London: Routledge.

Burgess, J. (2014), '"All your chocolate rain are belong to us?" Viral video, you tube and the dynamics of participatory culture', in N. Papastergiadis and V. Lynn (eds), *Art in the Global Present*, 86–96, Sydney: UTSePress.

Colman, F. (2011), *Deleuze and Cinema: The Film Concepts*, Oxford: Berg.

Dean, J. (2005), 'Communicative capitalism: Circulation and the foreclosure of politics', *Cultural Politics*, 1 (1): 51–74.

Deleuze, G. (1989 [1985]), *Cinema 2: The Time*-Image, trans. H. Tomlinson and R. Galeta, Minneapolis, MN: University of Minnesota Press.

Grosz, E. (2010), 'Feminism, materialism and freedom', in D. Cole and S. Frost (eds), *New Materialisms: Ontology, Agency, and Politics*, 139–57, Durham, NC: Duke University Press.

Horton, J. and Kraftl, P. (2006), 'Not just growing up, but going on: Materials, spacings, bodies, situations', *Children's Geographies*, 4 (3): 259–76.

Manning, E. (2016), *The Minor Gesture*, Durham, NC: Duke University Press.

Manning, E. and Massumi, B. (2014), *Thought in the Act: Passages in the Ecology of Experience*, Minneapolis: University of Minnesota Press.

Massumi, B. (2011), *Semblance and Event: Activist Philosophy and the Occurrent Arts*, Cambridge, MA: MIT Press.

Parsad, B., Spiegelman, M. and Coopersmith, J. (2011), *Arts Education in Public Elementary and Secondary Schools* 1999–2000 *and* 2009–10, Washington DC: U.S. Department of Education.

Rodowick, D. N. (1997), *Gilles Deleuze Time Machine*, Durham, NC: Duke University Press.

Rotas, N. (2016), 'Moving towards practices that matter', in N. Snaza, D. Sonu, S. Truman and Z. Zaliwska (eds), *Pedagogical Matters: New Materialisms and Curriculum Studies*, 179–96, New York: Peter Lang.

Sellar, S. and Zipin, L. (2018), 'Conjuring optimism in dark times: Education, affect and human capital', Educational Theory and Philosophy, [Online]. Available at: https://wwwtandfonline.com.ezproxy.mmu.ac.uk/doi/pdf/10.1080/00131857.2018.1485566?needAccess=true.

Shifman, L. (2011), 'An anatomy of a YouTube meme', *New Media & Society*, 14 (2): 187–203.

Springgay, S. (2016), 'Towards a rhythmic account of working together and taking part', *Research in Education*, 96 (10): 71–7.

Springgay, S. and Truman, S. (2018), 'On the need for methods beyond proceduralism: Speculative Middles, (in)tensions, and response-ability in research', *Qualitative Inquiry*, 24 (3): 203–14.

Steyerl, H. (2012), *The Wretched of the Screen*, Berlin: Stenberg Press.

Tsing, A. (2015), *The Mushroom at the End of the World: On the Possibility of Life in Capitalist Ruins*, Princeton, NJ: Princeton University Press.

Zeiher, H. (2003), 'Shaping daily life in urban environments', in P. Christensen and M. O'Brien (eds), *Children in the City: Home, Neighbourhood and Community*, 66–81, London: Routledge.

3

Experimental critical qualitative inquiry: Disrupting methodologies, resisting subjects

Travis M. Marn and Jennifer R. Wolgemuth

Introduction

In this chapter we demonstrate how the first author (Travis) drew on new materialist and posthumanist frameworks to conduct a philosophically informed, empirical study of 'black-white' biracial identity. In his study, Travis took up the philosophical frameworks of new materialism and posthumanism (e.g. Fox and Alldred 2015) to critique and evolve thinking about humanist qualitative methods to enable a novel account of 'biracial' identity distinct from previous research. Most qualitative (and quantitative) research on biracialism to date assumes a unified, stable 'biracial' sense of self (e.g. Fryer, et al. 2012) and neglects the important ontological role of research methodologies and methods in the instantiation of biracial identity. Posthumanist and new materialist theories offer important criticisms of this assumption, and, drawing on them, we sought to conceive of a different set of possibilities for this 'identity' in psychological research. To this end, we drew upon agential realism (Barad 2007) to provide a theoretical framework with which to: (1) view biraciality as a multiplicity of identity performances, (2) examine the materiality of both the experiences of participants and the research(er), and (3) account for the ways in which results are entangled with the means by which they were produced.

The purpose of Travis' study was to examine the identity talk and subject/ identity performances of five 'black-white biracial' individuals during semi-structured interviews and through psychological questionnaires. We present this study's methodology, Experimental Critical Qualitative Inquiry (ECQI) (Marn 2018), and the concept of 'purposeful entanglement' (Marn and Wolgemuth 2017) together as an exemplar of empirical posthumanist research.

Through ECQI and purposeful entanglement, we troubled human and non-human, and discourse and material binaries in transformative interview research (Roulston 2010) while still engaging in empirical inquiry; in so doing, we worked to evolve the interview method and qualitative methods more generally. We demonstrate through this chapter that empirical methods and philosophies like poststructuralism, new materialism and posthumanism are not incommensurable, but rather can be used together to facilitate research findings previously not possible. In the following section, we briefly explore the specific posthumanist and new materialist frameworks employed in Travis' study of 'black-white' biracial individuals.

Humanism, posthumanism, agential realism and post-qualitative research

Travis's 'biracial' study and our theorizing of ECQI and purposeful entanglements are grounded in posthumanism and new materialism. Posthumanism is not a unified framework and has been variously termed post-representation (MacLure 2013), new empiricism (Clough 2009), postconstructionism (Lykke 2010), feminist materialism (Rosiek 2013), ontological turn (St. Pierre 2013), among other labels. Authors who write in a similar vein, but predate the naming of these projects (e.g. Mol, Deleuze), have been retrospectively included in these traditions (Taguchi 2012).

The extent to which each of these terms describes the same tradition is uncertain as each of the component projects (e.g. Latour's Actor-Network Theory, Barad's Agential Realism, Bennet's Vibrant Materialism) employ their own methods, theorizations and individual ends. While the theoretical comparability of these projects is still under debate, these orientations all similarly seek to decentre the human subject as the sole agent and promote the role of material in the analyses of the social world (Mazzei 2013). For this chapter, we take up the terms posthumanism and new materialism to describe these current and oncoming theoretical frameworks and to facilitate communication while acknowledging in doing so, we risk suppressing important differences between these projects.

Humanism, historically, began as a boundary-making mechanism to draw a binary distinction between the human, seen as rational, agentive, and capable of self-reflexivity, and the non-human, seen as much less and without the power of agency (Bennett 2010). This distinction implied, and continues to sustain, an existing power relationship in which the human has rights of domination over the non-human. The humanist tradition centralizes agency in the individual and empowers the belief in the human self as an extant and constantly integrating entity with a 'set of static characteristics such as sex, class, race, sexual orientation' (Lather 1991, p. 5). Agency in humanist research is seen as 'an innate characteristic of the essentialist, intentional, free subject that enables him to act on and in the world' (Mazzei 2013, p. 733). This leads to the implication that an individual with agency is 'a voluntary actor making choices that are willed rather than determined' (p. 733).

The hegemonic belief in the human as the sole agent marginalizes the material world in the production of meaning, and beyond this, enacts a false separation of the human from its socio-material world (Barad 2007). In reaction to the imperialism of humanist thought, posthumanist scholars endeavour to contest the seemingly 'self-evident' nature of the human self and the human and non-human binary (Coole and Frost 2010). This enables a redistribution of agency from the human to the material, a movement that forms the foundation of posthumanism. Posthumanism is not synonymous with trans-humanism, where 'human' qualities are extended and amplified – a radical reification of humanism. Posthumanism is a rejection of the universality of human qualities, and is related to anti-humanism (e.g. Braidotti 2013) where the imperial and colonizing forces of humanism are awarded special scrutiny. This shift not only impacts the theoretical frameworks of social science research but also inspires a retheorization of qualitative methods and methodologies (e.g. Jackson and Mazzei 2012; Koro-Ljungberg 2016) under the umbrella term 'post-qualitative inquiry'.

To 'operationalize' posthumanist thinking for the study of biraciality, we drew upon Karen Barad's *agential realism* (Barad 2007), one of the most prominent new materialist frameworks. Barad developed agential realism out of quantum physics and an elaboration of the works of Niels Bohr's experimental physics. Formed partially as a reaction to the domination of language following the linguistic turn (2007), agential realism demotes the power of language as the primary unit of concern and amplifies the effect and impact of the material. In this framework, neither the human nor the non-human (matter) gains primacy in social analyses, but rather, the *intra-active* (2007) entanglements of the material and the discursive give rise to meaning – meaning that is in a constant state of iterative reconfiguration. This brings into question notions of 'matter, discourse, causality, agency, power, identity, embodiment, objectivity, space, and time' (p. 26). These retheorizations led to the conclusion that 'we are part of the nature we seek to understand' (p. 26).

Through Barad's (2007) theorizing, we imagine the research setting as a *phenomenon*, a particular material-discursive configuration, in which the design of the Travis's study served as an *apparatus*, the boundary-making force within a discreet phenomenon. As the phenomenon and apparatus of his study were materially contingent, Travis employed additional matter (e.g. questionnaires) to disrupt and reshape the boundaries of the research phenomenon by enacting a series of *agential cuts*, the material forces of resolution within a phenomenon (2007). As a result, the research setting, data, design, results, researcher and participants' physicality and potentially other elements unknown, entangled in ways to produce various (un)knowable 'biracial' identity performances.

Researchers have long employed traditional qualitative methods such as the interview to examine the 'authentic voices' and 'lived experiences' of their participants – what Lather (2013) called the liberal humanism of 'QUAL 1.0' (p. 634). Posthumanism and new materialist frameworks (e.g. Fox and Alldred 2015) assail these traditional methods and their taken-for-granted belief in an existing, stable, and reflective human self (Jackson and Mazzei 2012).In recent years, however, these theoretical and philosophical challenges to humanism turned back on qualitative inquiry itself and partially deconstructed traditional qualitative methods and methodologies (e.g. Koro-Ljungberg 2016). Scholars took up posthumanism to simultaneously problematize both the outcomes of humanist research and the means by which those outcomes were produced by qualitative methods and methodologies. The resulting post-qualitative inquiry takes up these challenges to ask what comes 'after' for qualitative research as well as to bring the agency of materiality into sharp relief (Lather and St. Pierre 2013).

As a result of the significant challenges raised by a posthumanist account of research epistemologies and ontologies, we sought to explore the possibilities created by combining both posthumanist theorizing and empirical qualitative research in one study. Rather than rejecting one or the other for the sake of research 'purity', we instead drew upon the space (Koro-Ljungberg 2016) opened by post-qualitative inquiry and layered posthumanist theorizing with traditional, humanist empirical qualitative research methods. We employed posthumanism to imagine qualitative inquiry differently – to affect how we design our studies and how we conceive our empirical research. In the following sections, we describe how we practically took the possibilities offered by posthumanism in education research to create the methodology ECQI and the conceptual tool purposeful entanglement.

'Biracial' study rationale

Research on biracialism has typically undertheorized 'biracial' identity and employed humanist assumptions in the study of that identity (Gilbert, D 2005). As posthumanism and new materialism offer strong criticisms of this assumption, we sought to conceive of a different set of possibilities for this 'identity' in psychological research. To this end, we drew upon agential realism (Barad 2007) to understand biraciality as both materially and discursively produced and performed in the conduct of empirical research.

Taking up posthumanism in an empirical study is difficult as these frameworks seek to decentre the human subject (both the researcher and researched). If posthumanism is a rejection of the stable, universal, always-integrating human self, then existing research methods (e.g. traditional qualitative interviews) may not be sufficient for a posthumanist account of subjects. Like Law (2004), we worried that 'standard methods are often extremely good at what they do, they are badly adapted to the study of the ephemeral, the infinite and the irregular' (p. 4). Certainly, posthuman accounts of identities and subjects, the topic of the 'biracial' study, are well described by the words ephemeral, infinite and irregular. Through Barad's agential realism, Travis employed methods to demonstrate how they entangle with their objects of study, repurposing them to focus on the processes of research and its methods on the performance of the 'biracial' identity.

Study outline

This study focused on the performance of the biracial identity in intra-activity with the research process in the study. Travis did not engage in this research assuming methodological purity or enforcing the supposed (in)commensurability of qualitative/quantitative, experimental/interpretivist paradigms, science/not-science. As a result, he was able to employ psychological questionnaires (e.g. Multigroup Ethnic Identity Measure; Phinney 1992), computer programs of implicit bias (Implicit Associations Test; Greenwald, Nosek, and Banaji 2003), cognitive interviewing (Willis 2004), and semi-structured interviewing to pursue a posthumanist analysis of biracial identity that illuminated the mechanisms through which methods reify and can be leveraged to destabilize the human self.

As no previously existing methodology could address the aims of his study, Travis created a novel post-qualitative methodology (Lather and St. Pierre 2013).

Attempting to provide an easy, unproblematic label to the overall design of this study was difficult as labels matter and bring a sense of determinacy to what is porous and messy. However, labels cannot and should not be avoided (Koro-Ljungberg 2016) as they connected Travis's work to the larger conversations of the field of biracialism and (post-)qualitative inquiry. As Travis engaged in semi-structured interviewing, this research could have been called 'qualitative inquiry'. As it employed tests, questionnaires, and interviews solely to provoke/invoke/observe identity performances, this research was *experimental* – not experimental in the postpositivist tradition of the 'gold standard' (e.g. Cartwright 2007), but in the colloquial meaning of a tentative, uncertain procedure (Merriam-Webster n.d) that produces an effect (e.g. focusing on how different questionnaire items produce different performances of biraciality under different interview conditions). As this research focused on power relations and performativity, this work was *critical*. Rather than attempting to ablate this unstable mangle of terms, Travis placed them uncomfortably together in a label under tension: ECQI.

ECQI adopts *informed ambiguity* (Koro-Ljungberg, et al. 2009) as it both provides space for the use of humanist methods without assuming those methods examine the 'lived-experiences' or 'reality' of participants. For example, in ECQI, the results of an identity questionnaire have meaning as they are performative enactment of participants' subjects, but those results cannot be decontextualized or generalized to any context beyond the entangled conditions of that questionnaire moment. Results must be solely interpreted through the intra-activity of the researcher body, participant body, the agency of the questionnaire itself, and other non-human elements of the research process. A score on an identity questionnaire is a performative enactment of the entangled materiality in which it was produced (e.g. in the presence of the researcher body, intra-acting with the agency of the questionnaire items, intra-acting with the material conditions of the interview space). As such, questionnaire results are neither meaningless nor represent transcendent knowledge (e.g. meaning the 'true' strength of a participant's identity). Instead, questionnaires become another way to examine the performance (process) of participants' subjects.

Humanist methods are thus repurposed in ECQI and enables an empirical account of a posthumanist conception of subjectivity/identity without sacrificing posthumanist assumptions. What is left of method in ECQI is the capacity to provoke identity performativity and facilitate identity talk during the research process. Drawing from the ECQI methodology, Travis created the following research questions:

1. How does the researcher, researched and interview intra-activity serve to instantiate the biracial subject?
2. Under what material alterations to the interview process do different subjects come to be?
3. Which subjects come to be or fail to come to be in the interview intra-action?
4. How does purposeful entanglement function during the interview process?

Five 'black-white biracial' individuals (under the pseudonyms Callie, Tony, Juliet, Michelle, and Anouk) were recruited for Travis's study.

Study methods

Travis's study employed three methods: interviewing, psychological questionnaires and the Implicit Associations Test. As the ECQI study was designed to examine biracial performativity during the research process, Travis employed a semi-structured interview format, a method familiar both to researchers and to participants. This familiarity enabled Travis to make material alterations to those interviews (e.g. by including psychological questionnaires) to provoke identities/subject performativity (black, white, biracial and others). This included drawing upon Travis's 'biracial' physicality (e.g. curly brown hair, tan skin-colour) as part of the interview apparatus. To provide space for those various subject performances, Travis employed a sequence of three interviews, each designed to prompt participants' identity performativity through different material alterations.

As the study explored sensitive issues (e.g. race, potential sources of conflict, childhood memories), the need to maintain the trust, rapport and confidence of participants was paramount. Therefore, for the initial interview, Travis employed Roulston's (2010) concept of *romantic* interviewing. The romantic interviewer seeks to 'generate the kind of conversation that is intimate and self-revealing' (2010, p. 217). This romantic style served the dual purpose of both establishing/maintaining rapport and prompting participants to perform subjects typical of a humanist, interpretivist interview.

The second interview employed what Roulston (2010) termed the 'postmodern' interview. This interview style differed from the romantic interview through a focus on the multiple meanings and the non-unitary selves (performativity) of interviewer and participants. The postmodern interview centralizes the 'belief that data collected is always partial, arbitrary, and situated, rather than unitary, final, and holistic' and serves to 'attempt to open up spaces for new ways of thinking, being, and doing' (2010, p. 220). Whereas the romantic interviewer was materially more passive and affirmative, the postmodern interviewer offered critical engagement with the participant and pushed back against the narratives provided by the participant. This more active interviewer included bringing the performativity of the biracial identity into the explicit awareness of participants.

For the third interview, Travis engaged in the process of *purposeful entanglement* (Marn and Wolgemuth 2017). *Purposeful entanglement* is a new materialist/posthumanist reinterpretation of what Roulston (2010) conceived of as transformative interviewing (e.g. Wolgemuth and Donohue 2006). This interview style was concerned with the responsibility of the researcher to be aware of the non-linear inculcation of their selves into the participant's entanglements – the researcher, being partially responsible for the subjects they render possible, impossible and differently possible, must centralize their ethical responsibility to the other. Purposeful entanglement was both the ethical aim of the overall study (to reveal the ways in which research 'findings' are entangled with methods) and the ethic that guided Travis's intra-actions with his 'biracial' participants. In this way, Travis sought to foster, within and across the interviews, opportunities for *critical resistance* (Hoy 2005) to categorization – to render the interview as a space in which all parties to the interview intra-actions might perform less entrenched social (biracial) identities (Wolgemuth 2014).

In addition to the overall structure of the interviews described earlier, Travis employed psychological questionnaires (MEIM; Multiracial Experiences Measure; Yoo, et al. 2016), computer programs of implicit bias (IAT), and cognitive interviewing (Willis 2004). Participants completed the IAT and identity questionnaires at the beginning of each interview, and Travis conducted a cognitive interview of their answers immediately after they complete the questionnaires. Throughout the interviews, as needed, Travis revisited participants' answers to the identity questionnaire and resulting cognitive interview when discrepancies arose in their identity talk or when elaboration was needed. For example, when a participant noted that races were 'not real', Travis would ask why they did not select the answers on the MEIM that most closely reflected that belief, regardless of which interview the participant completed that questionnaire. The resulting conversations with participants provided a window into the shifting process of subjectification as participants drew on their performative identities to defend, contradict or otherwise elaborate on their previous answers. In this way, Travis did not use these tools only once as a material alteration, but rather he employed these materials through the interviews (summarized in Table 3.1) as agential cuts to reshape (Barad 2007) the interview phenomenon and apparatus in the research process. That is, these material alterations changed the interview apparatus (Barad 2007) and in so doing, reshaped the research outcomes accordingly.

Travis sought to provoke a variety of identity performances through the design of the study, but what was recorded, transcribed and analysed was not the identity performances of participants, but rather linguistic enactments captured by the recording device, which has an agency of its own (Nordstrom 2015). This brought a variety of questions to the forefront. What escaped being recorded? What comprises a performative moment beyond identity talk (e.g. gestures, stylizations of the body, pauses, other behaviours/actions/thoughts not accessible by the researcher)? Where do identity performances start and stop?

Table 3.1 Study Design

Interview Number	Interview Style	Order of Material Alterations/Agential Cuts		Sample Interview Questions
1	Romantic	a)	Demographics Questionnaire	How much of your ethnic identity has been shaped by your family? Have you ever attempted to hide your mixed heritage?
		b)	Multigroup Ethnic Identity Measure	
		c)	Implicit Associations Test	
		d)	Cognitive Interviewing.	
2	Postmodern	a)	Implicit Associations Test (2nd trial)	Did the interview make you think about your racial identity after you left? Thinking back to past conversations you have had about race, how were they different from how we talked about it?
		b)	Multiracial Experiences Measure	
		c)	Cognitive Interviewing	
		d)	All previous interview material	
3	Purposeful entanglement	a)	Implicit Associations Test (3rd trial)	How did the interview make you rethink your racial identity? Why do you feel the need to identify with any racial group?
		b)	All previous interview material	

Do they start and stop? What materiality in the interview process that was not 'controlled' by the research had effects on participants' identity performativity? To what extent can the researcher directly control materiality? Does material during the interview process interact in ways not immediately obvious to researcher?

Despite these questions, Travis relied on a discursive analysis of interview transcriptions to view identity performances. For some performances, participants explicitly positioned themselves as part of a particular racial group. For other subject performances, participants distanced themselves from other groups by drawing on racialized discourses or stereotypes. Identity performances were not always clear with some instances of performativity seemingly not drawing upon explicit positioning or racialized discourses. For example, when asked about her racial identity, Juliet stated: 'I have a very limited racial identity. I am mostly just curious about my identities, but when it comes to picking one, I don't really have a preference for any of them; whichever one is easiest in the moment.' It is not clear what subject is being performed here as she seemed to express a mercenary attitude towards the act of explicit racial identifying. As such, what is presented in this chapter should not be thought of an exact accounting of identity performativity, but rather, these results should be viewed as a way reimagining identity through the tentative, uncertain posthumanist and post-qualitative frameworks.

Sample study results and discussion

The materiality of the questionnaires, the IAT, changing interview styles, and the intra-acting 'biracial' bodies of Travis and the participants seemed to render certain identity performances possible and others impossible. As Travis has the typical 'biracial' physicality (e.g. curly hair, light brown skin), his participants positioned him as 'biracial' as they believed themselves to be. This resulted in two 'biracial' individuals speaking and likely prompted participants to perform a 'biracial' identity in intra-active response. Travis could not remove his biracial body from the study and relied upon other interview materials to prompt other identity performances. As a result, any analysis of this study must include the intra-active effects of Travis's 'biracial' body on the results.

For example, one participant, Callie (a pseudonym), explicitly identified herself as 'biracial' during the interviews and when filling out questionnaires. When asked to elaborate on her questionnaire responses, she stated that she 'automatically' identifies as 'biracial' on all forms and when directly asked but thinks of herself as 'white'. Even as she thought of herself as 'white', this subject was rarely performed during the interviews in favour of her much more frequently performed 'biracial' subject. That is, rather than explicitly identifying as 'white', drawing on 'white' identity to distance herself from other racial groups, or otherwise positioning herself as white, Callie drew upon 'biracial' language during her identity talk. The materiality of the interview study itself may have thwarted her 'white' subject performance; Callie only intra-acted with 'biracial' questionnaires and Travis's 'biracial' body and these raced materials may have rendered her 'white' subject nearly impossible to perform. Callie seemed only able to perform a 'white' identity when she was not being examined or 'raced' by others. Travis and Callie had the following dialogue:

> Travis: If you had to just write down what race you consider yourself to be, what would you write down?
>
> Callie: Realistically it's white, but I always write down biracial.
>
> Travis: Do you feel like you must write down biracial?
>
> Callie: Yeah.
>
> Travis: Where does that feeling come from?
>
> Callie: I don't know. It's kind of always been, but you fill out the boxes when you take a test, and there's the 'other' [selection option] and I'm just 'so, I'm black and white and it's always just been my identity', just been biracial.
>
> Travis: Do you think I would have believed you if you're just written down white?
>
> Callie: I feel like if I write down white and someone sees me they'll think 'oh, why did she write down white'. You know what I'm saying? I don't want that kind of feeling either 'why the hell she write down white when she's not white'.

It is possible that in participating in a study on 'biracial' individuals, Callie may not have had access to a wider range of potential subjects, and as such, any study of her identity necessary would impact that identity and subsequent results of the study.

Like Callie, other participants performed a variety of raced subjects (e.g. black, white, biracial) and shifted between them as the material conditions of the interview changed (e.g. taking the IAT, change in interview style). For example, Tony frequently distanced himself from the concept of race in his identity talk (a type of 'human-race' performance), but when his IAT results in the first interview indicated a preference for 'black' faces as compared to 'white' faces, Tony began performing a 'black' subject by explicitly positioning himself as 'black' in stating that he 'claim[ed] black' as his primary racial identity when responding to his IAT score – the materiality of the IAT seemed to call his 'black' subject into being leading to him speaking of himself as 'black'. In the final interview, Tony's IAT score switched sides indicating a preference for white as compared to black, and for the first and only time during the study, Tony began to perform a 'white' identity by explicitly positioning himself as 'white'. This 'white' performativity was especially surprising as Tony directly stated earlier in the interviews that he would never identify as white. Tony seemed to resist typical raced performances, and seemed consciously aware that he was doing so, but when he intra-acted with the interview materials, his performances shifted and seemed to embrace racial classification.

Some participants rapidly shifted between raced subjects such as Juliet who stated that she drew upon multiple identities while taking a single questionnaire. During the cognitive interview of her responses to the questionnaire on racial identity, she stated that for some items she answered thinking of herself as 'white' whereas for other items she thought of her as 'biracial' or 'black' when responding – a surprising result for a questionnaire on racial identity strength. This was in sharp contrast to Callie who only performed her 'biracial' subject when answering the questionnaire. These results raise many questions. It is not clear why the questionnaire provoked multiple performances for some participants and only single identity performances from others. Is it possible that all participants performed multiple identities when taking the questionnaire but were not constantly aware of it or chose not to speak about it in the interviews? What intra-active effects did Travis's 'biracial' body have on participants as they completed the questionnaire? Did participants mobilize subjects beyond the typical raced subjects (e.g. black, white, biracial) to answer the questions? These questions, and many others, point to the complexity of not just the 'biracial' identity but to the intra-active agency of the research process itself.

The possibilities of ECQI and posthumanism research

As posthumanism, new materialism and poststructuralism each problematize notions of success and failure, it is not possible to fully appraise this ECQI study in such terms. However, we expect Travis's study met its goals of provoking certain identity performances through material alterations, in keeping with the agential realist framework, while examining those performances through the entangled researched/researcher inquiry process. This ECQI study demonstrated that it is likely not possible for researchers to know in advance what effects interview materials will have on identity performances or which performances will be rendered possible or impossible in studies. It is similarly unclear, or perhaps unknowable, the full extent of the intra-action of materiality of the research process. The material configuration of the research process itself was imbricated in the results of this research, and these results can only then be interpreted through an analysis that includes the intra-acting and entangled materiality of the interviews. If these 'identities' are diaphanous and ephemeral, new questions can be asked not only of biracial identity but of identity research in general. What other (research and non-research) materials are entangled in the performance of identity? Neither humanist qualitative methods, the questionnaires alone, nor pure philosophical engagement are capable of examining the inextricable intra-active nature of the 'biracial' identity and the research process. And research intra-actions extend beyond the artificial boundaries of research itself. Unless the participants discussed them in the interview spaces, Travis had no way of knowing what other intra-actions in the participants' worlds co-constituted their identity performances. What are the wider ways materiality is implicated in identity performance, and what research methodologies might be newly envisioned to research (elicit) them?

Humanist accounts of identity remain mired in dualistic thinking (e.g. black/white; biracial/monoracial, research/researched) and as such, these accounts, no matter how creative, are unable to account for the agency of materiality in identity performativity. ECQI enabled an examination of the process of identification and provided space for new, unpredictable results to occur (e.g. Juliet's rapid shifting of identity performances). In addition, ECQI and posthumanism allow researchers to examine how material alterations affect identity performances and how the research process itself is entangled with the results of that research. Rather than reducing identity down to answers on a questionnaire or interviews that reveal 'lived-experiences', ECQI enables researchers to conserve the messy, unstable, nature of identities and in this way, better understand the complexity of identity performances in social (research) spaces.

The post-qualitative methodology ECQI altered the assumptions underlining methods like interviewing and questionnaires. Whereas humanist methodologies look to methods for their 'data' and 'results', ECQI employs methods for their material alterations to the research process – a turn away from products to process. In EQCI, answers to questionnaires are not revealing of the inner beliefs of participants, but rather, participants, in answering the questionnaires, are performing their identities in real-time during the research. Through the premediated material alterations of the interview, a variety of materially contingent identity/subject performances become possible. ECQI, as a purposefully porous, messy methodology, allows researchers to draw on whatever methods are needed to provoke identify performances without regard to their supposed incommensurability. In this way, humanist methods and posthumanist philosophy can be employed to simultaneously imagine and examine identity differently and through that difference suggest a way forward for identity research after the ontological turn.

Posthumanism resists finality and evades simplicity. Despite the challenges of conducting ECQI or other configurations of philosophically informed empirical research, posthumanism opens inquiry to new possibilities, new areas of research, ethical principles beyond minimal risk, and repurposing familiar methods to open possibilities not previously conceivable. The cost of these new possibilities is, as always, the continuing loss of certainty in research – that 'results' in inquiry are and will always be tentative, partial and performative. We believe the risk of discomfort in ambiguity is well worth the knowledge gained when researchers creatively experiment with layering seemingly incompatible methods, methodologies and philosophies.

Glossary

Critical resistance A type of resistance that seeks to emancipate individuals from oppressive power relations and the need to be identifiable.

Humanism An Enlightenment boundary-making concept that centralizes agency solely in humans. With humanism comes the possibility of dehumanization.

New materialism A theoretical field that questions the privileging of discourse in postmodern and poststructural theorizing at the expense of material and bodily realities. New materialism entangles materiality and discourse in an account of ethics, reality, and knowledge (onto-ethico-epistemology) that respects the agency of the non-human.

Performativity The discursively generated acts and practices of particular identities and subjects; the social 'doing' of an identity.

Posthumanism Holds matter to be mutually articulated with humans and language. Seeks to disrupt the human and non-human binary.

Post-qualitative inquiry A methodology that deconstructs traditional, conventional qualitative methods (e.g. coding). It is without strict boundaries and conventions. Holds that the results of inquiry are always partial and situated.

References

Barad, K. (2007), *Meeting the Universe Halfway: Quantum Physics and the Entanglement of Matter and Meaning*, London: Duke University Press.

Bennett, J. (2010), *Vibrant Matter: A Political Ecology of Things*, Durham, NC: Duke University Press.

Braidotti, R. (2013), *The Posthuman*, Cambridge: Polity Press.

Cartwright, N. (2007), 'Are RCTs the gold standard?' *BioSocieties*, 2: 11–20.

Clough, P. T. (2009), 'The new empiricism: Affect and sociological method', *European Journal of Social Theory*, 12: 43–61.

Coole, D., and Frost, S. (2010), *New Materialisms: Ontology, Agency, and Politics*, Durham, NC: Duke University Press Books.

Fox, N. J. and Alldred, P. (2015), 'New materialist social inquiry: Designs, methods and the research-assemblage', *International Journal of Social Research Methodology*, 18: 399–414.

Fryer, J. G., Kahn, L., Levitt, S. D. and Spenkuch, J. L. (2012), 'The plight of the mixed-race adolescents', *Review of Economics & Statistics*, 94: 399–414.

Gilbert, D. (2005), 'Interrogating mixed-race: A crisis of ambiguity?', *Social Identities*, 11: 55–74.

Greenwald, A. G., Nosek, B. A. and Banaji, M. R. (2003), 'Understanding and using the implicit association test: I. An improved scoring algorithm', *Journal of Personality and Social Psychology*, 85: 197–216.

Hoy, D.C. (2005), *Critical Resistance: From Poststructuralism to Post-Critique*, Cambridge, MA: MIT Press.

Jackson, A. Y. and Mazzei, L. A. (2012), *Thinking with Theory in Qualitative Research: Viewing Data across Multiple Perspectives*, London: Routledge.

Koro-Ljungberg, M. (2016), *Reconceptualizing Qualitative Research: Methodologies Without Methodology*, Los Angeles, CA: SAGE.

Koro-Ljungberg, M., Yendol-Hoppy, D., Smith, J. J. and Hayes, S. B. (2009), '(E)pistemological awareness, instantiation of methods, and uninformed methodological ambiguity in qualitative research projects', *Educational Researcher*, 38: 687–99.

Lather, P. (1991), *Getting Smart: Feminist Research and Pedagogy within/in the Postmodern*, London: Routledge.

Lather, P. (2013), 'Methodology-21: What do we do in the afterward?', *International Journal of Qualitative Studies in Education*, 26: 634–45.

Lather, P. and St. Pierre, E. (2013), 'Post-qualitative research', *International Journal of Qualitative Studies in Education*, 26: 629–33.

Law, J. (2004), *After Method: Mess in Social Science Research*, London: Routledge.

Lykke, N. (2010), *Feminist Studies: A Guide to Intersectional Theory, Methodology and Writing*. Abingdon: Routledge.

MacLure, M. (2013), 'Researching without representation? Language and materiality in post-qualitative methodology', *International Journal of Qualitative Studies in Education*, 26: 658–67.

Marn, T. (2018), 'Performing the black-white biracial identity: The material, discursive, and psychological components of subject formation', Ph.D. University of South Florida.

Marn, T. and Wolgemuth, J. R. (2017), 'Purposeful entanglements: A new materialist analysis of transformative interviews', *Qualitative Inquiry*, 23: 365–74.

Mazzei, L. A. (2013), 'A voice without organs: Interviewing in posthumanist research', *International Journal of Qualitative Studies in Education*, 26: 732–40.

Merriam-Webster (n.d.), 'Experiment', viewed 10 December 2018, https://www.merriam-webster.com/dictionary/experiment.

Nordstrom, S. (2015), 'Not so innocent anymore: Making recording devices matter in qualitative interviews', *Qualitative Inquiry*, 21: 388–401.

Phinney, J. S. (1992), 'The multigroup ethnic identity measure a new scale for use with diverse groups', *Journal of Adolescent Research*, 7: 156–76.

Rosiek, J. L. (2013), 'Pragmatism and post-qualitative futures', *International Journal of Qualitative Studies in Education*, 26: 692–705.

Roulston, K. (2010), 'Considering quality in qualitative interviewing', *Qualitative Research*, 10: 199–228.

St. Pierre, E. A. (2013), 'The posts continue: Becoming', *International Journal of Qualitative Studies in Education*, 26: 646–57.

Taguchi, H. L. (2012), 'A diffractive and Deleuzian approach to analysing interview data', *Feminist Theory*, 13: 265–81.

Willis, G. B. (2004), *Cognitive Interviewing: A Tool for Improving Questionnaire Design: A Tool for Improving Questionnaire Design*. Thousand Oaks, CA: Sage Publications.

Wolgemuth, J. R. (2014), 'Analyzing for critical resistance in narrative research', *Qualitative Research*, 14: 586–602.

Wolgemuth, J. R. and Donohue, R. (2006), 'Toward an inquiry of discomfort: Guiding transformation in emancipatory narrative research', *Qualitative Inquiry*, 12: 1012–21.

Yoo, H. C., Jackson, K. F., Guevarra, R. P., Jr, Miller, M. J. and Harrington, B. (2016), 'Construction and initial validation of the multiracial experiences measure (MEM)', *Journal of Counseling Psychology*, 63: 198–209.

4

Troubling binaries: Gendering research in environmental education

Catherine Hart and Annette Gough

Introduction

The Future We Want, the outcomes document adopted at the Rio + 20 United Nations Conference on Sustainable Development (2012) reaffirmed the need for 'promotion of social equity, and protection of the environment, while enhancing gender equality and women's empowerment, and equal opportunities for all, and the protection, survival and development of children to their full potential, including through education' (Paragraph 11). These outcomes have been recognized, or at least acknowledged, or even updated since the 1992 United Nations Conference on Environment and Development. More recently, the Sustainable Development Goals of the 2030 Agenda for Sustainable Development (United Nations 2016) include Goal 5: 'Achieve gender equality and empower all women and girls'. Yet women, along with other marginalized groups such as those including persons who are poor, racialized, Indigenous, queer, differently abled and fat, have been overlooked in much environmental education practice, theory and research. Often those who occupy these subjectivities/positionings are subsumed under the notion of 'universalized people', or the 'norm' and the complexities of being in the world are lost or overlooked. Those who often find themselves 'othered' or marginalized have a distinctive contribution to make to environmental education as a form of anti-oppressive resistance. All needs must be foregrounded if humans, other more-than-human beings and the land are to flourish.

Applying feminist theory and research methods in many areas of education research is not new. Despite their obvious relevance, within the field of environmental education and environmental education research issues of unproblematized gendered and feminist and approaches have been rare (Gough 1999a, b, 2013). However, when they have been applied, there has been an enabled recognition of the absence of women from the discussions that frame the field and of the impact of environmental crisis, such as climate change, on the lives of women. This is particularly the case for women who are marginalized through their lack of education, poverty and powerlessness and constructed as victims of environmental degradation (Foster 2011).

Ecofeminist analysis 'emerged from the intersections of feminist research and the various movements for social justice and environmental health, explorations that uncovered the linked oppressions of gender, ecology, race, species, and nation' (Gaard 2011, p. 28). It is closely related to new materialist theory and can be employed as a strategy for disrupting normalized practices in environmental education. The term *ecofeminisme* was coined by Francoise d'Eaubonne in her book, *Le feminisme ou la mort* (1974). It was intended 'to represent women's potential for bringing about an ecological revolution to ensure human survival on the planet. Such an ecological revolution would entail new gender relations between women and men and between humans and nature' (Merchant 1990, p. 100). The focus of ecofeminism is on how, what Marti Kheel (2008) calls 'a culturally exalted hegemonic ideal' (p. 3), masculinity 'is promoted through a set of interrelated dualisms such as mind/body, reason/nature, masculine/feminine or human/nature' (Phillips 2016, p. 59). Ecofeminism challenges this dualistic thinking to alleviate the separation and promote a (re)connection with nature (Phillips 2016). Further, ecofeminism challenges the subordination of nature that seemingly has become intimately embedded with discourses that also promote the dominance of colonialism, racism and sexism (Phillips 2016).

The concept of 'agency' is also important in ecofeminism. For example, Alaimo (1994) argued for an environmental feminism that stressed a political alliance between women and nature and one that would not slide into essentialism. She argued that

> focusing on the agency of women and nature can help keep environmentalism in the political arena and can oppose the appropriation of nature as resource by stressing nature as an actor and by breaking down the nature/culture divide, thus undermining the systems of domination. (p. 150)

Ecofeminism suffered from a feminist backlash in the late 1990s, being criticized as essentialist, elitist and ethnocentrist, 'and effectively discarded' (Gaard 2011, p. 26). However, in recent times, studies at the intersection of feminism and environmentalism have seen a resurgence of the label ecofeminism (see, for example, Gaard 2011, 2015; Phillips and Rumens 2016a, b; Thompson 2006), as distinct from other labels such as 'ecological feminism' (Warren 1994; Warren and Cheney 1991), 'feminist environmentalism' (Seager 1993) or 'global feminist environmental justice' (Sturgeon 2009).

Gaard (2011) notes that materialist accounts of the woman-nature connection – such as those of Merchant (1992, p. 196) for whom 'nature is an active subject, not a passive object to be dominated, and humans must develop sustainable relationships with it' – 'described a socially constructed association among women (sex), femininity (gender), and nature that was contextual and fluid, not ahistorical and static'. Gaard (2011, p. 31) then argues that what is needed now, to address current environmental issues, is an intersectional ecological-feminist approach that 'frames these issues in such a way that people can recognize common cause across the boundaries of race, class, gender, sexuality, species, age, ability, nation – and affords a basis for engaged theory, education, and activism' (Gaard 2011, p. 44). Both ecofeminism and new material feminisms shift the emphasis from humans at the centre and 'propose that all manner of bodies, objects and things have agency within a confederation of meaning-making' (Taylor in press). That the binary between humans and nature need to be dissolved is a common theme across much new materialist and ecofeminist writings. As Merchant (2016) argues,

> Nature becomes postnature in ways that so thoroughly blur any human/nature differences as to make a single interactive, mutually influential, and mutually interdependent post-human-nature ... a new relationship between humanity and nature based on the idea of autonomous nature. (p. 161)

Like Barad (2007) and other new materialists, Merchant (2016) also refers to a posthuman world, and a different way of conceptualizing nature, where 'the creating force that brought about the world civilized by humans – becomes the chaotic, uncontrollable force that dismantles it' (p. 156). From this position, Merchant (2016) argues that a new paradigm requires new conceptualizations of concepts like nature. Working from a material feminism perspective, Alaimo (2010) describes the concept of 'environment' as being inseparable from ourselves and is part of our very being, rather than being an entity somewhere 'out there'. Alaimo and Hekman (2008) point out that nature 'is an active, signifying force; an agent in its own terms; a realm of multiple, inter- and intra-active cultures' (p. 12). These new perceptions of nature, 'a nature that is, expressly not the mirror image of culture – is emerging from the overlapping fields of material feminism, environmental feminism, environmental philosophy, and green cultural studies' (p. 12).

In the light of such assertions, this chapter engages such conceptually complex possibilities with a view to disrupting hegemonic practices with respect to subjectivity and agency in environmental education research. We discuss approaches to engaging the concept of subjectivity, consciously framed considering appropriate onto-epistemic groundings, that reflect new methodological and analytic approaches to gendered environmental research. These approaches contribute to ideas about problematizing simplistic approaches to qualitative research and the intersection and interweaving of the concepts of gender with environmental subjectivity and agency rather than the more positivist approaches that have been engaged in the past.

Using feminist theories and research methods in environmental education has enabled the generation of new questions and created possibilities for conceiving of and researching subjectivity, agency and identity. For example, Sandra Harding argues for a strong objectivity which 'requires that the subject of knowledge be placed on the same critical, causal plane as the objects of knowledge' (1998, p. 69), which creates opportunities for generating new questions. Engaging feminist poststructuralist and new feminist materialist theories critically presents possibilities for the ways in which concepts like subjectivity are framed. Such conceptualizations open opportunities to (re)consider approaches to issues of gender in environmental education research in credible and legitimate ways. We propose a challenge to methodological simplicity in gendered research that questions beliefs about the nature of reality and knowledge and assumptions about ontologies and epistemologies (McCoy 2012). Further we suggest a need to problematize normative approaches to research that produce knowledge devoid of contextual consideration and critical reflection (Koro-Ljungberg and Mazzei 2012).

Doing gendered environmental education research

So, how does one go about engaging in consciously gendered environmental education research? Historically speaking, there are examples of approaches to gendered environmental education research that, for a variety of reasons, have been more or less effective in responding to questions of gender. However, in spite of some clearly articulated research and thoughtful suggestions, there remains a 'gap' and seeming marginalization of issues of gender in both educational and environmental education research. Because the concept of gender itself is complex it is impossible to arrive at one particular answer for *how* to conduct gendered environmental education research. Instead, we argue that researchers must consider their interest and research question in order to develop a framework that demonstrates thoughtful consideration theoretically and methodologically so that the research is not dismissed due to concern of poor quality or legitimacy (McCoy 2012; St. Pierre 2013). Therefore, rather than be prescriptive, in the following section we provide examples of theoretical concepts recently taken up in an environmental education context. While not inherently or exclusive to inquiries related to gender nor specifically to environment, the examples offer openings that can be used to explore individuals' assemblages, including those related to both gender and environment (Taylor and Ivinson 2013). What is presented is not intended as formulaic for how to engage in gendered and feminist environmental education research at theoretical, methodological or methods levels. Rather we hope to provide examples of potential approaches that could be useful in a variety of environmental education research contexts as researchers feel are appropriate to their interests.

With theoretical and methodological levels of organizing foundations for research being continually (re)conceptualized, and new and returning concepts being presented, the possibilities for innovative approaches to research and new kinds of research questions are emerging within different fields of qualitative inquiry (Hart and Hart 2018). It is essential to move beyond the unproblematized use of research examining 'boys' and 'girls' 'environmental behaviours' and embrace the complexity of the concepts so that research can be done differently. It seems to us that possibilities are being explored that employ onto-epistemic framings that would be particularly helpful within the field of environmental education to problematize overly simplistic approaches to gendered environmental education research. However, implicated in any changes, and arguably advances, in approaches to qualitative research, researchers must, once again, consider what can count as evidence, as knowledge and as research itself. We are encouraged by trends within social and educational research that have, in some ways, turned towards posthuman and new materialist projects that support inquiries into issues of environment and gendered subjectivities (e.g. Brown 2017; Gough 2015; Hughes and Lury 2013; Willox 2012).

Framing and grounding research using concepts arguably provides opportunities for researchers to think differently not only about how research is conceptualized but also about the actual 'methods', or eschewing of methods, (anti-)analysis and (non-)representation which provide possibilities for how one can make sense of research. Jackson and Mazzei (2013) suggest use of concepts to read 'data' and illustrate the ways in which sense can be made by the researcher and readers based on the lens through which data is viewed. Not only must the ways in which research is conducted be problematized but also the ways in which sense is made and the acknowledgement of what can be said should be clearly and critically reflected upon.

One concept we believe to be key in a disruption of methodologies with respect to environment and gender is that of *subjectivity*. There are examples of environmental education research that consider gendered subjectivities, but the concept of gender has, in many cases in the past, been taken up unproblematically along with the concept of environmental subjectivity (see special issues of *The Journal of Environmental Education* on gendered environmental education research, 2017, 2018). Mostly, gender has been considered a simple binary (female vs. male) where one category is placed in opposition of the other (Gough and Whitehouse 2003). Further, given this classification, gender has been taken up as one of several variables that are engaged with respect to factors affecting environmental education programmes and individual environmental attitudes and behaviours. More conceptually complex engagements of the concept of gender using theoretical concepts such as subjectivity, becoming, and affect can challenge hegemonic norms and provide new conceptual and analytic tools when addressing questions of gender in environmental education research (Bazzul and Santavicca 2017; Gough and Gough 2003) (Gough and Whitehouse 2018; Hart 2017b; Russell 2013).

Environmental subjectivities: an embodied example

One example of an approach to research that sought to disrupt notions of how researchers might attempt to uncover and present aspects of who individuals are and how they come to position themselves as such is a recent doctoral dissertation about environmental subjectivities and processes of becoming (Hart 2017a). This dissertation attempted to open up discussion on implications of both theory and praxis that implicate (i.e. open and close) possibilities for emergent methodological perspectives and pedagogical applications. Here Hart took on challenges on two levels: first by exploring environmental worldviews using theoretical concepts which, until her work, had not been applied within environmental education research contexts, and second by challenging traditional approaches to the ways in which participants are positioned within research and the ways in which 'data' is presented, rather than analysed, whereby readers take responsibility for making their own sense about their environmental subjectivities as a result of their readings of participant narratives. Considering both of these goals, rather than retelling the story, we present a reflection on both the dissertation research itself and a critical reflection of the process and how, both during and after, the author has/continues to work within, against and beyond (Hart and Hart 2015). So while engaging with Hart's research, we will show, in parallel to the original research, how there is a reflection on both the process and product.

Hart (2017a) used the concept of *subjectivity* to pursue questions of environmental subjectivity and environmental discourses. Creating a theoretical framework using elements from poststructural and critical theoretical perspectives, the author assembled a collection of concepts through which she could pursue her research questions. Poststructuralist ideas present an attempt to examine fundamental assumptions of society. Authors such as Baudrillard, Barthes, Derrida, Foucault, Irigaray, Kristeva, Lacan and Lyotard have all been pivotal in developing *post* perspectives (McKenzie 2004). Concepts that contribute to poststructuralism come from a collection of theoretical positionings influenced by Althusser's theory of ideology, Lacan's reworkings of psychoanalysis, feminism, the new French feminists (Kristeva, Cixous, Irigaray), the work of Derrida, Barthes and Foucault (Gavey 1997) and more recently Lather (2007), Hekman (2008), St. Pierre (2013), and Davies (2013). Concurrently, and aligning with the aims of environmental education, critical perspectives drive a direction to the change that is of interest. Further, critical environmental education debates *what* is regarded as being important for future generations and should be carried out using approaches which can address their value-driven and socially constructed nature, and must be ongoing to accommodate their ever-changing nature (Stevenson 2007). Although not specifically attempting to directly address issues of gender, the framing presented opportunities for aspects of subjectivity in conjunction with environmental subjectivity (including gender) to be engaged should participants choose to identify it as critical to their being and becoming.

As one of the earlier components to be structured in a doctoral study, the theoretical framing of the dissertation is perhaps the section that might be most reconsidered were the study to be done again. While Hart does not argue that the fundamental theoretical framing might change, the nuances, advances and evolution of post-informed theoretical perspectives could support the application of additional concepts that could be described to help make meaning of the complexity of the overarching concept of subjectivity with respect to environment and gender. In particular, concepts from new material feminisms could deepen the reading of participant contributions (see for example, Grosz 2010; Hird 2009; Lenz Taguchi 2013) as well as examples of more recent connections being made directly to ecology and environment (see Brown 2017; Hughes and Lury 2013). While Weedon's (1987) description of subjectivity as being multiple and in an ongoing process of subjectification was taken up by Hart in her thesis, these ideas have more recently been expanded on to suggest the concept of schizoid subjectivities as deepening the complexity of understanding individual processes of being, continual becoming and overlapping with processes of de- and re-territorialization (Renold and Ringrose 2011). Likewise, critical consideration of the material, human and more-than-other-than-human while not throwing out post-critical theory does build on and expand the notion from that which is more language-focused to bodies entangled in their material surroundings. However, the concepts used, as informed by the theoretical perspectives highlighted do illustrate the ways in which more complex and nuanced illustrations and understandings of the complexity of humans evolving being in the world can be considered.

Hart's (2017a) work makes use of narrative methodologies and the concept of assemblage to illustrate the contributions of participants in the study. *Assemblage*, as a way of representing research, is described as 'a sort of anti-structural concept that permits the researcher to speak of emergence, heterogeneity, the decentered and the ephemeral in nonetheless ordered social life' (Marcus and Saka 2006, p. 101). Assemblage also, Hart argues, shows a closer connection to the theoretical framework she has assembled than other concepts used to represent participants. Likewise, in engaging *with* participants, she uses post-critically informed interview methods whereby conversations have topic 'areas' but no formal questions. Using rich narratives that are co-constructed with participants provides readers/listeners with the opportunity to witness an iterative and reflective process.

While Hart (2017a) made use of *assemblage* as an appropriate concept to be utilized within narrative methodologies, there are growing arguments to challenge the self-evident nature of research methodologies and calls for anti-methodology research (Jackson 2017). Interviewing is much more complex, particularly depending on the onto-epistemological considerations taken up theoretically and methodologically and continues to evolve as a means of engaging with participants in research. Roulston (2010) illustrates some differences in interview methods dependent on the theoretical considerations of the research and question and problematizes the sometimes overly simplistic and assumption-filled notion of more traditional interview methods. Jackson (2017) illustrates an approach to research without method, providing possibilities for emergent interactions and new possibilities for engagement with participants in research. In contexts where there is increasing acknowledgement of the need for individuals and voices to be heard, the potential for rethinking 'methods' and an opening to more disruption of research and established 'norms' of thinking and being demands a critical reflection on research choices made.

Hart (2017a) engaged, and frequently questioned throughout her doctoral process, the data from the co-constructed narratives in such a way that interpretation and analysis was left up to the reader. She rejected a static, hierarchical logic of representation and practices conventionally accepted as a technique of data analysis (MacLure 2013). Challenges were encountered as she, as Kuntz (2010) describes, attended to both the alignment with her theoretical framework and the determination to render cohesive participant narratives. Participants reading of the conversations and re-engagement with the narratives was essential to capturing, as fully as possible, the intentions and meanings each individual wanted to share. There were discourses of environmental education that became evident in reading the narratives but, and in keeping with the theoretical framing, the goal was not to distil and code to 'reveal' discourses. Although the valuing of differences in subjectivities and subjectification processes was at the forefront, the positioning of participants and similarities in world view meant that particular interests were expressed, in a variety of ways from several participants. For example, the clarification of the concept of environment was of particular interest and often a starting point for conversations as it would lay the groundwork for further discussion. It was not *what* discourses exist but rather *that* discourses exist among participants. This is, perhaps, the aspect of the dissertation that the author was most pleased with even if it did meet with resistance from her supervisory committee. She persisted, constantly grounding and supporting her approach in current and emerging research, to create to the greatest extent possible in her context, non-representations of participants as they wanted themselves to be seen.

Disrupting 'norms'

As Hart (2017a) found, disruption of research at any level of the framing and conceptualization can, particularly for a new researcher, present obstacles. She is very aware of the landscape. Her interests were to address research issues in critical areas of interpretation and representation in qualitative inquiry as examples of the larger shifts of thinking about worldviews and ways of knowing. She sought to open up rethinking social issues as ecological with the theory driving changes in educational and social inquiry. She used a significant critical reflection on the process of a doctoral study that took up questions of environmental subjectivity and subjectification processes. She introduced participants who contributed rich, thoughtful narratives co-constructed through conversations around environmental subjectivity. She grounded her work concepts informed by poststructural and critical theories and worked to convince a doctoral supervisory committee about different views of what counts as theory and practice within these frames. She described differences among doctoral committee members views on what counts as data and analysis as challenges of re-education. She encountered resistances to her legitimate approach to not interpreting 'results' and fought to keep the participant voices as they were presented to her and without over interpretation – the interpretation is up to the reader. While engaging in conversations specifically related to gendered subjectivities, the intention was not to separate 'threads' of individuals' subjectivities but consider the whole. She persisted across resistances to valuing the difference illustrated through the participant narratives and representations that in traditional approaches were seemingly impossible. From the 'other side' she now looks back at the aura of original work as poiesis, as worthy of challenges bringing into existence something that was not there before. While such disruption is necessary, it is not without challenges. However, she argues that the sometimes sceptical responses to a disruptive approach are worth the energy to engage as there is potential for very necessary changes to 'the way things are done'.

Critical environmental education demands responsibility on the part of those engaging it in their research as well as those, in public and private spheres, who engage it. It is up to the listener/reader to take responsibility to make sense of research and information, and to maintain a critical perspective and approach to how that sense-making translates into practice. Individuals must take an active role. Critical environmental education research is itself a form of activism and necessitates reflection on the process as well as what can come from that research *for* others. Hart's (2017a) research, and the ways in which the 'data' is presented, place the responsibility on the reader to make sense of what participants have said and how that relates to their own subjectivities and processes of becoming. Rather than indoctrination, relational ways of knowing provide opportunities and create spaces for individuals to come to begin to articulate and understand their sense of self and being-in-relation. Be it issues of environmental subjectivity, gendered subjectivities or subjectivities beyond, disruption of the concepts and approach to research of those concepts is necessary.

Conclusion

While consciousness and problematization of 'traditional' gendered research in other areas of education has grown in leaps and bounds, within the field of environmental education the growth has been slow, but slowly the flowers are now blooming – as evidenced by the previously mentioned two special issues of *The Journal of Environmental Education*. These new disruptions of the field are enabling more conceptually complex engagements of concepts that can challenge hegemonic norms and provide new conceptual and analytic tools when addressing gender in environmental education research.

However, as we have argued here, there is the bigger issue of binaries – particularly that of human/nature – that are still an issue that needs to be discussed. While gender was inherently part of the subjectivities discussed in Hart's (2017a) study, the theoretical framing created spaces to acknowledge the interconnectedness of gender with environmental subjectivities and therefore could serve as a model for how others interested more specifically in gendered environmental educational research could theoretically, methodologically and even ontologically frame research. Research related to posthumanism and the more-than-human is highlighting the complexity of the interrelationships between humans and nature/postnature. Disrupting these binaries and engaging with subjectivities and agency are challenges still facing the field of environmental education research. As Irving Berlin (1936) wrote nearly a century ago: 'There may be trouble ahead, But … while we still have the chance, Let's face the music and dance.' The need and opportunity are there to raise a challenge – courage is one key necessary to actually taking up that challenge and moving forward.

Glossary

Assemblage 'A sort of anti-structural concept that permits the researcher to speak of emergence, heterogeneity, the decentered and the ephemeral in nonetheless ordered social life' (Marcus and Saka 2006, p. 101).

Ecofeminism A term intended 'to represent women's potential for bringing about an ecological revolution to ensure human survival on the planet. Such an ecological revolution would entail new gender relations between women and men and between humans and nature' (Merchant 1990, p. 100).

Subjectivity 'Subjectivity' is used to refer to the conscious and unconscious thoughts and emotions of the individual, her sense of herself and her ways of understanding her relations to the world. Humanist discourses presuppose an essence at the heart of the individual which is unique, fixed and coherent and which makes her what she *is*. Poststructuralism proposes a subjectivity which is precarious, contradictory and in process, constantly being reconstituted in discourse each time we think and speak (Weedon 1987, pp. 32–33).

References

Alaimo, S. (1994), 'Cyborg and ecofeminist interventions: Challenges for an environmental feminism', *Feminist Studies*, 20 (1): 133–52.

Alaimo, S. (2010), *Bodily Natures: Science, Environment, and the Material Self*, Bloomington, IN: Indiana University Press.

Alaimo, S. and Hekman, S. (2008), 'Introduction: Emerging models of materiality in feminist theory', in S. Alaimo and S. J. Hekman (eds), *Material Feminisms*, 1–19, Bloomington, IN: Indiana University Press.

Barad, K. (2007), *Meeting the Universe Halfway: Quantum Physics and the Entanglement of Matter and Meaning*, London: Duke University Press.

Bazzul, J. and Santavicca, N. (2017), 'Diagramming assemblages of sex/gender and sexuality as environmental education', *The Journal of Environmental Education*, 48 (1): 56–66.

Berlin, I. (1936), 'Let's face the music and dance', in the musical film *Follow the Fleet*.

Brown, K. (2017), 'Global environmental change II: Planetary boundaries – A safe operating space for human geographers?', *Progress in Human Geography*, 41 (1): 118–30.

Davies, B. (2013), 'A feminist poststructural approach to environmental education research', in R. B. Stevenson, M. Brody, J. Dillon and A. E. J. Wals (eds), *International Handbook of Research on Environmental Education*, 480–6, New York, NY: Routledge.

d'Eaubonne, F. (1974), *Le feminisme ou la mort*, Paris: Pierre Horay.

Foster, E. (2011), 'Sustainable development: Problematising normative constructions of gender within global environmental governmentality', *Globalizations*, 11 (2): 135–49.

Gaard, G. (2011), 'Ecofeminism revisited: Rejecting essentialism and re-placing species in a material feminist environmentalism', *Feminist Formations*, 23 (2): 26–53.

Gaard, G. (2015), 'Ecofeminism and climate change', *Women's Studies International Forum*, 49: 20–33.

Gavey, N. (1997), 'Feminist poststructuralism and discourse analysis', in M. Gergen and S. Davis (eds), *Toward a New Psychology of Gender: A Reader*, 49–64, New York, NY: Routledge.

Gough, A. (1999a), 'Recognising women in environmental education pedagogy and research: Toward an ecofeminist poststructuralist perspective', *Environmental Education Research*, 5 (2): 143–61.

Gough, A. (1999b), 'The power and promise of feminist research in environmental education', *Southern African Journal of Environmental Education*, 19: 28–39.

Gough, A. (2013), 'Researching differently: Generating a gender agenda for research in environmental education', in R. B. Stevenson, M. Brody, J. Dillon and A. Wals (eds), *International Handbook of Research on Environmental Education*, 375–83, New York, NY: Routledge.

Gough, A. (2015), 'Resisting becoming a Glomus Body within posthuman theorizing: *Mondialisation* and embodied agency in educational research', in N. Snaza and J. Weaver (eds), *Posthumanism and Educational Research*, 254–75, New York: Routledge.

Gough, A. and Whitehouse, H. (2003), 'The "nature" of environmental education from a feminist poststructuralist viewpoint', *Canadian Journal of Environmental Education*, 8: 31–43.

Gough, A. and Whitehouse, H. (2018), 'New vintages and new bottles: The "Nature" of environmental education from new material feminist and ecofeminist viewpoints', *The Journal of Environmental Education*, 49 (4): 336–49.

Gough, N. and Gough, A. (2003), 'Tales from Camp Wilde: Queer(y)ing environmental education research', *Canadian Journal of Environmental Education*, 8 (1): 44–66.

Grosz, E. (2010), 'Feminism, materialism, and freedom', in D. Coole and S. Frost (eds), *New Materialisms: Ontology, Agency and Politics*, 139–57, Durham, NC: Duke University Press.

Harding, S. (1998), *Is Science Multicultural? Postcolonialisms, Feminisms, and Epistemologies*, Bloomington, IN: Indiana University Press.

Hart, C. (2017a), 'Exploring subjectification processes in environmental education: How environmental education researchers come to construct their environmental subjectivities', PhD thesis, University of Regina, Regina, Saskatchewan, Canada.

Hart, C. (2017b), 'En-gendering the material in environmental education research: Reassembling otherwise', *The Journal of Environmental Education*, 48 (1): 46–55.

Hart, C. and Hart, P. (2018), 'On seeing ones self being seen: Reconceptualizing EE research', Paper presentation at the American Educational Research Association Annual Meeting, New York, NY.

Hart, P. and Hart, C. (2015), 'Within, against … beyond? Exploring emerging methodologies in post-qualitative environmental education research', Research Workshop Presentation at the North American Association for Environmental Education Research Symposium, San Diego, CA.

Hart, P. and Hart, C. (2017), 'Activism, action and becoming: Taking action to learn what it means to embrace an activist/agentic research identity', in B. Shapiro (ed.),

Actions of their Own to Learn: Studies in Knowing, Acting and Being, 17–40, Leiden, The Netherlands: Brill | Sense.

Hekman, S. (2008), 'Constructing the ballast: An ontology for feminism', in S. Alaimo and S. Hekman (eds), *Material Feminisms*, 85–119, Bloomington, IN: Indiana University Press.

Hird, M. (2009), 'Feminist engagements with matter', *Feminist Studies*, 35 (2): 329–46.

Hughes, C. and Lury, C. (2013), 'Re-turning feminist methodologies: From a social to an ecological epistemology', *Gender and Education*, 25 (6): 786–99.

Jackson, A. (2017), 'Thinking without method'. Paper presented at the American Educational Research Association Annual Meeting, San Antonio, TX.

Jackson, A. and Mazzei, L. (2013), *Thinking with Theory in Qualitative Research: Viewing Data across Multiple Perspectives*, New York: Routledge.

Kheel, M. (2008), *Nature Ethics: An Ecofeminist Perspective*, Lanham, MD: Rowman & Littlefield.

Koro-Ljungberg, M. and Mazzei, L. (2012), 'Problematizing methodological simplicity in qualitative research: Editors' introduction', *Qualitative Inquiry*, 18 (9): 728–31.

Kuntz, A. (2010), 'Representing representation', *International Journal of Qualitative Studies in Education*, 23 (4): 423–33.

Lather, P. (2007), *Getting Lost: Feminist Efforts toward a Double(d) Science*, Albany, NY: SUNY Press.

Lenz Taguchi, H. (2013), 'Images of thinking in feminist materialisms: Ontological divergences and the production of researcher subjectivities', *International Journal of Qualitative Studies in Education*, 26 (6): 706–16.

MacLure, M. (2013), 'Researching without representation? Language and materiality in post-qualitative methodology', *International Journal of Qualitative Studies in Education*, 26 (6): 658–67.

Marcus, G. E. and Saka, E. (2006), 'Assemblage', *Theory, Culture & Society*, 23 (2–3): 101–6.

McCoy, K. (2012), 'Towards a methodology of encounters: Opening to complexity in qualitative research', *Qualitative Inquiry*, 18 (9): 762–72.

McKenzie, M. (2004), 'The "willful contradiction" of poststructural socio-ecological education', *Canadian Journal of Environmental Education*, 9: 177–90.

Merchant, C. (1990), 'Ecofeminism and feminist theory', in I. Diamond and G. F. Orenstein (eds), *Reweaving the World: The Emergence of Ecofeminism*, 100–5, San Francisco: Sierra Club Books.

Merchant, C. (1992), *Radical Ecology: The Search for a Livable World*, New York, NY: Routledge.

Merchant, C. (2016), *Autonomous Nature: Problems of Prediction and Control from Ancient Times to the Scientific Revolution*. New York, NY: Routledge.

Phillips, M. (2016), 'Developing ecofeminist corporeality: Writing the body as activist poetics', in M. Phillips and N. Rumens (eds), *Contemporary Perspectives on Ecofeminism*, 57–75, London: Routledge.

Phillips, M. and Rumens, N., eds (2016a), *Contemporary Perspectives on Ecofeminism*, London: Routledge.

Phillips, M. and Rumens, N. (2016b), 'Introducing contemporary ecofeminism', in M. Phillips and N. Rumens (eds), *Contemporary Perspectives on Ecofeminism*, 1–16, London: Routledge.

Renold, E. and Ringrose, J. (2011), 'Schizoid subjectivities? Re-theorizing teen girls' sexual cultures in an era of "sexualization"', *Journal of Sociology*, 47 (4): 389–409.

Roulston, K. (2010), 'Considering quality in qualitative interviewing', *Qualitative Research*, 10 (2): 199–228.

Russell, J. (2013), 'Whose better? (Re) orientating a queer ecopedagogy', *Canadian Journal of Environmental Education*, 18: 11–26.

Seager, J. (1993), *Earth Follies: Coming to Feminist Terms with the Global Environmental Srisis*, New York: Routledge.

St Pierre, E. A. (2013), 'The posts continue: Becoming', *International Journal of Qualitative Studies in Education*, 26 (6): 646–57.

Stevenson, R. B. (2007), 'Schooling and environmental/sustainability education: From discourses of policy and practice to discourses of professional learning', *Environmental Education Research*, 13 (2): 265–85.

Sturgeon, N. (2009), *Environmentalism in Popular Culture: Gender, Race, Sexuality, and the Politics of the Natural*, Tucson, AZ: University of Arizona Press.

Taylor, C. A. (In Press), 'Diffracting the curriculum: Putting "new" material feminist theory to work to reconfigure knowledge-making practices in undergraduate higher education', in K. Scantlebury, C. A. Taylor and A. Lund (eds), *Turning Feminist Theory into Practice: Enacting Material Change in Education*, Leiden: Sense Publishers.

Taylor, C. and Ivinson, G. (2013), 'Editorial – Material feminisms: New directions for education', *Gender and Education*, 25 (6): 665–70.

Thompson, C. (2006), 'Back to nature? Resurrecting ecofeminism after poststructuralist and third-wave feminisms', *Isis*, 97 (3): 505–12.

United Nations (1992), 'Rio Declaration on Environment and Development. Annex 1 in report of the United Nations conference on environment development, Rio de Janeiro, 3–14 June'. Retrieved from: http://www.un.org/documents/ga/conf151/a conf15126-1annex1.htm.

United Nations (2012), *The Future We Want: Outcomes document adopted at Rio + 20*. United Nations, Rio de Janeiro.

United Nations (2016), 'Sustainable development goals'. Retrieved from: https://sustain abledevelopment.un.org/sdgs.

Warren, K., ed. (1994), *Ecological Feminism*, New York: Routledge.

Warren, K. J. and Cheney, J. (1991), 'Ecological feminism and ecosystem ecology', *Hypatia*, 6 (1): 179–97.

Weedon, C. (1987), *Feminist Practice and Poststructuralist Theory*, Cambridge, MA: Basil Blackwell.

Willox, A. (2012), 'Climate change as the work of mourning', *Ethics and the Environment*, 17 (2): 137–64.

5

The shame of participation: Rethinking the ontology of participation with a stutter

Eve Mayes

This chapter constructs a conversation between retheorizations of the ontology of participation (Springgay 2016), the affect of shame (Deleuze and Guattari 1994/2009; Probyn 2004; Mayes and Wolfe 2018; Tomkins 1995), and an empirical 'participatory' research study in a school setting (Mayes 2016b). *Participation* in research conventionally presumes autonomous human subjects who choose to participate in research following processes of informed consent (Springgay 2016, p. 73). Understandings of participation in conventional qualitative and participatory research are defined in and through boundary-making practices: research 'participants' are assumed to be sovereign, rational, self-present human subjects, set apart from researchers who invite them into the participatory endeavour (Mayes and Wolfe 2018). Participation is conventionally framed according to liberal democratic notions of consensus decision-making and 'having a voice'. In the context of schooling, 'student voice' has become a widespread strategy taken up by schools to foster student–teacher engagement (e.g. Lodge 2005), to 'live' democracy at school (e.g. Fielding and Moss 2011), and to transform institutions through student/ teacher partnerships (e.g. Beattie 2012).

In this chapter, I rethink the notion of participation in research, as well as in school efforts to encourage student voice. Attending to disruptive moments where *shame* – an ambivalent affect that disturbs the (presumed) boundaries between autonomous human subjects – materializes (Mayes and Wolfe 2018; Wolfe amd Mayes 2019), the boundary-making practices of conventional notions of participation are reworked. Shame intrudes in and through a particular moment when the researcher stutters:

> Eve: [*Pause*] Have you tho – like have you – like then – have you – an, an – has
> tha tha – has [*Pause*]. Let me start again. Has that made you reflect on how

you might [*Pause*] talk to people? [*Pause*] Or has that just made you ju –
feel like [*Pause*] upset that [*Pause*]. Yeah. How do you how do you–

This embodied stutter physicalizes the researcher's entanglements, complicity and response-ability (Mayes and Wolfe 2018) – and insinuates a researcherly *shame* that is of interest. I do not use the term 'shame' in the sense that it is conventionally used in relation to education: as associated with moral breaches to (and, indeed, abuses of) social, cultural, religious and institutional norms, as individualized and as intrinsic to the self, even if entangled with institutional corruption (e.g. Benade 2015; Stearns and Stearns 2017; see Mayes and Wolfe 2018 and Wolfe and Mayes 2019). Rather, this chapter takes up theories of shame as inextricable from interest (Tomkins 1995; Probyn 2004) to consider its potential to unsettle the boundaries of participation – of borders demarcating 'participant' from 'non-participant'. This chapter examines particular flows of interest and shame in concrete configurations where bodies 'have a voice'– the 'immanent modes of existence of people provided with rights' (Deleuze and Guattari 1994/2009, p. 107). My interest is in the shame that is *in* and *of* the researcher's stutter in its entanglement with the research event and past classroom events. Exploring this intrusion of shame, it becomes what Miessen (2011) calls, in his proposition for participation without consensus, an 'uncalled participator'. I consider researchers' methodological participation in the constitution of shame as interest(ing) (Deleuze and Guattari 1994/ 2009, pp. 107–8; Mayes and Wolfe 2018), and rethink the 'lived relational[ity]' of participation (Springgay 2016, p. 72). Through analysing the relations between this embodied stutter, other 'data' and theory, I further rethink the ontology of participation itself.

In the following section, I introduce previous critiques of participation and contextualize an empirical study of student participation in schools (in which I foreground a student voice initiative), before constructing an account of affect and shame in research. Within this account of affect and shame in research, I include words spoken during participatory encounters in this research study about the disruptive e/affects of participating in student voice work. 'Data' and theory participate in re-forming the presumed boundaries between them. This rewriting of participation is influenced by St. Pierre's (2008) refusal of the 'primacy of voice' (i.e. the separation of participants' voices into a separate data section of a piece of writing, with participants' voices distinguished from the voices of other theorists and researchers quoted in the research text). I do not view data as separated from the field, nor the researcher, nor texts written about data. Participatory 'data' are thus enfolded into this chapter, as voices among the other voices (of researchers and theorists) that I read and engaged with in assembling an alternative account of participation.

Shameful participation?

The logics of participation, particularly assumptions that the power relations of participatory endeavours are necessarily more 'equitable', have been previously critiqued as paternalistic and as instrumentally mobilized in neoliberal practices of governance. In development studies (e.g. Cooke and Kothari 2001), critics of participatory approaches have tracked the inherent authority and domination in participatory enterprises. Such critiques have been extended to participatory research with children and young people; Gallacher and Gallagher (2008) caution about the overenthusiasms of assertions that participatory research will necessarily *empower* participants. In youth studies, arguments that participation neutralizes or equalizes power relations have been critiqued as overlooking the significance of increasing inequalities and differences between groups of young people (Wierenga, et al. 2003); participation may even create new inequalities (Black 2011).

These critiques suggest the stultifying potential of invitations to 'participate': the ostensibly benevolent aims of participatory work may generate unanticipated and ambivalent affects. In an evocative description of the 'imperative to participate' in participatory art, Brian Massumi (2011) describes the command to the sea cucumber to 'express' itself '"truly" or "authentically"' (p. 42). The 'prodded sea cucumber that spits its guts', becomes 'viscerally exposed', 'exposed down to [its] inmost sensitive folds, down to the very peristaltic rhythms that make [it] what [it is]' (Massumi 2011, p. 42). Thinking with the affective force of Massumi's exposed sea cucumber, I extend these previous critiques of conceptualizations of power in participatory research to consider the ontology of participation – participation's *being* and *relationality*.

This chapter attends to affective disruptions to such notions of participation, through examining moments where participation is unsettled. By *affective disruptions*, I am not referring to emotional perplexities, though these may be an outworking of affect. My use of the term 'affect' is indebted to Deleuze's (1988) work on Spinoza's affect: the capacities of human and more-than-human bodies to affect and to be affected. Affect is different from 'emotion': emotions are subtractive linguistic labels (Clough 2007, p. 2); there is always a remainder that exceeds or escapes participants' and researchers' consciousness or capture

(Massumi 2002, p. 30). A participant may speak of their 'fear', or 'resentment', or 'delight' – but the account cannot fully account for the intensities of the moment that they narrate. Affective intensities are social, mobile, sticking to bodies and worlds (Seigworth and Gregg 2010): relations between entangled entities – students and teachers, participants and researchers – are constituted in and through the ways in which affect is apprehended and narrated. Affect is dynamically co-constructive of phenomena (including, for example, the subject positions of 'student', 'teacher', 'researcher' and 'participant').

Disrupting participation in a research study

This chapter thinks with what happened during a research study concerned with one secondary school's adoption of student voice as a school reform strategy. The school where this study was undertaken is a public coeducational secondary school in the south-west of Sydney, with approximately 87 per cent of students from a language background other than English. This school incorporated a student voice initiative into a four-year school reform process funded through the Australian federal and state governments' *National Partnership for Low Socio-Economic Schools* (Australian Government [DEEWR], National Partnership for Smarter Schools, & NSW Department of Education and Communities 2012). Each year between 2010 and 2013, a group of approximately twenty students in Year 9 were apprenticed as co-researchers to devise, design and conduct their own research inquiries, working with a teacher-facilitator and an academic partner (see Mayes 2016a; Mayes 2016b). This group was known in the school as the 'Steering Committee'. Students became familiar with qualitative and participatory research methods including interviews, focus groups and participant observation, the development and analysis of surveys, visual and embodied methods, and participatory data analysis. General research topics guided the students' inquiries each year: The school I'd like (2010), The teachers I'd like (2011), The learner I'd like to be (2012), and What I'd like to learn (2013). I was a full-time teacher at this school from 2007 to 2011 and was part of proposing and then facilitating the student voice group in 2010 and 2011. In 2013, I returned to the school as a researcher, interested in how, over time, students, teachers and parents made meaning of these experiences of participation in student voice work and participatory research.

Throughout the year of my research fieldwork, teachers and students gave accounts to me of the participatory research work that they had been part of (e.g. their experiences of interviewing other students and teachers), the student research presentation events where students reported their research findings to staff (e.g. at staff meetings), and the aftermath of these encounters (e.g. back in individual classrooms). Participatory events – where, for example, students interviewed teachers about their experiences – were sometimes associated by students and teachers not only with feeling 'appreciat[ion]', 'comfortable' and 'understanding each other' but also with feeling 'weird' or interpreting teachers to be 'nervous'. Student research presentation events, similarly, were described in dissonant terms. A member of the school's senior leadership team[1] said that she had felt 'goosebumps'. For other teachers, the students' presentations had 'triggered' a response of 'oh, yes, yes' and of 'oh yeah that's really good'; it 'open[ed] my eyes', 'made me sit up', that it was 'enlightening' and 'beautiful'.

Other teachers spoke about 'the mood' in the room, of other 'teachers getting their back up' as they listened to students present their research about the importance to students of 'mutual respect'. What followed these participatory events and research presentation events – back in individual classrooms and in the broader terrain of the school – was also narrated divergently. Some accounts from students and teachers foregrounded renewed relationships – a greater sense of 'understanding' between students and teachers. Others foregrounded subsequent conflicts between particular teachers and particular students. The dissonances between different accounts of past events and their accompanying feelings were striking; accounts of past events did not easily fit within the sorts of school reform progress narratives that contemporary accountability requirements compel teachers and schools to construct (Lingard, Sellar and Lewis 2017).

In particular, I was surprised by the disruptive intrusion of ambivalent affective intensities associated with classroom encounters between students and teachers during and after their involvement not only in student voice work but also in participatory research encounters. 'Student voice"', a school reform strategy usually celebrated as fostering dialogical understanding, empowerment and school improvement, was associated with ambivalent feelings. I was unnerved by drawings and puppet productions created by students when we spoke about past student voice encounters. I was unsure how to write about my positionality in the study – as a former teacher of student participants in the

[1] I use this term to include the school principal and three deputy principals. I do not specify whether it is the principal or a deputy principal for reasons of preserving anonymity. By signalling that these statements are made by a member of the senior leadership team, I foreground that these statements are uttered from positions of relative power within the school.

study, as a former facilitator of the student voice group, and as a colleague and friend of teachers who participated in the study. Theories of shame and interest (see following section) became participants in these sense-making endeavours.

Feelings in participatory research – and shame

Liberal humanist understandings of participation are conventionally associated with affirmative feelings – for example, the recognition, mutuality, and joy that comes with honouring the 'rights' of others and engaging in dialogue (e.g. Cook-Sather 2002; Fielding and Moss 2011). Alongside descriptions of positive feelings are descriptions of uncertainty and anxiety (Rudduck and Fielding 2006, p. 225), and 'fear [of] the misuse of "voice"' (Bragg 2007a, p. 516). In these accounts, however, feelings are localized: properties (emotions) of the individual teacher or student. Bragg (2007b) has previously raised concerns that such explanations of feelings in participatory work are 'overly psychologizing' (p. 344); felt responses remain individualized rather than situated in discursive and institutional contexts.

To extend Bragg's (2007b) critique, participants' discursive accounts of feeling, and researchers' interpretations of these accounts, reduce and betray the fluxing intensities of relational encounters that exceed any account that can be made of them.

> Teacher: When you're working with other people, you don't actually have that much control over them and what they're doing and what they're thinking. But as a teacher you're kind of told that you should have this level of control … And I'm sure the kids can pick up on your emotions.

What participants name as their feelings in particular participatory encounters (e.g. 'joy', 'fear') suggest the affective significance of what has happened to them (Ducey 2007, pp. 192–3). Yet, ungovernable feelings continue to surge and escape, elusive, unable to be stopped or paused to analyse (Thrift 2008, p. 206). How a participant gives an account of feelings in motion also depends on the actions and reactions of others; 'it is through such re-actions that we most often see what we are doing' (Thrift 2008, p. 176).

> Eve: I've heard other people talk about the resentment that some teachers felt when the students presented to staff …
>
> Teacher: I certainly felt that … because the kids were actually – at the time – sorry …

Eve: It's okay.

Teacher: They were actually bullying me in a way, with those statements.

Eve: Right.

Teacher: [*Loudly*] 'Respect. We want respect.'

Eve: When they come back here [the classroom]?

Teacher: Yeah, and the thing is like, and I'm thinking like, 'I have never seen respect from you.' In my mind I'm thinking, 'these kids who have – who don't know what respect looks like.' They are now like throwing, throwing it around like a weapon. Like, 'we've got a weapon, we are throwing it at you.' … We were never getting respect and then they came in and accused us of not giving them what we were dying for.

Spurred on by the smile and nod of the researcher, a participant may continue speaking of what they have felt. Apprehending a dark, inscrutable shadow across the face of the researcher, a participant may regret their choice of words, and stop mid-sentence.

Sometimes, something surges forth that breaks the boundaries of the skin; the guts become emphatically involved in the participatory encounter: a blush springs to the surface, tears spill out, rage burns up, laughter breaks out, a stutter intrudes (Katz 2000, p. 322). The 'corporeal sense of the communicative act' (Thrift 2008, p. 208), the language used to describe this sense, the response sensed from the other about what has been said, generates further feelings that move in potentially infinite directions.

Probyn (2004) and Deleuze and Guattari's (1994/2009) theorizations of shame became productive interlocutors with these ambivalent affects.[2] For Probyn, following Tomkins (1995), shame is entwined with interest. According to Probyn (2004), interest involves 'a desire for connection' (p. x). Holding out one's interest entails vulnerability, a laying bare of one's desires, in a way that puts oneself at risk. 'Interest is always hedged by the conditional *if* (Probyn 2004 p. xi):

> If you enjoy communicating your experiences and ideas and aspirations and I enjoy being informed about the experiences, ideas and aspirations of others, we can enjoy each other. (Tomkins 1995, p. 5)

---

[2]   Silvan Tomkins and Deleuze's approach to affect differs. Affect theorizing influenced by Tomkins' work has been described as starting with bodily drives, following a quasi-Darwinist 'innate-ist' frayed wiring that works from the 'inside-out' (Coleman 2013, p. 31), as biology interacts with social relations. Affect theorizing influenced by Deleuze, after Spinoza, analyses affect 'in the midst of things and relations (in immanence)' and 'in the complex assemblages that come to compose bodies and worlds simultaneously' (Seigworth & Gregg 2010, p. 6).

In the moment where interest is held out, there are seeds for communion, for engagement, for friendship. But the conditional *if* 'contains the seeds for shame' (Probyn 2004, p. xi) – *if* the interest, the vulnerability is not reciprocated, one may feel undone, unwound and raw – ashamed.

> Savannah Smith[3]: When you're trying to do something and then someone –
>
> Hagrid: – Cuts you down.
>
> Savannah Smith: – yeah, you feel hopeless, useless, like you're trying your best but then there's that someone telling you that you're not good enough. It gets to you.
>
> Hagrid: Aaah [*breathing out heavily*]. Amen to that.
>
> John Citizen Smith: It just makes you give up because you think, 'oh well like what's the point? Stuff it.'
>
> Ayman: Sometimes you don't have the energy to keep on going. Sometimes there is no next time … There's no more.
>
> John Citizen Smith: You can't go back. Once you leave you're out. You're not into it.

The moment where 'desire for connection' (Probyn 2004, p. x) is held out is precarious. When met with a blank stare, or with censure, the 'little moment of disappointment – "oh, but I was interested"' may be 'amplified' (Probyn 2004, p. 13). You feel 'hopeless, useless … It gets to you … You don't have the energy to keep on going.' As Deleuze (1988) puts it, the capacity of your body to act is 'diminished or blocked; your body is separated from its capacity to act' (p. 27). Probyn (2004) argues that shame is an 'ambiguous state of feeling, emotion, and affect'; a 'fine line or border between moving forward into more interest or falling back into humiliation' (p. xii). In its physical manifestation (a blush, a flood of sensation, a stutter), shame makes 'visible' what we care about (Probyn 2004, p. xii); it 'alerts us to things, people, and ideas that we didn't even realise we wanted' to engage with (p. 14).

I extend Tomkins and Probyn's work on shame with Deleuze and Guattari's interest in shame, articulated in the context of a critique of the democratic state and of human rights. This context of their discussion seems, to me, particularly pertinent for considerations of participation in student voice, as a movement that is concerned to honour students' rights to 'have a voice' on matters affecting them. For Deleuze and Guattari (1994/2009), 'the shame of

---

[3] All student names are pseudonyms created by the students.

being human' is experienced 'not only in ... extreme situations',[4] but also 'in insignificant conditions': 'before the meanness and vulgarity of existence that haunt democracies, ... and before the values, ideals, and opinions of our time' (pp. 107–8). After Deleuze and Guattari, I view shame as a '"composite" feeling': a 'shame that [humans] could do this, shame that we have been unable to prevent it, shame at having survived, and shame at having been demeaned or diminished' (footnote 17, 1994/2009, p. 225). Returning to Probyn (2004), shame might be 'hidden away', 'corrected' or 'denied' (p. xiii), but may also be 'positive in its self-evaluative role' (p. xii). Interest, in its micropolitical movements, may flow in ambivalent affective directions, depending on the response to its display in a particular configuration.

A stutter

A stutter and a blush – shame, perhaps? – intruded into this study of experiences of participation – in a particular focus group with four Year 11 students. Before this focus group, I had spoken with a number of teachers and members of the school leadership, who had given accounts of how student 'participation' in school reform processes became an opportunity for teachers to encourage students to take responsibility for their 'behaviour'. As a member of the senior leadership team put it in an interview:

> Senior leadership: This [Steering Committee] has also been good for the kids because it's put back the responsibility on them about their behaviours.
>
> Eve: Mmm.
>
> Senior leadership: And I think it's only then that the teachers started to have – that was the turning point.
>
> Eve: And when was that, do you think – that that happened?
>
> Senior leadership: ... The initial stuff was hard and then it was only when they [teachers] got to the discussions about – 'yes, that's fine, I hear what you're saying, but what about the kids?' [It was] when the teachers felt they had this opportunity ... to say to the kid, 'well, what's your responsibility?' Cause we always talk about the rights of people and the rights of kids – But then attached to that is some responsibility as well.

---

[4]   Deleuze and Guattari are discussing living after Nazism. They stress that it is 'not only in the extreme situations' associated with Nazism that 'we experience the shame of being human' (1994/2009, p. 107).

This statement troubled me, as an example of student voice inciting 'students to constitute themselves as active, responsible and choosing subjects' (Bragg 2007b, p. 355). I was disturbed, as I have written elsewhere, at how participation had become an 'instrumental strategy for governing students, with the focus of intervention remaining squarely on the student's learning and behaviour in school rather than on processes of transformation involving adults and young people' (Mayes 2018, p. 3).

During a focus group with four Year 11 students who had been part of the Steering Committee when they were in Year 9, they created a scenario using cloth puppets. This scenario enacted a classroom conversation between a particular teacher and a group of students. The scenario's events echoed the kind of interaction that the member of the senior leadership team had described: a student questions a teacher, and a teacher responds by speaking to the student about their responsibility to 'change' their behaviour. After the students created this puppet scenario, our conversation turned to a particular classroom example connected to this scenario:

Ayman: [In a particular class] Every single lesson if there's anything like talkativeness or whatever, [the teacher] always goes back to the Steering Committee. She goes, 'this is what I get from my Steering Committee kids.' Everything that happens, if we're talking – whatever, it's, 'this is what Steering Committee has done to you guys' or if we say, 'miss, I think we should be doing this or we should do' – 'this is what the Steering Committee has made you into.' …

Hagrid: Oah. What?

John Citizen Smith: So they blame everything on the Steering Committee. Even if you're trying to give advice on how you could do something so that everyone can enjoy it –

Hagrid: Are you serious? [*Whispering*] Wow.

John Citizen Smith: It's like – 'Oh no Steering Committee has made you – not better or worse but some kind of – [*indecipherable*]'

Ayman: They made you, they made you question –

John Citizen Smith: Think.

Ayman: Question how to learn or question how to – or try to do things different ways or something: 'Oh that's what the Steering Committee's done to you guys. They've given you a big ego.' Or stuff like that.

[*Overlapping*] John Citizen Smith: A big ego.

[*Overlapping*] Eve: Right? 'A big ego.'

[*Overlapping*] Hagrid: Is that – [*whispering*] whaaaaat?

John Citizen Smith: Also, some teachers, if you try to give them advice about how we can do something, they think that you're trying to teach them how to do their job.

Ayman: All the time.

Eve: Yep.

John Citizen Smith: And they get really defensive.

Eve: [*Pause*] Have you tho– like have you – like then – have you – an, an – has tha tha – has [*Pause*]. Let me start again. Has that made you reflect on how you might [*Pause*] talk to people? [*Pause*] Or has that just made you ju – feel like [*Pause*] upset that [*Pause*]. Yeah. How do you how do you–

Hagrid: [*Quietly*] If that happened to me, I would be upset and I'd probably be suspended or expelled. I would argue. [*Eve laughs. No one else laughs*] I would argue. But uh, I need to come to school. [*Eve laughs*]

Ayman: I do that. I do that when she does it to me now. I'm not just going to say that I sit there and take it. No – I say, 'no that's not true. That's not fair.'

Eve: Yeah. So it does lead sometimes to a bit of a –

Ayman: Confrontation sort of thing.

I stutter.[5]

The researcher is caught in micro-perceptible moments of participatory paralysis.

The eventual question that she asks is about whether or not this group of students 'reflect[ed]' on how 'you might talk to people'. Her question is spoken in the common-sense terms that she is quietly questioning (cf. Mayes and Wolfe 2018). She (re-)produces what she has heard that others say to the students. 'Well what's your responsibility?' 'Has that made you reflect on how you might talk to people?' '[A]ll manner of voices in a voice, murmurings, speaking in tongues' (Deleuze and Guattari 1980/1987, pp. 76–77) whisper around her question. In this question, perhaps she suggests that it should be the students who reflect on their words and attempt to express themselves more diplomatically. That, perhaps, students should apologize. That students should be silent rather than suggest how things could be better. She laughs at Hagrid's quiet response that he would be 'upset' and would 'probably be suspended or expelled'.

---

[5] I deliberately employ the present tense here because this stuttering is still occurring. I also deliberately switch from the first person pronoun to the third person in the paragraphs that follow.

The researcher is forcefully attuned to her *comprehensive participation* in these assemblages, unable to step outside them. She is not the benign but distant researcher who invites 'participation' – and who steps away to write up the 'data'. She is not a former teacher who has stepped outside of her former roles, affiliations and affections. She is not separate from participants, nor her research methods, nor the data that are generated in these 'participatory' research encounters.

The shame of colleagues – entrusted in gentle moments of vulnerability – is present in this stutter. The wounds of students that they collectively shared in focus groups in quiet rooms in the library reopen. The shame of being a teacher. The shame of being a student. The shame of being a researcher listening to it all. The shame of saying too much. Or saying too little. The shame of not doing enough – or doing too much. Not feeling 'outside of [this] time' but continuing 'to undergo shameful compromises with it' (Deleuze and Guattari 1994/2009, pp. 107–08). Affecting and being affected, enfolded, implicated. Participating.

Stuttering participation

Have you tho –	*When you're working with other people, you don't really have that much control over them and what they're doing and what they're thinking.* [Whose words are these? The teacher who the researcher spoke to, or the researcher's?]
like have you –	*But as a teacher* [a researcher?] *you're kind of told that you should have this level of control.* [Who tells her? Or do I tell myself/ herself? Where did it come from?]
like then –	*They* [Teachers?] *came in and accused us* [Students?] *of not giving them what we were dying for.*
have you –	*What's your responsibility?*
an, an –	*They were actually bullying me in a way, with those statements.*
has tha tha –	*Cuts you down.*
has [Pause].	*Has that made you reflect on how you might talk to people?* [And 'do' research?]

This rupture, where quotations from multiple transcripts are brought into arrangement in the moment of a transcribed stutter, is not a performance of sympathy or pity for students and/or teachers. Bringing these words into relation is not to substitute places – as if to suggest that the researcher had grasped the standpoint of another, stepped into their shoes. It is also not imitational, appropriating students' and teachers' words. This rupture is not a moment of mutual understanding between the students and the researcher, or the teachers and the researcher, or teachers and students. This rupture is not a moment where the researcher 'empowers' the voices of others by letting their 'raw voices' 'speak for themselves'.

The reader's task is not to wonder what this stuttering *means*. Rather, the task is to widen the cracks between words and amplify the common-sense logics that subjectivate students and teachers. Rhizomatically connecting transcribed stuttering with other utterances from students and teachers is a production of a 'zone of exchange between [students, teachers, the researcher] in which something of one passes into the other' (Deleuze and Guattari 1994/2009, p. 109). A zigzagging through the cracks.

> *This is not a feeling of pity*, [still less an identification]. It is a composition of speeds and affects involving entirely different individuals, a symbiosis; it makes the [student] become a thought, a feverish thought in the [teacher/researcher], at the same time as the [teacher/researcher] becomes a [student] ... The [student] and the [teacher/researcher] are in no way the same thing, but Being expresses them both in a single meaning in a language that is no longer that of words, in a matter that is no longer that of forms, in an affectability that is no longer that of subjects. *Unnatural participation.* (Deleuze and Guattari 1980/1987, p. 248, their emphasis)

This is a participation in the collective shame of our time: 'the shame of being human' experienced in and beyond schools:

> ... before the propagation of these modes of existence and of thought-for-the-market, and before the values, ideals, and opinions of our time. The ignominy of the possibilities of life that we are offered appears from within. We do not feel ourselves outside of our time but continue to undergo shameful compromises with it. (Deleuze and Guattari 1994/2009, pp. 107–08)

Deleuze and Guattari (1994/2009) write, concerning the shame of being human: 'We are not responsible for the [others] but responsible before them' (p. 108). In changing the preposition from 'for' (*pour* in the original French) to 'before' (*devant*), they shift the notion of responsibility: not acting for others or acting as if one were the other in a manner that would presume that one is set apart from the other as an autonomous and discrete subject. Instead, one is 'responsible before others, facing them, and in relation to them' (Gilson 2011, p. 79). In *Difference and Repetition*, Deleuze (1968/1994) explains 'the situation of being before' as supposing 'a swarm of differences, a pluralism of free differences' (p. 55). According to Lawlor (2008), their use of *devant* 'refers neither to an experience of being over and against, outside of one another, nor to the subject-object relation' (pp. 175–6). This is to become something other than 'teacher' or 'researcher' 'in proximity' with the students and the teachers: 'among the others and they are in me' (Lawlor 2008, p. 178). *Participation.* Springgay (2016) writes that participation is always already part of any relation, 'rendered in affective terms as co-composition' (p. 75). This is a becoming-*response*-able to the 'zone of exchange' between bodies (Deleuze and Guattari 1994/2009, p. 109).

To think *participation* in this way is to break with relations that judge and seek to remediate the Other's (student or teacher or researcher) lack, but to instead attend to the conditions and processes of *becoming*. Bodies affect and are affected in the zone of exchange, enfolded, entangled and co-implicated in the constitution of shame (and interest) in schools and in research. This movement is not the liberal democratic 'responsibility' of the rights-bearing subject as he/she participates in school reform processes. Nor is it the responsibility of the individual of neoliberal education reform logics. Rather, it is 'a *response*-ability between interdependent, interrelated bodies differentially positioned through relations of power, who affect and are affected by each other' (Mayes and Wolfe 2018, p. 13). Participation, then, is '*inescapable*' (Springgay 2016, p. 73, her emphasis); ethical questions about the particular mode of relations that research encounters generate are also inescapable.

Acknowledgements

I thank the anonymous peer reviewers and the editors for their supportive and constructive feedback on an earlier draft of this chapter. Conversations and previous collaborative work with Melissa Wolfe have informed and enriched the discussion of affect, shame-interest and ethics in this chapter.

Glossary

Affect Affect is a relation – the capacity to affect and to be affected. Affect is different from 'emotion': emotions can be understood; emotions are subtractive linguistic labels. A remainder exceeds or escapes participants' and researchers' consciousness or capture.

Participation: Participation, according to liberal democratic conceptualizations, is conventionally understood to be an agentic action: taking part in an activity (such as research). Sovereign, rational and self-present human subjects are assumed to be set apart from researchers who invite them into the participatory endeavour. Mayes's chapter rethinks the ontology of participation as lived relation; interdependent, interrelated bodies affect and are affected by each other in all relations, including those described as 'participatory'.

Shame-interest Conventional notions of shame conceptualize it as an individualized emotion. Mayes's chapter draws on the work of Silvan Tomkins, Elsbeth Probyn, Gilles Deleuze and Félix Guattari, to rethink shame as inextricable from interest. Shame materializes when you are interested in establishing and/or maintaining a connection – for example, when you think that a person has smiled at you, and you smile back, only to realize that the person was smiling at someone beyond you.

References

Australian Government [DEEWR], National Partnership for Smarter Schools, & NSW Department of Education and Communities. (2012), *National Partnerships for Low Socio-Economic Schools: Information Package for Schools*. Available at: http://www .lowsesschools.nsw.edu.au/Portals/0/upload/resfile/Low:Socio-economic_Status_Sch ool_Communities_National_Partnership_Information_package_for_National_ Partnership_schools.pdf (Accessed 17 September 2018).

Beattie, H. (2012), 'Amplifying student voice: The missing link in school transformation', *Management in Education*, 26 (3): 158–60.

Benade, L. (2015), 'Shame: Does it have a place in an education for democratic citizenship?' *Educational Philosophy and Theory*, 47 (7): 661–74. doi:10.1080/001318 57.2014.880644.

Black, R. (2011), 'Student participation and disadvantage: Limitations in policy and practice', *Journal of Youth Studies*, 14 (4): 463–74.

Bragg, S. (2007a), '"But I listen to children anyway!" – teacher perspectives on pupil voice', *Educational Action Research*, 15 (4): 505–18.

Bragg, S. (2007b), '"Student voice" and governmentality: The production of enterprising subjects?' *Discourse: Studies in the Cultural Politics of Education*, 28 (3): 343–58.

Clough, P. T. (2007), 'Introduction', in P. T. Clough with J. Halley (eds), *The Affective Turn: Theorizing the Social*, 1–33, Durham and London: Duke University Press.

Coleman, R. (2013), *Transforming Images: Screens, Affects, Futures*, Oxon and New York: Routledge.

Cook-Sather, A. (2002), 'Authorizing students' perspectives: Towards trust, dialogue, and change in education', *Educational Researcher*, 31 (4): 3–14.

Cooke, B. and Kothari, U., eds (2001), *Participation: The New Tyranny?* London: Zed Books.

Deleuze, G. (1968/1994), *Difference and Repetition*, Columbia: Columbia University Press.

Deleuze, G. (1988), *Spinoza: Practical Philosophy*, San Francisco: City Lights Books.

Deleuze, G. and Guattari, F. (1980/1987), *A Thousand Plateaus: Capitalism and Schizophrenia*, Minneapolis: University of Minnesota Press.

Deleuze, G. and Guattari, F. (1994/2009), *What Is Philosophy?* London and New York: Verso.

Ducey, A. (2007), 'More than a job: Meaning, affect, and training health care workers', in P. T. Clough with J. Halley (eds), *The Affective Turn: Theorizing the Social*, 187–208, Durham and London: Duke University Press.

Gallacher, L. A. and Gallagher, M. (2008), 'Methodological immaturity in childhood research? Thinking through "participatory methods"', *Childhood*, 15 (4): 499–516.

Gilson, E. C. (2011), 'Responsive becoming: Ethics between Deleuze and feminism', in N. Jun and D. W. Smith (eds), *Deleuze and Ethics*, 63–88, Edinburgh: Edinburgh University Press.

Fielding, M. and Moss, P. (2011), *Radical Education and the Common School: A Democratic Alternative*, London and New York: Routledge.

Katz, J. (2000), *How Emotions Work*, Chicago: University of Chicago Press.

Lawlor, L. (2008), 'Following the rats: Becoming-animal in Deleuze and Guattari', *SubStance*, 37 (3): 169–87. Available from Project MUSE: https://muse.jhu.edu/ (Accessed 17 September 2018).

Lingard, B., Sellar, S. and Lewis, S. (2017), 'Accountabilities in schools and school systems', *Oxford Research Encyclopedia of Education*, 1–27. doi:10.1093/acrefore/9780190264093.013.74.

Lodge, C. (2005), 'From hearing voices to engaging in dialogue: Problematising student participation in school improvement', *Journal of Educational Change*, 6 (2): 125–46.

Massumi, B. (2002), *Parables for the Virtual: Movement, Affect, Sensation*, Durham, NC: Duke University Press.

Massumi, B. (2011), *Semblance and Event: Activist Philosophy and the Occurrent Arts*, Cambridge, MA and London: MIT Press.

Mayes, E. (2016a), 'Shifting research methods with a becoming-child ontology: Co-theorising puppet production with high school students', *Childhood*, 23 (1): 105–22. doi:10.1177/0907568215576526.

Mayes, E. (2016b), *The Lines of the Voice: An Ethnography of the Ambivalent Affects of Student Voice*, PhD thesis, University of Sydney. Available at: https://ses.library.usyd.edu.au/handle/2123/15274?mode=simple (Accessed 17 September 2018).

Mayes, E. (2018), 'Student voice in school reform? Desiring simultaneous critique and affirmation', *Discourse: Studies in the Cultural Politics of Education*. doi:10.1080/01596306.2018.1492517.

Mayes, E. and Wolfe, M. (2018), 'Shameful interest in educational research', *Critical Studies in Education*. doi:10.1080/17508487.2018.1489871.

Miessen, M. (2011), *The Nightmare of Participation*, Berlin: Sternberg Press.

Probyn, E. (2004), *Blush: Faces of Shame*, Sydney: University of NSW Press.

Rudduck, J. and Fielding, M. (2006), 'Student voice and the perils of popularity', *Educational Review*, 58 (2): 219–31. doi:10.1080/00131910600584207.

Seigworth, G. J. and Gregg, M. (2010), 'An inventory of shimmers', in M. Gregg and
     G. J. Seigworth (eds), *The Affect Theory Reader*, 1–25, Durham and London: Duke
     University Press.

Springgay, S. (2016), 'Towards a rhythmic account of working together and taking part',
     Research in Education, 96 (1): 71–7. doi:10.1177/0034523716664603.

St. Pierre, E. A. (2008), 'Decentering voice in qualitative inquiry', *International Review of
     Qualitative Research*, 1 (3): 319–36.

Stearns, P. N. and Stearns, C. (2017), 'American schools and the uses of shame:
     An ambiguous history', *History of Education*, 46 (1): 58–75. doi:10.1080/00467
     60X.2016.1185671.

Thrift, N. (2008), *Non-representational Theory: Space | Politics | Affect*, Oxon and New
     York: Routledge.

Tomkins, S. (1995), *Exploring Affect: The Selected Writings of Silvan S. Tomkins*, edited
     by E. V. Demos, Cambridge, New York, Melbourne and Paris: Cambridge University
     Press & Editions de la Maison des Sciences de l'Homme.

Wierenga, A., Trenbath, G., Kelly, J. and Vikakovic, O. (2003), 'Sharing a new
     story: Young people in decision-making', A report for the Foundation for Young
     Australians, Australian Youth Research Centre, The University of Melbourne,
     Melbourne.

Wolfe, M. J. and Mayes, E. (2019), 'Response-ability: Re-e-valuing shameful measuring
     processes within the Australian Academy', in M. Breeze, C. Costa and Y. Taylor
     (eds), *Educational Futures and Fractures: Time and Space in the Neoliberal University*,
     277–98, London: Palgrave Macmillan.

Part Two

Frontiers: Possibility, times-pace and materiality

6

Posthumanist poetics and the transcorporeal, hypercorporeal chronotope

Robin Bellingham

Introduction

In an attempt to provide a meaningful yet brief description of my approach to the term 'posthumanism' I draw from Braidotti's (2018) discussion of the posthuman. The posthuman is a transdisciplinary field of scholarship and a conceptual tool drawing on the generativity of intersecting critiques of humanism and of anthropocentrism. It aims at how we might better understand the processes of becoming that make reality, including human–non-human linkages. These aims are framed by a major problem of our times that Braidotti terms: 'the opportunistic commodification of all that lives, which … is the political economy of advanced capitalism' (Braidotti 2018, p. 5).

Researchers have used posthumanist concepts to reimagine social science inquiry (e.g. Fox and Alldred 2015; Ulmer 2017) and educational research (e.g. Lenz Taguchi and Palmer 2013; Rosiek 2018; Rousell 2016; Snaza et al. 2014) for a number of years and with a range of approaches. In this chapter, I am concerned specifically with a reimagining of research writing poetics – the ways in which different elements and techniques of a written text come together to co-constitute affects and phenomena. An early experience of my fascination with the capacities of language occurred as a child in reading the episode at the water pump in Helen Keller's story (Keller 1903/1996) in which she makes the visceral–ontological connection between sign and the world, manifestly transforming for her the nature of being and reality. Later, through school and in teaching at high school and university levels, I developed concerns about the implications, uses, and abuses of concepts of the true and the normal in human existence, and interest in the function and agency of discourse and language in both the closing down and the opening up of unique potentials in thinking, justice, the ontic and relations.

Following this interest, in this chapter I am concerned with research writing poetics read through Barad's theory, as a technoscientific practice (Barad 2007) that can work to enable new education narratives, ontological understandings and ontic unfoldings. Research writing methods are part of the material-discursive entanglements that make a difference to what can be co-constituted in education. I argue that an onto-epistemology that takes up indeterminacy rather than uncertainty is required to recognize and trouble the dangerous banality of normalized reductivism and managerialism in education. I take up MacLure's (2010) argument that we need to theorize in order to offend and interrupt, and Haraway's (1999, 2016) suggestion that the SF genre (inclusive of Science Fiction, Speculative Fiction and Fantasy) can be an enactment of philosophy, experimental thought and investigation.

A diffractive reading is a reading of insights through rather than against one another, undertaken not to critique one view with the use of another but to attend and respond to 'the details and specificities of relations of difference and how they matter' (Barad 2007, p. 24). Here, the central texts are not read intertextually to make comparisons between them as individual and stable works. Texts are becoming in their entanglements with/in other phenomena and the key texts here are engaged in a process of emerging together through this reading. In effect, this means noticing the entanglements in which the texts and their ideas and other texts are *already* participating, the ways they sound new discordant and resonant notes together, prompt sudden rememberings, and surface different materials (Van der Tuin 2016). This diffractive reading engages with Chapters Five and Six of *Meeting the Universe Halfway* (Barad 2007), with Bakhtin's 'The Dialogic Imagination' (1981), and with the SF novel *Naked Lunch* (Burroughs 1959) to consider the implications of their entanglement for writing educational research in a posthuman world.

Stories of uncertainty and indeterminacy

It matters what … thoughts think thoughts, what descriptions describe descriptions, what ties tie ties. It matters what stories make worlds, what worlds make stories.

(Haraway 2016, p. 12)

Haraway has written many times that the stories we tell about our world and knowledge shape the possibilities of these things in material ways (e.g. Haraway 1999, 2016; Haraway et al. 2016). In posthumanist conversations, the sophisticated and various arguments made by Haraway, Barad (2007), Braidotti (2013), and others that the separation of 'human' from 'nature' is seriously problematic in Western ontology and epistemology are familiar ones. Humanist 'Hero's Journey' (Campbell 1993) and Bildungsroman type narratives are entrenched in Western knowledge (Smethurst 2000) and research, enacting material-discursive forms wherein the world and its objects are a comparatively passive backdrop and resource for the revelation of human capacity, transformation and growth, typically occurring in an individualized, event-driven, linear fashion (Smethurst 2000). These assumptions have historically been aspects of an onto-epistemological metanarrative common to both traditional scientific inquiry and conventional qualitative social science inquiry (Fox and Alldred 2015). Humanism and its coproduct capitalism (Haraway 2016) entrench the dominant view of nature as a passive economic resource for humanity, and the logics of colonial and imperialistic power. Ontology, epistemology and the political economy are linked in an apparatus that co-constitutes a reality that is characterized by human competitive self-interest, capitalism and consumption, which differentiates and restricts the possibilities of agency for different human and non-human phenomena in particular ways (Barad 2007). This reality, referred to by some as the Anthropocene (Haraway et al. 2016), is an era in which the extent of impact made on the planet by the human species is historically unprecedented by any other single species (Crutzen 2006). As the implications of this reality become more impossible to ignore, a co-emergent and ubiquitous story is that of a world also haunted by the crisis of global uncertainty (Clough 2009).

A prominent rationale for education produced in this context says that education is an instrument important to our competitiveness and survival in this increasingly uncertain and chaotic world. Education research agendas in many Western countries urge an imperative to develop the 'gold standard' (Lather 2006, p. 48) neo-positivist research practices through which we will know 'what works' in education (Biesta 2016, p. 6). This includes how best to manage schools and to commodify knowledge and instructional strategies to serve as the foundations for the greatest yield of investment (Biesta 2016; Connell 2013). Powerful in this narrative is an ontology that holds that the world is uncertain and the reasoning that if uncertainty is the challenge, then this must be countered with movement towards certainty.

However Barad (2007) makes an argument that an ontology of uncertainty is momentously misguided. Drawing on the physicist Bohr, she explains the distinction between two notions in quantum theory: the uncertainty principle and the indeterminacy principle. What is shown in the iconic quantum physics double-slit experiment is that the world is neither ontologically uncertain in that its essence and laws are random nor epistemologically uncertain in that we do not yet know how to access the full extent of its objective truths. It is instead *indeterminate* in that its reality only emerges via entities in relations and the particular ways of (human and non-human) knowing that are brought to these relations.

In this way, the apparatuses of education research are already politically and ethically implicated in the phenomena they seek to understand. Apparatuses of rationalism and capitalist progress are attuned to the atomization and measurement of supposed certainties and the commodification and quantification of economic growth and power. In the urgency of global crisis, further imperatives are placed on education and education research to attend to methods for the optimization of competition and minimization of uncertainty. The logic and rhetoric of technocratic models for pedagogy and curriculum that include objective and well-defined fields of knowledge; normative human learning stages; standardized testing; measurement of 'effect size' in instructional strategies (Hattie 2012); ranking; and other forms of auditing of processes, outcomes and success, are positioned as moral responses to the need for common-sense action in uncertain times (Riddle and Apple 2019).

Against banality as a matter of ethics

Apparatuses that are finely attuned to defining, measuring and managing objects in the world cannot be at the same time well attuned to examining their own ontological, axiological and structural entanglements or to other more rich or unstable forms of knowledge. Widespread education discourses reinforcing the reductive and the competitive have co-produced erosion of the capacity to know through social connection, political agency and social justice (Apple 2001; Biesta 2016; Freire 2000; Giroux 2011). Other diminished opportunities are knowing through experiences of the arts, risk-taking, and creativity (Connell 2013). Education and learning become means to achieve narrowly defined outcomes rather than experiences of new potentialities. The unproblematized objectification inherent to these education narratives means a loss of ethical discourse, of connectedness and of imagination and wonder. Together these are the conditions for the kinds of everyday banality that become dangerous (Deleuze 1989) including sanctioned racism, human and animal rights abuses and other violence on and to the planet.

In education, research, policy and practice are entangled in many standardized classifications and normative notions including those often challenged through critical education research, for example, disability, gender, sexuality, ethnicity, indigeneity, history, knowledge and curriculum. Posthumanism further challenges the categories and dichotomies associated with these terms, and involves more than human relations including the material, the ecological and the geopolitical (Ulmer 2017), in considerations of the ethical implications of these and other constructions. Research narratives that attend to the prodigious possibilities yielded by these relations and that reimagine these constructions and norms are critical to developing the capacity to respond ethically and imaginatively to complex and serious local and global concerns (Barad 2007).

The SF author Le Guin argued that 'it is above all by the imagination that we achieve perception, and compassion, and hope' (1979, p. 58). The texts used in this diffractive reading are chosen in response to these concerns about apparatuses of certainty, indeterminacy, banality, imagination and hope. Chapter Five of Barad's text *Getting Real: Technoscientific Practices and the Materialization of Reality* develops a discussion of how observational instruments are involved in relationships with the discursive, co-producing bodies and reality. Chapter Six, *Spacetime Re(con)figurings: Naturalcultural Forces and Changing Topologies of Power*, focuses on ways that space, time and society are not given but are mutually constituted and are agents of change in the unfolding of reality.

The second text drawn on in this diffractive reading is Bakhtin's '*The Dialogic Imagination*' (1981). Bakhtin's chronotope offers a productive means towards thinking through rather than about entangled human–non-human phenomena, including space and time, by attending to the material-discourses through which ontic entanglements express themselves. The chronotope indicates the configuration of time and space that emerges and congeals within a literary text via its particular expression of relations of narrative, plot, discourse, being, epistemology, spatiality and temporality (Bakhtin 1981). '[S]patial and temporal indicators are fused into one carefully thought-out concrete whole. Time, as it were, thickens, takes on flesh, becomes artistically visible; likewise, space becomes charged and responsive to the movements of time, plot and history' (Bakhtin 1981, p. 84). The chronotope determines what is possible within the world of that text: how reality is experienced and by whom or what, how time is shaped, and what kinds of interactions are possible between people, animals, space and objects. Further, Bakhtin held a view of the reciprocal rather than unidirectional relationship of texts with the world. While his argument for this centres on the social world, it sounds a note of resonance in relation to considerations of texts in entangled ontic human–non-human worlds. Texts co-enact open-ended reality in the process of its unfolding (Bakhtin 1981). The chronotope has an entangled and agentic rather than a unidirectional relationship with the world itself.

The previous texts are read through *Naked Lunch* to imaginatively attend to how text is both a practice that describes observations of reality and an instrument in the co-production of that same reality, and to wonder about the range of possibilities of reality and agency that different texts could enable. Burroughs's SF novel *Naked Lunch* (1959) is a seminal experiment with the question posed by Gomel (2012): How can humans create a narrative voice that represents/constructs a post/inhuman subjectivity? Burroughs can retrospectively be considered an early author in the posthumanist tradition. He explored an absence of boundaries between humans, worlds, language and machines. He 'cut-up' text, randomly rearranging it (McHale 2004) and enabling its mutation, bringing attention to the 'materialities of inscription' (Land 2005, p. 451). In *Naked Lunch*, the writing, involving the experiences of the junk (heroin) addict William Lee, and including extreme depictions of drug use and of sex, simultaneously heightens attention to text, bodies and worlds, while dissolving them, shifting between voices and blurring boundaries. The collective voices both come into being via, and subvert, humanist discourse as they produce something radically Other (Gomel 2012), enabling a disturbing reimagining of the world and relations with/in the world.

I can understand Lovell's opinion that '(i)f a text can be dismissed as speculative, radical, or titillating, it remains safe, voyeuristic fiction of limited use for persuading readers to consciously recognise already existing posthuman configurations of subjectivity' (2018, p. 58). I nonetheless view texts such as *Naked Lunch* as valuable precisely for their capacity to work against the banality of objective realism, the genre conventionally understood as appropriate for research texts. SF modes of philosophy such as those deployed in *Naked Lunch* offer alternatives to both the neo-positivist and the humanistic. SF is not premised on supposed fixed, objective empirical truths that stand outside of the text to be discovered and represented. Nor is it premised on subjective, individualized human experience as the source of truth (Gomel 2012; Le Guin 1979), as it often deals with a distanced view of humans as a species. It can assist in destabilizing binary understandings of the radical, the normal, the real and the unreal. Both humanism and posthumanism are *already there* in the forms of and relations with the world (Lovell 2018). It is a matter of ethics for researchers to remain open to the different ways genre choices 'glow' (MacLure 2013) for the co-constitutions, situated risks and/or generativity they might yield.

The facets of the poetics that emerge through this chapter, transcorporeality and hypercorporeality, work against banality by attending to indeterminacy and enabling wonder. In naming these principles I draw on Alaimo's concept of transcorporeality, indicating a site of theoretical-material mingling and a 'time-space where human corporeality ... is inseparable from "nature" or "environment"' (2008, p. 238). Transcorporeality is about how matter and knowledge move through non/human bodies, ideas and forms. In this diffractive reading transcorporeality manifests in dissolved boundaries between human and non-human, real and unreal, reality and textual representation. This diffractive reading also suggests the significance of hypercorporeality: a poetics that enthusiastically embraces embodiedness. Hypercorporeality emerges here in the dissolution of pathologizing and corporeal classifications such as organic and inorganic, sensuous and disgusting, inner and outer and living and dead. This diffractive reading surfaces the idea that transcorporeality and hypercorporeality in writing assist to actualize certain posthumanist ideas: The congealing of text, world and human subject, the confusion of human and non-human boundaries and the openness of reality to possibility. Transcorporeality and hypercorporeality enact the materiality of discourse, and the discourses of materiality. The remainder of this chapter considers these diffracting ideas, along with some of their implications for research writing that can challenge and transform reductive and instrumental stories of education.

A transcorporeal, hypercorporeal chronotope

I propose an understanding of reality that takes account of the exclusions on which it depends and its openness to future reworkings.

(Barad 2007, p. 205)

Barad's (2007) account of reality holds not that this is made up of pre-existing and individualized phenomena with distinct boundaries, but that reality is an entanglement of inseparable phenomena, and is constantly emerging via ongoing and shifting relations. Reality is therefore limited by the possibilities of the particular relations involved in its creation. But because entities in relations are themselves emerging and contingent, not fixed and individualized, and because relations have ongoing, dispersive agency in the universe, reality is also open to possibility. How can posthumanist poetics enact the fact that reality is dependent on the exclusions created in particular relations and is at the same time open to future reworkings? In this diffractive reading, a transcorporeal and hypercorporeal chronotope (Bakhtin 1981) emerges as a form for these enactments.

Attention to the chronotope (Bakhtin 1981) – the configuration of time and space that is constructed within a text – draws attention to the entangled discourses of materiality, and materiality of discourses, and what they do, and might produce, together. The particular chronotope enacted in *Naked Lunch* is characterized by a vitalism and dynamism of space, objects, place and time. Assemblages of living/dead materialities, sensory, imaginative, hallucinogenic and technological landscapes, and a narrative structure of loosely connected, non-linear episodes are evoked in this excerpt:

> Chicago: invisible hierarchy of decorticated wops, smell of atrophied gangsters, earthbound ghosts hit you at North and Halstead, Cicero, Lincoln Park, panhandler of dreams, past invading the present, rancid magic of slot machines and roadhouses. (Burroughs 1959, p. 24)

This confusion of space, time and im/materiality are achieved via a particular and fluid kind of heteroglossia. Heteroglossia is a Bakhtinian term indicating the representation in a text of multiple discourses without authorial preference (Bakhtin 1981). Burroughs's discourses are not tied to particular and human subjects. Rather, the voice, agency and vitality of author, narrator, characters, space-time and text are an undifferentiated, fluid element of the assemblage of the text. An example approaching a similar transcorporeal, hypercorporeal chronotope in research is found in Snaza et al.'s (2014) description of the assemblage of a school site. In traditional notions of education the school is a site for human management and knowledge deals primarily with the conceptual, which is in turn conceived as largely separate from materiality and physical bodies. In the writing of Snaza et al (2014), humans are displaced from the centre of the narrative and attention is distributed through linkages of small or often-overlooked material things and their relations with one another:

> Networks of wire and pipe linking the buildings' architecture to the subterranean infrastructures of cities and beyond that to the swirls of the oceans and global deposits of prehistoric dead organisms waiting to be mined and refined; dead

nonhuman animals on plates in cafeterias, as well as on feet, human bodies, athletic equipment, and biology dissection trays. (Snaza et al. 2014, p. 40)

The assemblage approaches posthumanist writing in that it enables curious attention to the corporeal and to the fluidity of its boundaries. The banal in schooling is made unfamiliar, creating openings for curiosity about how school meanings, bodies, boundaries, knowledge and power are produced (Snaza et al. 2014).

The hypercorporeality enacted in *Naked Lunch* baulks at notions of normal, safe, clean, managed bodies, as forms of social control (Land 2005). Instead it frees expression of a range of embodied realities that are alternative to those that are socially sanctioned, revelling in non-normative bodily transgressions, aggressions, pollutions, obscenities, parodies, penetrations and inscriptions with needles in/on bodies. This includes the dissolution of pathological classifications, for example a blurred distinction between living and dead. The junky's surrender to the bodily need of his habit simultaneously and paradoxically means a dissolution of the boundaries of the body:

> Look down at my filthy trousers, haven't been changed in months. The days glide by on a syringe with a long thread of blood … I am forgetting sex and all sharp pleasures of the body – a grey, junk-bound ghost. The Spanish boys call me El Hombre Invisible. (Burroughs 1959, p. 63)

The chronotope radically and disturbingly confronts us with the fact that death and decay are indistinct from life. Braidotti (2010) argues that a significant challenge provoked by posthumanism is the recognition that the labelling of the outcomes of particular relations as either generative or pathological in a binary sense is problematic and is linked to our lack of understanding that degeneration is always integral to life and relations. The notion of generative benefit is always problematic, is dependent on context and on point of view, and can never be fully evaluated (Colebrook 2006). Fox and Alldred's (2017) research on pro-ana (pro-anorexic) social media groups illustrates the possibilities afforded when pathologizing classifications are decentralized from the research writing apparatus. For the participants of the pro-ana groups, freedom from socially sanctioned notions of embodiment and from classifications that labelled them destructive enabled new freedoms via new transcorporeal assemblages involving body, school, fashion, hunger, identity, social media, diagnosis and sexuality. A transcorporeal, hypercorporeal chronotope can enact the breaking open of conventional classifications of the body. It reminds us that conceptualizations with the power to crack open deeply entrenched thinking about material boundaries, good and bad bodies, life and death, must necessarily be radical and disturbing for some.

This reading suggests the value of writing by thinking through the dynamism and materiality of the times and spaces that are the settings of research, removing them from banality, noticing them as agentic and provocative and as involved in the constant co-production of life and death. Such a poetics moves towards posthuman realities, limited by the possibilities of the particular material-discursive relations involved in their creation, but also open to transformation. The next section of this chapter emphasizes the agency of language in this emerging poetics.

Language as virus

Agential realism takes into account the fact that the forces at work in the materialization of bodies are not only social and the bodies produced are not all human.

(Barad 2007 p. 225)

Barad (2007) rejects the assumption that humans are the only species with the intelligence and agency to produce knowledge. Agency is not a quality possessed by particular subjects and enacted on objects but is an inherent capacity throughout the universe. All entities have the capacity to intra-act with other entities (Barad 2007) and co-produce affects: material or immaterial intensities or shifts in experience (Fox and Alldred 2015). A poetics for posthumanist writing then is concerned with how things come into being via relations, and with noticing new kinds of agency and knowing in these relational entanglements.

Burroughs work breaks the dichotomy that says that language belongs only to the human. Burroughs's language is not a human, social tool or construction, but a virus: an organism with the purposeful agency to replicate itself (Land 2005). *Naked Lunch* emphasizes a hypercorporeal, copulating, infecting, relationship between discourses, humans, and worldly objects, in which the agency of language is emphasized, as is made explicit here:

> The Word is divided into units which be all in one piece and should so be taken, but the pieces can be had in any order being tied up back and forth, in and out fore and aft like an innaresting sex arrangement ...

> Gentle reader, the Word will leap on you with leopard man iron claws, it will cut off fingers and toes like an opportunist land crab, it will hang you and catch your

jissom like a scrutable dog, it will coil round your thighs like a bushmaster and inject a shot glass of rancid ectoplasm. (Burroughs 1959, p. 181)

Like Stengers (2008), who argues for the use of language for 'efficacious propositions' (p. 40), Burroughs's language is material force. Language does not belong to humans; it is its own life force, engaging with and provoking the world. Language, organisms and landscapes are arresting and sexual, engage in lewd acts, grab readers, characters and scenes, infect, spill on and soil them. The potential of language as virus includes its capacity to problematize representational discourse, to emphasize the agency and materiality of words and non-human expressions, to optimize ironic meaning and to open possibilities of new, complex, dynamic forms of reality. In the previous quotation, 'the Word' is vitally alive, and language itself is defamiliarized, shedding its reductive, representational banality. Binaries of the passive and the agentic, representation and reality, subject and object, material and conceptual, human and non-human are troubled. In neo-positivist education, measured objects are passive entities that can be 'known', objectively described in texts, and are subject to education interventions. But in posthumanist writing, all phenomena might engage with language, and vice versa. Multiple ironies are enabled, and communications take on further performative qualities.

In support of his deployment of aggressive, agentic language Burroughs drew again on heteroglossia. The use of heteroglossia – multiple discourses without authorial preference – produces in a text the capacity to face outward, away from itself (Bakhtin 1981), as intrinsic to its indeterminate meaning is an expectation of interaction with the world and readers. In Burroughs's text a multitude of characters including the junky William Lee and a blurred range of landscapes, machines, dealers, users, police, informants and bystanders, subvert and question systematized norms, institutionalized practices and normative bodies (McHale 2004). Their discourses are provocative and dialogic; they bring contentious ideas, bodies and realities to attention with an expectation of reaction. Parody is one example: 'Straight' norms, discourse and ways of living (McHale 2004) are given condescending translations of specialized counterculture vocabulary. The subtle forms of oppression that lurk in the everyday banal (Deleuze 1989) of our institutions are also given parodic treatment. In this example, Doctor Benway, adviser to the 'Freeland Republic' on the management of citizens, explains how institutions achieve 'total demoralization' by subtle means:

prolonged mistreatment, short of physical violence, gives rise, when skilfully applied, to anxiety and a feeling of special guilt. A few rules or rather guiding principles are to be borne in mind. The subject must not realize that the treatment is an attack of an anti-human enemy on his personal identity. He must be made to feel that he deserves any treatment he receives because there is something (never specified) horribly wrong with him. (Burroughs 1959, p. 31)

Language as virus also deploys a deadpan, flat, descriptive voice used equally to describe bizarre, disturbing events and banal everyday minutiae, as demonstrated here:

> Several Meat Eaters lay in vomit, too weak to move (The Black Meat is like a tainted cheese, overpoweringly delicious and nauseating so that eaters eat and vomit and eat again until they fall exhausted) (Burroughs 1959, p. 55)

This provokes an uneasy ontological hesitancy (Todorov 1975) in the reader. In contravention of other genre norms, the deadpan voice provides no suggestion as to what might safely be understood to be metaphor, what is representative of the 'real', and what is supposed to sit within the realms of 'fantasy'. Without authorial guidance about how to interpret the narrative, the reality of the text becomes multiple and indeterminate (Klapcsik 2012; Mendlesohn 2008). The world seems loaded with irony, and cracked open to the possibility of new, complex, dynamic, non-reductive, ultimately unknowable forms of reality.

Examples and arguments for the above kinds of defamiliarization of language and genre exist in poststructural literature (e.g. Deleuze and Guattari 1987; Latour 1993). Haraway, in her Cyborg Manifesto (1999), takes seriously the notion of the use of language for serious play, humour and irony for political ends. MacLure, drawing on Latour's work, theorizes 'the recalcitrance of the object' (2006, p. 734) that occurs when 'the object' is defamiliarized. If language as 'the object' is made recalcitrant and vital, the onlooker is '*gripped*' (MacLure 2006, p.734). The text looks back, throwing doubt on our trust in language and our assumed knowledge and drawing attention to the inherent irony of reality. In *Naked Lunch* language asserts itself recalcitrantly, defamiliarizing itself, provoking responses and making conventions, norms and binaries absurd.

In education research such uses of defamiliarization, parody or irony could harness as an agentic force the frustration and concern that many learners, educators and researchers feel in an increasingly managed and surveilled environment, and direct this into 'forging efficacious propositions' (Stengers 2008, p. 40) that highlight absurdity and unrecognized harm, reimagine chronotopes and can transform. The rhetorics and practices of 'safe schools' and 'safe spaces'; notions of 'engagement in learning'; performance auditing; 'value-free curriculum'; pathologized youth experiences; the positioning of children as citizens-to-be rather than citizens (Murris 2016); or the 'othering' of children, animals, plants or objects might be useful targets.

Significantly, while parody is deployed to question systems and the agency of social controls, a commitment to heteroglossia in *Naked Lunch* enables more subtle understandings of power and agency, than do the unidirectional models of power often manifest in conventional research writing genres. Just as heteroglossia means discourses are dynamically dispersed and intra-acting in the novel and do not belong to phenomena, it also means agency and power are similarly fluid. This characteristic of heteroglossia allows for attention to a range of agencies in the flows of capitalism including Lee's own exploitation and dehumanization of his junk market:

> The junky does not sell his product to the consumer, he sells the consumer to the product. He does not improve and simplify his merchandise. He degrades and simplifies the client. (Burroughs 1959, p. 8)

Power is not unidirectionally exerted downward from macro agents who hold it to micro levels lacking in power, but is a dynamic relationship produced by all phenomena in/emerging with the apparatus (Barad 2007). There are no first or second order agents or effects of capitalism or post-positivism in education and research. Rather, geographies, creatures, plants, objects, ecosystems, knowledges, desires, laws, histories and onto-epistemologies produce these material-discursive phenomena in their multiple, shifting manifestations. In illustration, Barad discusses Fernandes's research about relations of power in a Calcutta jute mill:

> Fernandes maintains that the spatiality of capitalism is produced not merely through actions of managers who carve up the production process but through the workers' own exclusionary practices as well. That is, while the mill is perhaps most obviously an ongoing process of the materialization of capital, the iterative materialization of the mill is also the outcome of the exclusionary practices of the workers themselves, but not via some linear additive dynamics. Rather, the exclusionary practices of the workers need to be understood to be part of the technologies of capitalism. (Barad 2007, p. 237)

Rational argument as a discursive form is not well equipped to attend to such complexities of power, being premised on humanism, linearity, cause and effect, stable and final conclusions and static understandings of phenomena. Language as virus in the transcorporeal, hypercorporeal chronotope can enable more nuance in writing the workings of power, allowing for the ways in which researchers are both deeply marked by and involved in the co-production of the marks and realities of class, violence, exploitation, neo-liberalism, consumerism, and capitalism and so are co-responsible for the research stories and structures that they might simultaneously argue are banal, risk-averse, unjust or anthropocentric.

Some concluding thoughts

Barad's agential realism and the indeterminacy at its heart provoke profound disturbances to Western ontology and epistemology. In this chapter I have aimed to experiment with diffractive reading to consider how an ontology of indeterminacy and an epistemology of wonder might manifest in ways that are not readily available from conventional qualitative inquiry genres. Entangled in the poetics for a transcorporeal, hypercorporeal chronotope that emerges in this diffractive reading is a particular epistemology, a principal of which is the subversion of reductive banality and the opening up of indeterminacy and wonder with/in the world. Wonder in MacLure's (2006) notion of the term is a corporeal experience involving interaction with, confusion and horror in, worldly bodies (Daston and Park 2001). It is at the same time an unbounded experience involving the emergence of liminal ideas and glimpses of alternative possibilities. This poetics might assist in enabling the conditions for creative activism against education narratives of technocratic and reductive objectification, and for reimagining and engaging with the world, language, research and education as non-normative, wondrous and dynamic.

Glossary

Defamiliarization A literary technique for making the strange seem familiar and the familiar seem strange, having the effect of providing an altered view of realties, ideas, habits, practices and morality.

Hypercorporeality The enthusiastic embracing of corporeality and the dissolution of pathologizing and embodied classifications such as organic and inorganic, sensuous and disgusting, inner and outer and living and dead.

Language as virus The defamiliarization of discourse and use of language to emphasize its virus-like symbiosis with life and its agency.

Transcorporeal, hypercorporeal chronotope A textual time-space that blurs and confuses multiple subjectivities, im/materialities, spaces and times.

Transcorporeality The notion that 'bodies' are complex networks of entities through which materiality and knowledges move. Boundaries such as those between human and non-human matter, and between the real, the representational and the unreal are contingent.

References

Alaimo, S. (2008), 'Trans-corporeal feminisms and the ethical space of nature', in S. Alaimo and S. Hekman (eds), *Material Feminisms*, 237–64, Bloomington, IN: Indiana University Press.

Apple, M. W. (2001), *Educating the "Right" Way: Markets, Standards, God, and Inequality*, New York, NY; London: RoutledgeFalmer.

Bakhtin, M. (1981), *The Dialogic Imagination*, Austin, TX: University of Texas Press.

Barad, K. (2007), *Meeting the Universe Halfway: Quantum Physics and the Entanglement of Matter and Meaning*, Durham, NC: Duke University Press.

Biesta, G. (2016), *Good Education in an Age of Measurement: Ethics, Politics, Democracy*, New York: Routledge.

Braidotti, R. (2010), 'The politics of "Life Itself"', in D. Coole and S. Frost (eds), *New Materialisms: Ontology, Agency, and Politics*, 201–18, Durham and London, UK: Duke University Press.

Braidotti, R. (2013), *The Posthuman*, Cambridge, MA: Polity.

Braidotti, R. (2018), 'A theoretical framework for the critical posthumanities', *Theory, Culture & Society*, 1–31.

Burroughs, W. (1959), *Naked Lunch*, Paris: Olympia Press.

Campbell, J. (1993), *The Hero with a Thousand Faces*, London: HarperCollins.

Clough, P. (2009), 'The new empiricism: Affect and sociological method', *European Journal of Social Theory*, 12 (1): 43–61.

Colebrook, C. (2006), *Deleuze: A Guide for the Perplexed*, London: Continuum.

Connell, R. (2013), 'The neoliberal cascade and education: An essay on the market agenda and its consequences', *Critical Studies in Education*, 54 (2): 99–112.

Crutzen, P. J. (2006), 'The "Anthropocene"', in E. Ehlers and T. Krafft (eds), *Earth System Science in the Anthropocene*, 13–18, Berlin, Heidelberg: Springer Berlin Heidelberg.

Daston, L. and Park, K. (2001), *Wonders and the Order of Nature*, New York, NY: Zone Books.

Deleuze, G. (1989), *Cinema II*, Minneapolis, MN: University of Minnesota Press.

Deleuze, G. and Guattari, F. (1987), *A Thousand Plateaus: Capitalism and Schizophrenia*, Minneapolis, MN: University of Minnesota Press.

Fox, N. J. and Alldred, P. (2015), 'New materialist social inquiry: Designs, methods and the research-assemblage', *International Journal of Social Research Methodology*, 18 (4): 399–414.

Fox, N. J. and Alldred, P. (2017), *Sociology and the New Materialism*, Los Angeles, CA: Sage.

Freire, P. (2000), *Pedagogy of the Oppressed*, 30th anniversary edition edn, New York: Continuum.

Giroux, H. (2011), *Education and the Crisis of Public Values: Challenging the Assault on Teachers, Students, & Public Education*, New York: Peter Lang Publishing.

Gomel, E. (2012), 'Posthuman voices: Alien infestation and the poetics of subjectivity', *Science Fiction Studies* 2: 177.

Haraway, D. (1999), 'A cyborg manifesto: Science, technology, and socilaist-feminism in the late twentieth century', in *Simians, Cyborgs and Women: The Reinvention of Nature*, London: Free Association Books.

Haraway, D. (2016), *Staying with the Trouble: Making Kin in the Chthulucene*, Durham, NC: Duke University Press.

Haraway, D., Ishikawa, N., Gilbert, S. F., Olwig, K., Tsing, A. L. and Bubandt, N. (2016), 'Anthropologists are talking – about the Anthropocene', *Ethnos*, 81 (3): 535–64.

Hattie, J. (2012), *Visible Learning for Teachers: Maximizing Impact on Learning*, London: Routledge.

Keller, H. (1903/1996), *The Story of My Life*, New York: DoubleDay, Page & Co/Dover Publications.

Klapcsik, S. (2012), *Liminality in Fantastic Fiction: A Poststructralist Approach*, e-book edn, Jefferson, NC: McFarland & Company.

Land, C. (2005), 'Apomorphine silence: Cutting-up Burroughs' theory of language and control', *Ephemera: Theory and Politics in Organisation*, 5 (3): 450–71.

Lather, P. (2006), 'Paradigm proliferation as a good thing to think with: Teaching research in education as a wild profusion', *International Journal of Qualitative Studies in Education (QSE)*, 19 (1): 35–57.

Latour, B. (1993), *Aramis: Or the Love of Technology*, Cambridge, MA: Harvard University Press.

Le Guin, U. (1979), *The Language of the Night: Essays on Fantasy and Science Fiction*, New York: G.P. Putnam's Sons.

Lenz Taguchi, H. and Palmer, A. (2013), 'A more "livable" school? A diffractive analysis of the performative enactments of girls' ill-/well-being with(in) school environments', *Gender & Education*, 25 (6): 671–87.

Lovell, S. (2018), 'Toward a poetics of posthumanist narrative using Ruth Ozeki's a tale for the time being', *Critique: Studies in Contemporary Fiction*, 59 (1): 57–74.

MacLure, M. (2006), 'The bone in the throat: Some uncertain thoughts on baroque method', *International Journal of Qualitative Studies in Education*, 19 (6): 729–45.

MacLure, M. (2010), 'The offence of theory', *Journal of Education Policy*, 25 (2): 277–86.

MacLure, M. (2013), 'Researching without representation? Language and materiality in post-qualitative methodology', *International Journal of Qualitative Studies in Education*, 26 (6): 658–67.

McHale, B. (2004), *Postmodernist Fiction*, London: Methuen.

Mendlesohn, F. (2008), *The Rhetorics of Fantasy*, Middletown, CT: Wesleyan University Press.

Murris, K. (2016), *The Posthuman Child*, London: Routledge.

Riddle, S. and Apple, M. (2019), 'Education and democracy in dangerous times', in S. Riddle and M. Apple (eds), *Re-imagining Education for Democracy*, 1–9, New York: Routledge.

Rosiek, J. L. (2018), 'Agential realism and educational ethnography', in D. Beach, C. Bagley and S. Marques da Silva (eds), *The Wiley Handbook of Ethnography of Education*, 547–69, John Wiley & Sons, Proquest Ebook.

Rousell, D. (2016), 'Dwelling in the anthropocene: Reimagining university learning environments in response to social and ecological change', *Australian Journal of Environmental Education*, 32 (2): 137–53.

Smethurst, P. (2000), *The Postmodern Chronotope: Reading Space and Time in Contemporary Fiction*, Atlanta, GA: Postmodern Studies, Rodopi.

Snaza, N., Appelbaum, P., Bayne, S., Carlson, D., Morris, M., Rotas, N., Sandlin, J., Wallin, J. and Weaver, J. (2014), 'Toward a posthumanist education', *Journal of Curriculum Theorizing*, 30 (2): 39–55.

Stengers, I. (2008), 'Experimenting with refrains: Subjectivity and the challenge of escaping modern dualism', *Subjectivity*, 1: 38.

Todorov, T. (1975), *The Fantastic: A Structural Approach to a Literary Genre*, New York: Cornell University Press.

Ulmer, J. (2017), 'Posthumanism as research methodology: Inquiry in the anthropocene', *International Journal of Qualitative Studies in Education*, 30 (9): 832–48.

Van der Tuin, I. (2016), 'Reading diffractive reading: Where and when does diffraction happen?' *Journal of Electronic Publishing*, 19 (2). doi:10.3998/3336451.0019.205.

Who is in my office and which century/ies are we in? A pedagogical encounter

Mary Dixon

I am seated in my office, my back to the window looking across the computer desk to my door. Over the day it will open for three doctoral supervision meetings. Rebecca's thesis concerns the pedagogical positioning of secondary teachers. She is finalizing her colloquium document but still struggling for a theoretical frame. Tom is finishing his thesis on the pedagogical networks of higher education online students. He is putting Dewey to work along with Van Manen and Maggie MacLure. Finally, Zoya will come later today. Her work regards the educational opportunities for teenage girls in newly developed areas of Melbourne. She insists on engaging Foucault and Bourdieu and Butler. Each meeting will last at least an hour and will also involve an associate supervisor.

Researching pedagogical encounters

What follows here is a two-step analytical experiment in pedagogical encounters. Here 'black holes' are engaged as analytic devices to discern the 'event'(Deleuze 2003) of learning in these encounters. The experiment then involves a pedagogical mapping that is discerned through a black hole perspective. I have chosen to locate this exploration in pedagogical encounters in doctoral supervision. The chapter is not intended to provide an analysis of doctoral study and supervision although located in those spaces and some attention is given to it. Nor are the encounters here from an actual research study. The imagined encounters are offered to provide a site for a new form of pedagogical analysis. The reading of pedagogical encounters offered here draws on overlapping concepts from both Barad and Deleuze. There has been considerable discussion around the problematics of using Barad and Deleuze together. Hein (2016) argues that 'Deleuze's is a philosophy of immanence and difference, whereas Barad's is a philosophy of transcendence and identity' (p. 132). Hein draws on the distinctions of immanence (from Deleuze) and transcendence (from Barad). These concepts call up issues of interiority and exteriority which lend themselves to a binary reading of these ontological positions. Several scholars have taken up this problematic (Sheldon 2016; Davies 2016) with a significant contribution from Kathrin Thiele (2016) who argues the relationship between Deleuze-Guattarian immanence and Barad's agential realism. Barad and Deleuze share an interest in different understandings of thought and being. The lively agency of Barad's posthumanism overlaps with what St. Pierre (2016, p. 101) names 'the vitalist proclivities of Gilles Deleuze'. I use this chapter as an opportunity to read pedagogical encounters diffractively into each other (Barad 2007 p. 30; Jackson and Mazzei 2012, p. 11) putting to work Barad's 'timespacemattering' (2007) and Deleuzian 'becoming' (2003).

Pedagogy is the study of learning, of learner, of knowledge, of place and, on occasion, of teacher. The pedagogical encounter is their dynamic intra-action (Barad 2007, p. 141). The nature of their dynamic intra-action is a critical component in reading this encounter. As Barad argues, these entangled agencies, in this case the learner, knowledge, place and teacher are in mutual constitution. They each emerge through their intra-action. In this research, I am looking to more fully recognize and map the 'events' of learning in these encounters.

In current educational discourses learning is commonly addressed within the fields of psychology and neuroscience with particular attention to the links between brain activity and learning. Significant attention is also paid to the provocations to learning by sociologists, by cultural theorists and of course by pedagogues. The reading of learning here is as 'event' and sits outside those readings and addresses instead the nature of the learning beyond the individual subject. As philosophy is for Deleuze (2003), so learning, for this author, is an event through which the movement of life becomes. This understanding of event opens up the conceptualization of learning and the pedagogical encounter.

In the initial section of the chapter I consider Deleuze's reading of event (2003) and engage with these event attributes as they pertain to learning. I then turn attention to the doctoral meeting as a site of this analytical work. This analysis is put to work with three doctoral encounters. The 'black hole' structure of the pedagogical encounter is presented as a way of analysis of the encounter. The possibilities of mapping these black hole encounters are considered. Finally, suggestions are made for the possibilities this analytic experiment offers not only for researchers but also for those inside the encounters.

The Deleuzian event

In the 'Logic of Sense' (2003, pp. 8–9) Deleuze asserts the event is unlimited becoming. Events are produced in a chaos of multiplicity. The event of learning is produced in the chaos of knowledge, knowing, being, becoming, experiencing and living. Events are actualized within us (Deleuze 2003, p. 148).

> The event is not what occurs (an accident), it is rather inside what occurs, the purely expressed. It signals and awaits us … it is what must be understood, willed and represented in that which occurs. (2003, p. 149)

The event in this reading is the learning, and it may not even appear, regardless of willing it. It is the learning, the becoming of each in the encounter: the candidate, the supervisor, the knowledge and the place. The doctoral candidate wills the event of learning. The supervisor wills the event of learning for the candidate. The knowledge wills the event. Learning awaits us – it awaits the candidate, the knowledge, the place and the supervisor. We seek/summon/will the event as 'Willing the event is to release its eternal truth' (Deleuze 2003, p. 149). However, we may be blind to the event, unable to see what it reveals, what we may not be able to bear, what we may desire. We may not be sure of when the learning occurs.

Events and, in this case, learning are not the essential unified quality of things. Deleuze argues events really are irreducible to material reality: 'Events are the only idealities' (2003, p. 53). They are real, but their reality is not material. Learning is a reality which is not essential or unified nor reducible to material reality and nor is it located in specific time or action. The event of learning as a vibration of intensities – the vibrations of knowing and understanding and knowledge – slips through learner, knowledge, place and teacher. When these come together, willing the event, a pedagogical encounter is the state of affairs.

Structure of event

The event of learning has a double structure – the moment of its actualization and the moment in which the event is in – a state of affairs which is the pedagogical encounter. The spatio-temporal realization of the event is in a state of affairs.

> there is the present moment of its actualisation, the moment in which the event is in a state of affairs, an individual or a person … The future and the past of the event are evaluated only with respect to this definitive present …. But on the other hand, there is the future and the past of the event considered in itself, sidestepping each present, being free of the limitations of the state of affairs impersonal and pre-individual. (Deleuze 2003, p. 151)

Deleuze asserts the event is Unlimited becoming (2003, pp. 8–9) and is always that which has just happened and that which is about to happen but never that which is happening. Learning is a synthesis of the past and future. It is an unobservable space – personal and private space. The event of learning is at once located within a time and at the same time expresses a new time. Like the great pyramid, as Deleuze states of an event, the duration of learning 'may be for a period of one hour thirty minutes five minutes or a life time' (Deleuze 1992, p. 76). This temporal nature of learning is felt relentlessly and poignantly in the doctoral work spanning years of engagement between learner, knowledge, place and supervisor. The pedagogical nature of these relationships is heavy in its presence and insistence but elusive in the recognition and management of the event of learning.

Deleuze (1992) argues that a component of the event is extensions. Extension exists when one element is stretched over the following ones, such that it is a whole and the following elements are its parts. Such a connection of whole-parts forms an infinite series that contains neither a final term nor a limit. It is critical to note that the element stretches or is stretched – this is more than connected. In the learning event, extensions are stretched over knowing, understanding, knowledge, becoming. It is a dynamic intra-action with time and space moving in the extension. It is 'a vibration with an infinity of harmonics or submultiples, such as an audible wave, a luminous wave' (Deleuze 1992, p. 77).

Learning as event is a vibration coursing through knowledge, learner, place, teacher. Events do not directly cause anything, but provide the problem, structure or orientation to a given state of affairs around which it changes. For Beck and Gleyzon (2016, p. 229)

> Deleuzian events are rhizomatic and part of an ever-changing, ongoing process. … Deleuzian micro-Events can occur within individuals or small groups. Nevertheless, these events spur change; they reshape the conceptual and material fabric of connectivity, relationships, path-ways and institutions.

The analytic site – Doctoral meetings

The pedagogical work which is the subject of this chapter is located inside doctoral supervision. The supervisory meeting becomes a pedagogical encounter when the event of learning occurs. The thickness and uneven movement of learning and understanding in doctoral work is a common experience for social science doctoral candidates. The protracted time of doing this work from up to four years for full-time candidates to eight years for part time exacerbates this already intense and charged endeavour. The encounter with the supervisor is chosen for this analytical experiment not because it is seen as the significant, pivotal or critical learning point in thesis work. It may well be, but it is not necessarily intended or actualized that way. In Australia this is a supervisory relationship. The academic is named as a supervisor, neither a teacher nor a mentor. The candidate is not named as a student. The work is research. Yet this work, this research, is definitely a learning project. The candidate learns to do research and learns the field of their research. The encounter with the supervisor is chosen for this engagement because it is a recurring encounter over many years with largely the same participants and these are the major thesis structural points with the candidate's learning as the focal point of the encounter. I have put to work fragments of an imaginary of various candidate and supervisor meetings. These encounters are drawn from a large bank of supervision meetings with an array of candidates over my academic career. This imaginary method of representation is deployed as it offers an opportunity to open up the thesis learning intra-actions of supervisors, candidates, theorists, knowledge, time and place. Further, it offers the possibility of problematizing the temporal nature of research and research learning.

There have been very productive poststructural readings of supervision across a range of relevant issues. Fullager, Pavlidis and Stadler (2017), for example, provide a rhizomatic reading of supervision in order to create new knowledge practices in doctoral supervision. Supervision research also does much to attend to identity formation work inside academia (e.g. Barnacle 2005, Green 2005). This chapter, however, is an engagement with the broader concept of pedagogy and its manifestation in a state of affairs known as a pedagogical encounter. Herein are entanglements of people, spaces and knowledge which are summoned to produce new knowledge. The encounter includes addressing theorists and knowledges from the past and the future. The relationship between supervisor and candidate and the pedagogical encounter has traditionally been seen as very private and personal (Lee and Green 1998) and conducted behind closed doors (Mc William and Palmer 1998). I follow the position of Fullager et al. who challenged both the technical rational viewing and 'the mystique that traditionally enveloped the PhD supervisor and student in a shroud of hierarchical, transcendent knowledge relations' (2017, p. 24). In my interrogation of this encounter I provide an intra-active analysis which allows us to reveal what we as candidates and as supervisors cannot bear and what we desire. The drama and the resistance of the encounter is represented in an architectural reading of the office as meeting place.

> *My office is large enough for a desk as well as a table for discussion. There is a white board on the wall and I still have a small book case. However, I chose to forego the usual meeting table and chairs. I purchased for this space, instead, a second hand three-seater, gold brocade, very small Victorian lounge suite. The dark wooden arms and feet are slender and curved. The suite is low to the ground with straight backs. First time visitors are often taken aback. However, the supervision meetings require seating for a growing number of people who come and go but often stay for long and sometimes uncomfortable conversations.*

The supervisor's office itself is not read through a modernist idea of architecture which proffers that design can be representational of occupation and provide a fit between human behaviour and space (Boys 2011, p. 62). Indeed, my office did include the usual venetian blinds, computer desk, office chairs and a single bookshelf. The large bookshelves had been removed by the university in the light of the prevalence of digital readings and resources. In a resistant move to consider the office as a container for speaking from the desk, I (the supervisor) used the empty bookshelf space to fill the office with a gold brocade Victorian lounge suite – though not large enough for Hannah Arendt to recline in (*Hannah Arendt* 2013) but comfortable enough for long conversations and with room for all who may enter. Indeed, the provocative furnishing was seen to enable an activity akin to a European literary salon. The making of the learning space is done through action (Mulcahy, Cleveland and Alberton 2015) and is not a backdrop to the action of learning but co-constitutes the learning.

'Black holes' for analysis

The doctoral engagement is a heated site of pedagogy extending as it does over many years with intense relationships between knowledge and learner (candidate). These doctoral encounters summon us to see the thickness of pedagogy. They are also deeply perspectival constructs. When faced with the complexity of the teaching and learning relationship, Roy argues that 'sensation in the smallest interval must be watched in a pedagogic relationship' (2003, p. 174). The matter between the bodies (and here I include humans, non-humans, objects and spaces) is pedagogic matter. The body of each extends beyond its material boundaries. In these extensions, bodies reach out to the other – these extensions are felt by others, seen by others. Pedagogical readings pull in to focus Ellsworth's 'rickety space' between self and other (Ellsworth 1997, p. 163) – the area of the bodily between. For Deleuze the physical extension of bodies in assemblages is embodied as 'matter-energy' (Deleuze and Guattari 1987, p. 408). Through a Deleuzian understanding of 'energies' Zembylas argues these 'produce new affective and embodied connections' (2007, p. 20). Pedagogical encounters are embodied in matter energy manifestations in the bodily between.

I seek to 'analyze' the supervisory meeting when it is a pedagogical encounter. I want to bring the unthinkable into representation, to see the familiar anew and to use that familiar to make it strange. I seek to map the event of learning in these encounters through what can be offered in a black hole reading. To do this I put to work the structure of black holes for what they offer in opening up these pedagogical encounters. A fabulation is a story in the style of magical realism (Scholes 1967; Haraway 2016; Truman 2018). In this section the fabulation of a black hole is explored to realize that pedagogical encounter in the supervisor's office which can now be seen to contain all mass but has zero volume and where the space-time curvature becomes infinite.

Black holes have been the subject of fiction writers and have come to the screen in the likes of Star Trek and the Voyager series (Wertheim 1999). Black holes are also the concern of scientists. As the theoretical physicist Rovelli asserts, 'Today they {black holes} are observed in the sky in their hundreds and studied in great detail by astronomers' (2015, p. 8). Closer to the black hole space-time starts to deform. There are more paths going towards the pedagogical black hole than paths moving away. Of significance in understanding the pedagogical encounter is the centre of a black hole in which lies a region where the space-time curvature becomes infinite. This region contains all mass but has zero volume. Time and space are collapsed and this is of critical importance for this reading. Its boundary is a mathematically defined surface – an event horizon through which matter and light can only pass inward towards the mass of the black hole. Nothing, not even light nor information, can escape from inside the event horizon making it impossible to identify to an observer if anything even happened. The certainty of the learning in this black hole is not apparent and may not even have occurred. It is a matter of time. In this collapsed time and space, those inside the black hole – the supervisor and the learner, the knowledge, the place – are surrounded by now, befores and possible afters. To a distant observer, clocks near a black hole appear to tick more slowly than those further away from the black hole. Due to this effect, known as gravitational time dilation, an object falling into a black hole appears to slow down as it approaches the event horizon, taking an infinite time to reach it. At the same time, all processes on this object slow down, for a fixed outside observer, causing emitted light to appear redder and dimmer, an effect known as gravitational redshift. Eventually, at a point just before it reaches the event horizon, the falling object becomes so dim that it can no longer be seen. For Deleuze and Guattari, black holes work as the norm in the social fabric – the points around which structure is organized (1987, p. 40). Deleuze and Guattari put to work a black hole in 'A Thousand Plateaus' (1987) as a place from which there is no escape. The black hole holds great promise and great danger. Everything resonates with everything else inside a black hole.

The pedagogical encounter

I am not alone as the meeting time draws near. I feel the presence of those who inform the supervisory role. I hear the cautionary words of Elizabeth St Pierre (2016). I am reading Barad (2007) and feel the mattering of knowledge. Rebecca is agitated. She has entered with her knowledge firmly in her control with answers to her research well established from her practice before entering the PhD. She is an advocate for teacher reform and is impatient with the doctoral process as she wants her knowledge documented and active in the field. She does not want to engage with theorists of any kind. She knows what they will say to her.

Tom comes later. Tom hails Dewey to appear. Tom refuses the lounge and sits at an upright office chair. He is confident of his entanglement of digital networks with Dewey, Van Manen and MacLure.

Zoya enters the office. Her face conveys her determination to control the theorists she calls upon. She sits on the lounge and spreads her notes and computer. The associate supervisor enters and sits in the armchair across from me. We are all willing learning to occur. Foucault, Bourdieu and Butler are summoned by Zoya. The knowledge work around the young women in the project also summons them.

The learning event with its structure of a black hole awaits. In this encounter, bodies of supervisors, candidates, knowledge, learning objects and learning spaces may inhabit this black hole to come. 'Inside a black hole, space is so deeply distorted (so curved) that anything crossing the threshold – known as the 'event horizon' – is sucked into the maw below and eviscerated' (Wertheim 1999, p. 179). In this space of all mass and no volume, there are the bodies, objects and spaces summoned and unsummoned from candidates/supervisor/knowledge pasts and futures. Time is collapsed here and so the bodies from knowledge, summoned and unsummoned, are here. Philosophers, methodologists, pedagogues, curriculum theorists, identity theorists, cultural theorists all come into the encounter in the hole. In this pedagogical encounter the histories of learner and teacher are present. In pedagogical encounters with children the people from the learner's history are often readily apparent and 'seen' – the families, the communities, the past teachers, the peer groups. In the adult encounter of doctoral work, the histories of candidate and of supervisor are present but rarely named or spoken. This place is densely populated with bodies that are enfolded in each other. All bodies from past, present and the future and from near and far must be recognized in the fullness of their physicality including the very atoms of their being and also the fullness of their being beyond physicality. The pedagogical relationship between self and other is not metaphorical. It is not only that the learning and teaching are bodily but also that the form of the relationship is bodily. In her book *Meeting the Universe Halfway*, Barad (2007) draws on Bohr's work in arguing that the visual clues about the borders of bodies may be misleading. For Bohr things do not have boundaries. He asserted that if we look closely at an 'edge' what is seen is not a sharp boundary but rather a series of light and dark bands in a diffractive pattern – allowing or revealing an exteriority within (2007, p. 97). For Barad the nature of the production of bodily boundaries, human and non-human, is an ontological issue. It is not only how bodies are positioned materially and discursively in the world; it is a matter of how they are constituted as being-of-the-world. There is no independent existence. Barad argues, 'To figure matter as merely an end product rather than an active factor in further materialisation is to cheat matter out of the fullness of its capacity' (2007, p. 66). Barad argues the active performance of matter in the world's becoming, in its intra-activity. Matter is not passive. Rather matter is a substance in its intra-active becoming, not a thing but a doing, a congealing of agency.

The black hole is provoked by the event of learning. The supervisors and candidate are brought into an encounter with new knowledge and with old acquaintances – Foucault/Deleuze/MacLure/Dewey/Bourdieu/Butler. They are all summoned here in new configurations reaching out to each other, resisting being present, entangled, becoming and becoming. The knowledge is present in the encounter not as some inert stable object waiting to be found but as matter entangled with all that is present material and non-material. These bodies (human and non-human) from the past and in the present are entangled in each other. The body of each extended beyond their material boundaries. In these extensions, the matter of these bodies reach out to the other. These entangled pedagogical bodies are not equivalent to entwined objects. Entangled bodies are always in a dynamic relationship (Barad 2007).

Mapping

The black hole perspective opens up the complexity and the becomings of the event of learning. This reading calls for a mapping which is responsive to this time-space collapse and to the presence of intra-active bodies.

> *Rebecca brings large sheets of paper with Venn diagrams of data processes she wishes to pursue. She has already determined participants and processes of data collection. I bring her back to the field of pedagogy she is engaging. She is resisting the multiple readings of the field. She attempts to dismiss alternate readings. She falters as she is brought back from methods to methodology by the associate supervisor. She comes undone when asked what she does not know of the site of her research. This conversation has recurred over several meetings.*

> *The meeting with Tom is matter of fact – almost procedural. He directs the meeting with plans for finalisation of the thesis argument. Earlier in his thesis work he had a brief encounter with MacLure and her post humanist readings of Deleuze. I had brought Deleuze to the table via MacLure to bridge the embodied work of Dewey and Van Manen. These latter theorists have been in the office at every meeting. Tom brought them in early in the work. I sought to find a way to read the digital networks which would satisfy these pre-digital pedagogues.*

> *The last meeting for the day erupts as Zoya seats Butler and Bourdieu on the couch. Zoya wants the structure Bourdieu offers in reading the educational world of young women. She also wants what Butler's performance by these young women can offer. She is struggling bringing these two into conversation with each other.*

Our attention in the black hole is now fully on 'learning'. Learning is at the heart of this encounter. The intra-active analysis must attend to that which is willed and summoned by the participants, the knowledge and the place. A pedagogical mapping of this learning environment calls upon us to read *from* the smallest intervals or moments of bodies reaching out to others to the wider surfaces of the office, to the corridors of the university, to the candidate's desk. Our mappings of this encounter in this black hole must follow these flows capturing the bodily between. As we follow these flows between those in the office and out into the imagined world of the candidates' thesis making we begin to make pedagogical maps. Deleuze and Guattari urge the making of maps as opposed to the tracing of action:

> The orchid does not reproduce the tracing of the wasp; it forms a map with the wasp, in a rhizome. What distinguishes the map from the tracing is that it is entirely oriented toward experimentation in contact with the real. (1987, p. 12)

Following Deleuze and Guattari, the map that is discerned and evoked is 'always detachable, connectable, reversible, modifiable and has multiple entry ways and exits and its own lines of flight' (1987, p. 21). As the researcher I draw ambient, reflected and radiant (Rodaway 1994) lines of flight mapping the shape or contours of embodied pedagogy. Maps reveal the smooth and the striated spaces of the learning environments. For Deleuze and Guattari the smooth space is occupied by intensities and events. It is haptic rather than optic. The maps evoke the constant interchange between the striated university spaces where everything is arranged and disciplined in closed systems and the smooth spaces of the candidate's thesis life where everything is chaotic, sensate and undisciplined.

The mapping analysis – with its ambient, reflected and radiant lines, identification of longitude and latitude of the striated spaces, its contours of smooth space and striated space, the circling of hot pedagogical spots, and the layering of mapping artefacts reveal the flows between candidate knowledge and supervisors and place/s and those theorists summoned from afar and from the past. This practice of mapping compels me to focus my eyes on the very space around/between bodies. Inside of the event horizon all paths bring the particle closer to the centre of the black hole. It is no longer possible for the particle to escape. We do not escape from a pedagogical encounter unchanged. It is not a matter of escape.

I map these shapings, the becomings, the event and learning. I follow the flows of bodily assemblage of theorists, supervisors, places and times, of Rebecca, Tom and Zoya and indeed all the others brought here. Are they eviscerated in these black holes? In a sense they are. Each of those in the black holes is undone. This is experienced most by those who enter as learners – the candidates.

Rebecca is coming undone as today she comes with a question – not her research question but a question to which she does not know the answer. She has given up the safe place of knowing and the doctoral work has summoned her to go into unsafe places of not knowing. Becoming nomad 'is giving up a place that is safe, that is home' (O'Riley 2003, p.29). She is becoming the offspring of her learning event.

Tom resisted the meetings with Deleuze and MacLure. It has been Tom's deep knowledge of the digital world and of pedagogy that has brought me, and also Dewey, into a digital pedagogical reading.

The supervisors are quiet in the room when Zoya is in conversation with Butler and Bourdieu. There are already many voices claiming to be heard. All those present – Zoya, the young women, the supervisors, Butler, Bourdieu, knowledge – are willing the event of learning.

It is often uncomfortable in this black hole where space and time are collapsed and bodies from the past are present. The doctoral work is full of cracks and voids and is always in the middle. O'Reilly reminds us nomadic becoming 'grows from the middle, the crack, the voids, the hyphens, the slashes and the outcrops' (2003, p. 29). However, these bodies are not here in the way they were. They are reconstituted as well as re-represented by the knowledge that is becoming, by the candidate and by the new place and by the supervisors. The mapping reveals bodies that are spatially and temporally dislocated are pulled into this place – Butler and St. Pierre are in the room. Dewey is in conversation with Tom and myself and with Van Manen as new knowledge is made around digital learning. Dewey is becoming a theorist of digital learning. Occasionally, these bodily spectres turn on the others here and leave or are even sent away. They, too, are becoming in the encounter – these bodies that are summoned from other times and other places. These intra-actions produce paradoxical becomings of all and each – the candidate becoming the knowledge, becoming the supervisor; the supervisor becoming the candidate, becoming the knowledge; the knowledge becoming the candidate and becoming the supervisor; the candidate becoming Foucault, and Foucault becoming the candidate.

From black holes and mapping

For candidates and supervisors this reading of learning and of the pedagogical encounter does not offer a method of approach to doctoral learning or to doctoral supervision. Learning as event offers us a way of experiencing and knowing learning. The learning is an event which is a vibration with intensities. It is that which has just happened and that which is about to happen but never that which is happening. Learning is a synthesis of the past and future. A learning event is at once located within a time and at the same time expresses a new time. The duration of the learning event in the black hole is immeasurable. The intensities of learning move through learner, knowledge, place and sometimes supervisor. The learning event is not only for but also of the learner. The learning event is a vibration through knowledge and through place and objects and supervisor and all those summoned to the pedagogical encounter.

We can will learning to occur but that does not mean it *will* occur. We may not recognize it when it does occur. It is not located in time. We cannot locate our doctoral learning in a specific moment, and it may last over an extended period or for just a moment. We cannot cause it to come. We set up numerous actions to provoke the event – reading, experimenting, writing, discussing, viewing, listening. These actions are not randomly chosen. However, they cannot be clearly identified as causal for the event of learning nor are they directly linked in time and space to learning. However, the event of learning does move through us. The black hole offers a productive approach to researching the pedagogical encounter that stands in stark contrast to the blunt instrument of measurement of teacher action and learning outcomes

Through this black hole fabulation, paradoxical encounters between diverse theoretical embodiments are interrogated. For the researcher, mapping black holes offers the opportunity to discern a dynamic intra-action of theorists, supervisors, knowledge, candidate and place. Learning is materialized in this dynamic intra-active becoming. The meaning of this learning matter is the performance of the world as this space, the candidates, the researchers and the theorists from past and from far away make the world known to each other.

Glossary

Black Hole An area of space-time and in the centre lies a region where the space-time curvature becomes infinite. This region contains all mass but has zero volume. Time and space are collapsed. Its boundary is a mathematically defined surface. This is an event horizon through which matter and light can only pass inward towards the mass of the black hole.

Deleuzian Event In the 'Logic of Sense' (2003, pp. 8–9), Deleuze asserts the event is unlimited becoming. Events are produced in a chaos of multiplicity. The event of learning is produced in the chaos of knowledge, knowing, being, becoming, experiencing and living. Events are actualized within us (Deleuze 2003, p. 148).

Pedagogy Pedagogy is the study of learning, of learner, of knowledge, of place and, on occasion, of teacher. The pedagogical encounter is their dynamic intra-action (Barad 2007, p. 141). The nature of their dynamic intra-action is a critical component in reading this encounter. As Barad argues, these entangled agencies, in this case the learner, knowledge, place and teacher, are in mutual constitution. They each emerge through their intra-action.

References

Barad, K. (2007), *Meeting the Universe Halfway: Quantum Physics and the Entanglement of Matter and Meaning*, Durham, NC: Duke University Press.

Barnacle, R. (2005), 'Research education ontologies: Exploring doctoral becoming', *Higher Education Research & Development*, 24 (2): 179–88.

Beck, C. and Gleyzon, F. (2016), 'Deleuze and the event(s)', *Journal for Cultural Research*, 20 (4): 329–33.

Boys, J. (2011), 'Where is the theory?' in A. Boddington and J. Boys (eds), *Re-shaping Learning- A Critical Reader*, xi–xxii, Rotterdam: Sense.

Davies, B. (2016), 'Ethics and the new materialism: A brief genealogy of the "post" philosophies in the social sciences', *Discourse: Studies in the Cultural Politics of Education*, 1–15. doi:10.1080/01596306.2016.1234682.

Deleuze, G. (1992), *The Fold: Leibniz and the Baroque*, trans. T. Conley, London: The Althone Press.

Deleuze, G. (2003), *The Logic of Sense,* trans. M. Lester with C. Stivale, New York: Columbia University Press.

Deleuze, G. and Guattari, F. (1987), *A Thousand Plateaus: Capitalism and Schizophrenia*, trans. B. Massumi, Minneapolis: University of Minnesota Press.

Ellsworth, E. (1997), *Teaching Positions: Difference, Pedagogy, and the Power of Address*, New York: Teachers College Press.

Fullager, S., Pavlidis, A. and Stadler, R. (2017), 'Critical moments of (Un)doing doctoral supervision: Collaborative writing as rhizomatic practice', *Knowledge Cultures*, 5 (4): 23–41.

Green, B. (2005), 'Unfinished business: Subjectivity and supervision', *Higher Education Research & Development*, 24 (2): 151–63.

Hannah Arendt (2013), film, Zeitgeist Films, USA.

Haraway, D. (2016), *Staying with the Trouble: Making Kin in the Chthulucene*, Durham, NC: Duke University Press.

Hein, S. (2016), 'The new materialism in qualitative inquiry: How compatible are the philosophies of Barad and Deleuze?' *Cultural Studies Critical Methodologies*, 16 (2): 132–40, DOI: 10.1177/1532708616634732.

Jackson, A. and Mazzei, L. (2012), *Thinking with Theory in Qualitative Research*, New York: Routledge.

Lee, A. and Green, B. (1998), 'Introduction postgraduate studies/postgraduate pedagogy', in A. Lee and B. Green (eds), *Postgraduate Studies Postgraduate Pedagogy*, Sydney: University of Technology Sydney.

McWilliam, E. and Palmer, P. (1998), 'Teaching tech(no)bodies: Open learning and postgraduate pedagogy', in A. Lee and B. Green (eds), *Postgraduate Studies Postgraduate Pedagogy*, Sydney: University of Technology Sydney.

Mulcahy, D., Cleveland, B. and Alberton, H. (2015), 'Learning spaces and pedagogic change: Envisioned, enacted and experienced', *Pedagogy Culture and Society*, 23 (4): 575–95.

O' Riley, P. (2003), *Technology, Culture and Socioeconomics*, New York: Peter Lang.

Rodaway, P. (1994), *Sensuous Geographies*, London: Routledge.

Roy, K. (2003), *Teachers in Nomadic Spaces: Deleuze and Curriculum*, New York: Peter Lang.

Rovelli, C. (2015), *Seven Brief Lessons on Physics*, trans. S. Carnell and E. Segre, London: Allen Lane.

Scholes, R. (1967), *The Fabulators*, New York: Oxford University Press.

Sheldon, R. (2016), 'Matter and meaning Rhizomes', *Cultural Studies in Emerging Knowledge*, 30, https://doi.org/10.20415/rhiz/030.e03.

St Pierre, E. (2016), 'The empirical and the new empiricisms', *Cultural Studies Critical Methodologies*, 16 (2), DOI: 10.1177/1532708616636147.

Thiele K. (2016), 'Of immanence and becoming Deleuze and Guattari's philosophy and/as relational ontology', *Deleuze Studies*, 10 (1): 117–34.

Truman, S. (2018), 'SF Haraway's situated feminisms and speculative fabulations in english class', *Studies in Philosophy and Education*, https://doi.org/10.1007/s11217-018-9632-5.

Wertheim, M. (1999), *The Pearly Gates of Cyberspace: A History of Space from Dante to The Internet*, Sydney: Doubleday.

Zembylas, M. (2007), 'The spectres of bodies and affects in the classroom: A rhizo-ethological approach', *Pedagogy, Culture & Society*, 15: 19–35.

8

Disturbance and intensive methodology in capitalist ruins

Jesse Bazzul

I remember when a good friend, Meghan Cheng, told me she was doing her master's thesis on skin. We had met in a poststructural feminist class at the University of Toronto, where I was a relatively new graduate student. Meghan needed a laptop to do a presentation (I think it was about Audre Lorde), and I was able to give her mine. She never sat next to me, even after the whole laptop thing, but would meet me in the hallways and study rooms of New College and OISE – two modern buildings straight out of a Kafka story. Through things like skin, and places like 'the common' on Dufferin St., Meghan tried to teach me that worlds could be built outside of the references given to us. And though I wanted to dwell more on her story of skin, Meghan told me I just needed a little more faith in *topics-like-skin* that were already taking shape. Following Meghan, this chapter suggests that scholarship in education needs to increasingly becoming decentred from pre-given taken-for-granted disciplines, methods and dominant narratives, and give more attention to concepts like *disturbance*.

Instead of always beginning research with 'majority[1]' concepts that can overcode, prescribe and occlude – like achievement, success and outcomes – educators might enable different vistas and ways of living by shifting what Donna Haraway (2016) calls the *stories we use to tell stories*. In other words, using rich, yet incomplete, stories that are not just about one protagonist or one singular event (even creation stories are never really about one lone act). Anna L. Tsing (2015) draws from science fiction writer Ursula Le Guin (2017) to show how good stories should remain unfinished:

---

[1] Research that enables becomings from majority to minority (Deleuze and Guattari 1988; Deleuze 1994) might become the stakes of research that aims to provoke a different ethics of living and being.

In 'The Carrier Bag Theory of Fiction', Ursula Le Guin argues that stories of hunting and killing have allowed readers to imagine that individual heroism is the point of a story.

Instead, she proposes that storytelling might pick up diverse things of meaning and value and gather them together, like a forager, rather than a hunter waiting for the big kills. In this kind of storytelling, stories should never end, but rather lead to further stories. (p. 287)

From this perspective, gathering threads becomes the general work of scholars and educators; instead of proclamations, moralizations, repeatability and confident endings. Entangled research, in an Anthropocene context can be seen as both material and discursive assemblages with both actual and virtual entrances and exits. Seen this way scholars and researchers might choose to use these entrances and exits in ways other than how they were intended to be used – or make different ones. Remaining open to different imperatives, desires, and relations may lead to endless possibilities that a scholar, traveller or sojourner might take. For Deleuze and Guattari (1986), this is the onto-political hope of Franz Kafka's body of work, whose optimistic message goes something like: *Fear not, nothing is totalized. There are infinite possibilities, and not even oppressive powers themselves really know what they are doing!*

Figure 8.1 is a provocation figure of this idea using a drab Kafkaesque building.[2]

When academics do their work, do they accept the entry ways and exits given to them? Or do they look and hope for different ones? When they hit an impasse or wall, is it really an impasse or can they find a way though?

In endeavouring to relate research-as-assemblage and methodology in a broad sense, I feel it important to develop this notion of disturbance within the context assemblages. Working with assemblages involves trying to relate, trace and entangle different material parts, living entities, stories and discourses, ethics and politics, as well as different forces such as desire and collective action (Bazzul and Kayumova 2016). Anna L. Tsing's ethnographic (2015) work *The Mushroom at the End of the World: On the Possibility of Life in Capitalist Ruins* helps bring forth different and more imaginative assemblages of livability involving more-than-human beings, flows of care and ethico-political arrangements

---

[2]   Deleuze and Guattari (1986) point to the lack of coherence in the charges laid against Joseph K in Kafka's *The Trial* (Kafka 1998 [1914]). One lesson of the novel is that no disciplinary power or institution can totalize. Considering the fact that educational institutions are apparatuses of governance, educators and researchers should be wary of what is deemed appropriate and successful by nebulous organizational entities and institutions.

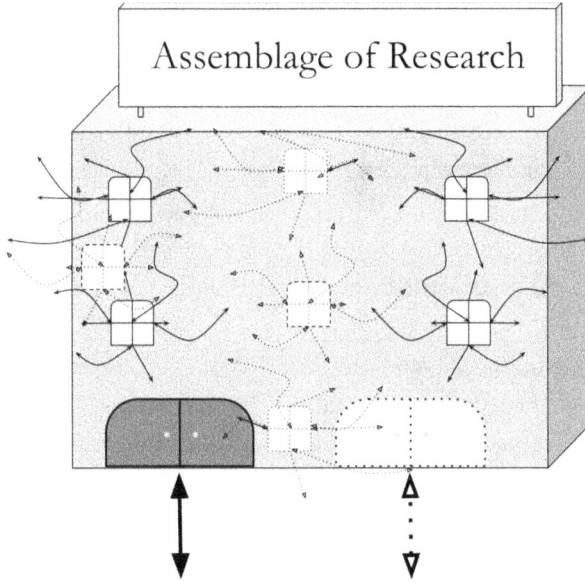

Figure 8.1 Provocation: Research as Kafkaesque Assemblage with virtual and actual doors.

in the context of an irreversibly disturbed planet. Tsing's work succeeds in simultaneously recognizing that different ways of living together are needed in precarious times, and that the wicked and persistent problems of capitalism and neocolonialisms are currently the major context for these forms of life. That is, not forgetting that our desire for collective forms of life necessarily involves multispecies justice and emancipation. Science and science education from a perspective of living with entanglement and precarity can perhaps be thought of as specific kinds of translation machines that leave behind messy indeterminate entities (Carbon emissions, plastic wastelands, extinctions) alongside other material manifestations (electronics, mechanical marvels, bioengineered crops) people often associate with science. As I piece together the methodological concept of disturbance my intent is not to outline a method but to provoke an ontologically rich approach to transdisciplinary justice-oriented educational research. As a reader how might you understand disturbance or concepts like disturbance? After all, disturbance may entail a range of possibilities, from subverting heteronormative sensibilities to bulldozing an urban landscape. How might you assemble a research agenda that attends to the more-than-human and multispecies justice? How is the call to disturbance an ethical and political act?

Some years later I am beginning to follow Meghan's lead: attention to seemingly minor things like skin might just shift human thinking and do our species a lot of good. So too, I argue, would attention to disturbance as a definitive feature of life in the Anthropocene, where economic insecurity and traditional social and ecological relationships are changing. To put it in Anna L. Tsing's terms, the eco-social reality of disturbance is integral to understanding the responsibility of living-in-relation among capitalist ruins.

Disturbance, assemblage and the work of Anna L. Tsing

All environmental, social and psychic disturbances operate as queer(ing) forces because they disrupt normativity, coherence and safety, unleashing multiplicitous ecological potentials.[3] The understanding that queer forces are in fact 'natural' forces of the universe is what physicist and philosopher Karen Barad's (2011) work painstakingly tries to make clear. Barad (2007) encourages a renewed love for realism(s) that can account for phenomena in a specific time, place, name, agency and ethos, all of which are completely entangled and co-emergent. From the perspective of entanglement, life is concomitant with social and ecological disturbance: historically, geologically, developmentally, psychologically and socially. Understanding disturbance as a characteristic of life in the Anthropocene is vital for engaging our peculiar political moment and creating different forms of ethical (and educational) life. Disturbance is part and parcel of the politics of dissensus in Jacques Rancière's (2015) terms – a disruption of the taken-for-granted status quo that shifts the aesthetic dimensions of what is sensible, doable and thinkable in the name of radical equality. In this way, disturbance is not only an essential ontological backdrop to democracy but also key to navigating the current eco-political state-of-things that will increasingly come to orient life in capitalist, neocolonial ruins. As far as the work of caring and conscientious educators and scholars is concerned, the long-held boundary between geological/political/biological/cultural can no longer be seriously defended in educational research. Educational communities are thirsting for more relational ways of being/thinking to comprise everyday ethical living and communal life. Researchers such as Dwayne Donald (2012), through Indigenous land-based education, effectively nurture a relational ethics in ways that allow ethical reflexivity in the form of relationships to accompany multiple forms of collective politics. The question of ethics is vital to our current

---

[3] It is worth dwelling on the idea that modern disciplinary distinctions are becoming increasingly useless when tackling large-scale problems – for example, European colonization has led to the destruction of much of the planet's biodiversity.

moment of entanglement, because ways of being are inherent to any politics; though it is often the case that either politics or ethics are forgotten in justice-oriented research (Bazzul 2018).

In new-/neo-materialist philosophies that attempt to dislocate agency from a human(ist) subject and discourse, the concept of assemblage has been a productive way of entangling a more-than-human world together[4] (Bazzul and Santavicca 2017). Assemblages are conglomerations of forces, materials, and discourses that have shifting relations and capacities (Delanda 2006; Deleuze and Guattari 1988). Books, cells, ecosystems, and political projects are assemblages, and need to be understood in terms of specific dynamic relationships and capacities or, to put it more simply, 'how they work'. Understanding assemblages as multiplicitous and dynamic is necessary because it renders assemblages as open, with no definitive entry, exits, capacities, codings or purposes. However, it is also useful for educators to recognize that assemblages can also be rigid and restrictive like bureaucracies and geological formations, and indeed sometimes we may even desire this as the material and coded assemblies of military institutions would demonstrate (Deleuze and Guattari 1988). However, creativity in assembling, relating, and allowing for difference is needed in educational research in order to address the problem of how to live together in precarious times. Assemblages are a helpful concept when complex questions of ontology and their accompanying ethico-political questions are privileged in research. Here, in the form of figures and diagrams, they help construct a practical backdrop by which to understand disturbance on an ontological and relational level. The relevance of assemblages for research is that provide 'scenes for considering livability' (Tsing 2015, p. 163).

Disturbances, histories and landscapes

All disturbances have multifaceted and detail-rich histories and stories embedded in their events and processes. To get a better sense of what these might be, Anna Tsing (2015) advises gathering all the possible learning practices available: crime novels, colonial geographics, geological surveys, foundational stories, scientific studies, as well as pieces of art. Noel Gough (2017) exemplifies this approach in science teacher education through the infusion of science fiction, social theory, the arts and various media into pedagogy and curriculum design. Layering them and looking for clashes and points of connection can

---

[4] Networks, clouds, the commons, intra-active agencies, and ethical relationality are just some of the ways diverse materialist scholars are trying understand the entangled 'nature' of our shared existence.

help educators understand their current relational space and realize an ethically and politically relevant pedagogy and methodology of *noticing*. Disturbance as methodology and pedagogy involves an entanglement of story, life and matter – a creation event of immense sadness and/or happiness like when an ecosystem changes virtually forever. However, disturbances do not tacitly infer or signify any kind of garden-of-eden state prior. Rather, disturbances always follow other disturbances: political change follows love, fire follows climate change and fascisms follow failed socialisms. The outcome of disturbance, for better and for worse, is possibility and encounter. Disturbance helps contextualize Haraway's (2016) notion of the Chthuluscene, an era of multi-storied tenticular life on a damaged planet, and Jason Moore's (2015) Capitalocene, an era of eco-social destruction by capital – each is simply another side of anthropocentric catastrophe. On one side, the modern pursuit of capital is disturbing millions of years of evolution and diversity, and on the other Chthulucenic creatures take up the work of rearranging the threads of ecological disturbance in order to learn how to live on a damaged planet.

Any meaning of a disturbance is formulated retroactively according to the relations, structures, and forms/assemblages of life that come forward. This is true for ecologists and biologists and who study the heterogeneity of an environment, and it is also true when researching political protest, and socio-technological change. Disturbances, like ethics, can never be completely characterized or evaluated because they are relational and situated. What is a disaster to a 'natural' bee community may not be to competing human-honey bee kinships in the production of sustainable foods. For Anna Tsing, a key reason to pay attention to disturbances is not to prevent each and every one from happening, but rather to call attention to very specific histories and heterogeneity. It will become increasingly productive to think about how organisms, including humans, mediate disturbances and also create media(tions) by disturbing. Humans have managed to both cause and mediate grand geographic disturbances, from adapting to glaciation periods to forcing bird and insect displacements through climate change. Climate education, Indigenous ways of living in nature, and socio logical/environmental/anthropological studies that examine such disturbances will become increasingly valuable. Moreover the various ways our other kin, such as horses, whales, dolphins, trees, mediate disturbances by communicating, sharing and forging new relationships will also become valuable knowledge for life on a damaged planet. In this way, disturbances come with ethical potentials that can be assessed by their power to make things grow and their avoidance of destructive encounters. Disturbances are forces/events that each have their own ethics. However, the stakes are high because disturbances are not reversible – there is no going back. In disturbed ecological times it may be time to look for possibilities that are hopeful, yet realistic. As Tsing put its, 'In this time of diminished expectations, I look for disturbance-based ecologies in which many species sometimes live together without either harmony or conquest' (p. 5).

Unpredictability and difference: What is disturbance?

Educational research has arguably crossed a threshold into transdisciplinarity, making traditional disciplinary research less relevant. However, the widespread erosion of strict modern disciplinary boundaries like science and history, geology and politics was well underway in the early twentieth century. Anna Tsing draws inspiration from work that brings the social and ecological into a visceral encounter, such as Laura Cameron's (1999) essay 'Histories of Disturbance'. Cameron's historical analysis follows the career of Arthur Tansley and his conservation work with diverging ecological succession patterns of Wicken Fen in Cambridgeshire, UK. Tansley's transdisciplinary career allowed him to see how disruptions in a person's life, the ones 'disturbed' into popular existence by Freud's psychoanalysis, to some extent resembled particular aspects of ecological succession in disturbed environments.[5] That is, how traumatic disturbances in childhood, like the disturbances of industrialization, urbanization, and agriculture on 'natural environments', create conditions of emergence and possibility that sidestep normalized expectations of development, growth and even how the future might unfold. Human beings act and think not only predictably but also unpredictably because of their histories. Likewise, the 'natural' succession of disturbed landscapes, nature reserves, parks and fallow fields, do not necessarily follow predictable patterns, but can 'veer off' to unpredictable arrangements of life and environment. In other words, like human reactions to trauma, the unfolding of a particular space, once disturbed or significantly altered by humans or other organisms, can take on an entirely different set of contingencies outside of basic succession ecology. Similarly, the visceral experiences of a person affects what happens in their present and/ or future. Studying unique responses to disturbance might better inform how human communities develop responsibilities towards/for disturbances (again,

---

[5] A close relationship between Freud and Tansley also helped forge a bridge between psychology and botany

ecological, social or psychic). As Cameron (1999) puts it: 'Wicken Fen contained anomalous successions, but in the study of ecology, as in Freudian analysis, one could study the disturbed to study mechanisms at work in the normal' (p. 17).

Attention to disturbances therefore carries a larger methodological and ontological implication: in ecological, social and psychic life, disturbances fundamentally change how beings thrive (in response to these disturbances). Not all ecological spaces follow a prescriptive flow of succession, and neither does/ will multispecies survival on this planet. There is no 'natural' or normative way of being in relation, and there never has been. Furthermore, it may be detrimental to pursue multispecies flourishing outside of a context of disturbance. Entanglement with/in disturbance is therefore not just an epistemic-onto-ethical practice but a shift in methodological focus towards intensive relationalities.[6] Intensive here entails dependency on context and relationships, not something discrete. Intensities are forms/aspects of being and existence that escape quantification and singularity. An overall goal of studying concepts/events like disturbance is a more relational account of how lives might be lived differently. Like Tansley's unwitting 'botanical politics', educators and researchers might develop transdisciplinary methodologies based on a creative politics of disturbance as they pay attention to forces that are silent before and after a disturbance. 'Paying attention' might then become a bridge to transdisciplinary for a researcher. If there is no obvious way to attend to disturbances, it makes sense that an ethical turn in research would develop these different knowledges and practices.

A more creative ontological approach to research would view reality as the emergence and repetition of difference in the world (Deleuze 1994). Every teacher experiences this difference year after year as different beings and different ways of living manifest differently in educational spaces. The repetition of difference is also evident in biological evolution as well as histories of media (Peters 2015); a relational world is made possible only through the repetition of difference. In this way, disturbances are the emergence of difference, especially if we understand differences as a form of intense relation to other entities.[7] This brings us again to one of the fundamental problems of disturbances, and for that matter assemblages: it is never absolutely clear what constitutes a disturbance or assemblage. An earthquake and the release of 'seismic potential' might destroy several ecosystems

---

[6] The biological sciences give us a great example through the study of holobionts, which act as 'hosts' or spaces for multiple symbiotic relationships. Humans and their immune systems are holobionts (Gilbert 2017). The ontology of 'the individual' may simply be insufficient in a world of relationships.
[7] In Deleuzian terms difference is located less in a static comparison between two entities, and more in the intensities that flow out of the relation between these entities. As such difference is always in a state of becoming.

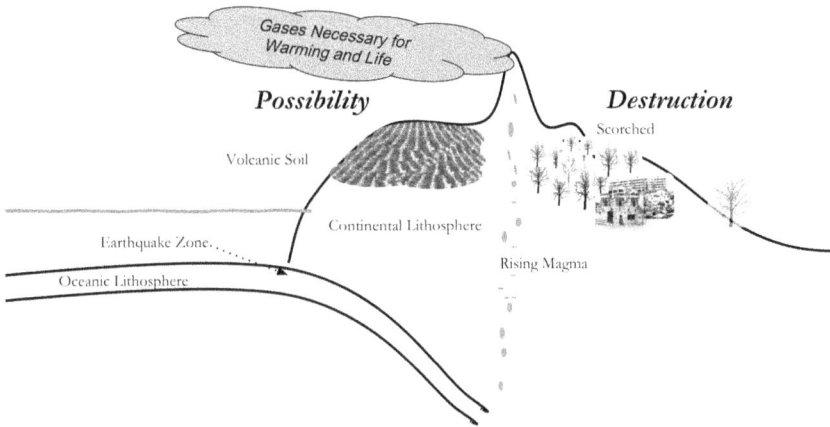

Figure 8.2 Provocation: The dual side of disturbance: possibility and destruction.

or communities, yet create crevasses for new life (see Figure 8.2). Student resistance to educational initiatives can be both healthy and problematic. This is why awareness of the observer's perspective is vital when using disturbance as an analytical tool/concept (Tsing 2015). There are no universal measuring tools, rather disturbances need to be seen in heterogeneous relation to the lens and experiences used to view them. Whether a disturbance is 'good or bad' is largely determined by the life-affirming socio-material assemblages that flow from the disturbance. In this way disturbances initiate not only research but life callings. Why begin a project, a career, a passionate inquiry in the first place (here my mind flows to Meghan)? Is it the un-livability of many lives? If we do not acknowledge 'the disturbing', are researchers simply being duped into not disturbing life under late capitalism, white supremacy and anthropocentrism?

In Deleuzian-style, the next section proposes a series of assemblages or diagrams intended to provoke some understanding(s) of disturbance. Diagrams are simultaneously non-discursive and discursive 'machines' that are meant to generate thought – and if they do not they fail (Deleuze and Parnet 2007). Since anything might disturb, how might educators and researchers view disturbances? This is a primary methodological question, one that must engage local and global realities of entanglement, difference and relationality. It is an inherently materialist question because local contexts and histories, as well as the distribution of the more-than-human are fundamental to approaching disturbance and its relation to life. As researchers go forth creating methodologies for better futures, how might they ontologically think through these methodologies as they move forward without overly relying on prefabricated methods (and theory).

If prefabricated methods become the norm for researchers the most critical question becomes what in the world is being assembled from these 'prefab' parts.

Figures of disturbance

It might be appropriate now to try and imagine what disturbance might mean in relation to educational research writ large. Methodologically, the goal of diagramming is to provoke creative thought, break down disciplinary boundaries, and different directions for educational research (Bazzul, Wallace and Higgins 2018). The provocation figures in this section are diagrammatic material-discursive assemblages that might also be considered as thought-machines. They are intended to compliment discussion in way a written text cannot, and provide different ways to think about the more-than-human, and how our shared worlds might be arranged. Figure 8.2 illustrates the ambiguous and ambivalent nature of disturbance through volcanic activity.

On one hand volcanic activity is reported in the news media as a terrifying event, and for good reason. The scorched path of destruction is notable and signals other seismic activity that could destroy many communities. However, in geological time, volcanic activity was necessary to release gases needed to heat the earth's surface sufficiently for life and provides water and nutrients to make extra-rich soil. Similarly the presence or absence of gases such as CO_2 helps determine how and if life thrives today, and some argue that grand disturbances such as climate change and the carbon economy should be central to science policy and science education (Bazzul and Tolbert 2017; Sharma 2012). For educational researchers these multiple sides of disturbance determine the emergent conditions for educational life; whether it be through war, inequality or even big social changes, it is imperative that we examine the way disturbances gather together new collectivities. This multidimensional side of disturbance also allows educators to avoid myopic moral questions that often do not allow for different forms of analysis. Instead, the ethics in-relation emerges between various entities affected by disturbances.

Colonization, genocide and *Eyininiw mistatimwak* (horse-based healings)

Where I live in Saskatchewan, Canada, and also across most of the planet, the disposability and genocides of humans and the more-than-human through (neo) colonization and capitalism, currently comprise the most stark disturbances to multiple forms of life. Indigenous scholars are leading the way with research that entangles colonization, healing and resurgence. Angela Snowshoe and Noel Starblanket's (2016) work with culture-positive history and healing entangles two massive disturbances: the systematic genocide of Indigenous peoples and the erasure of the Lac Lacroix Indigenous Pony in North America. By giving First Nations youth direct access to *eyininiw mistatimwak* (horse-based healings), where horses cease to be objects of healing and instead are central to healing and learning. While Lac LaCroix Indigenous Ponies have been decimated and obscured through colonization, revitalization efforts in response to this genocide has given rise to revitalized entanglements and kinship relations with/of First Nations peoples. Figure 8.3 illustrates some of these resurgences and historical entanglements.

Assemblages arising from these relationships are rather bleak and terrorizing for Indigenous youth and threatened species, though also rich in ethico-political possibility. Snowshoe and Starblanket's work outlines how oral histories about the Lac La Croix Indigenous Ponies, histories which contradict the widespread myth that all horses in North America were introduced by Spain's colonial enterprise, were characterized as insignificant because colonial narratives and scant scientific evidence could not validate them (remembering Tsing's call to collect many forms of data). Denial of the ponies' heritage acted as justification for the seizure of wild Lac La Croix Indigenous Ponies as white European private property. The Lac La Croix Indigenous Pony is now thought

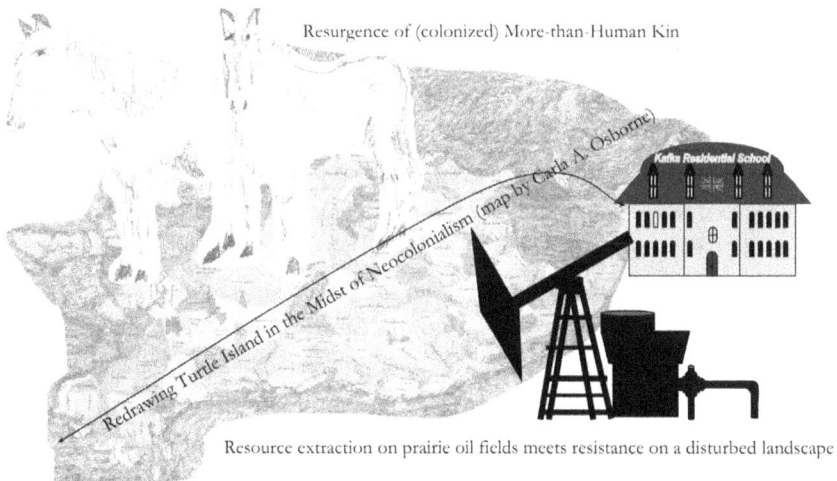

Figure 8.3 Provocation Natural History, colonization and disturbance.
Source: Map of Turtle Island provided by Carla A. Osborne (2018).

to have existed well before European arrival. In addition to the efforts to decolonize the history of these Ponies, they are now central to renewed forms of decolonized healing involving spirituality, community involvement, and more-than-human kin (the Indigenous and clinical aspects of this healing are beyond the scope of this chapter but are highly recommended reading). Snowshoe and Starblanket's entangled Indigenous healing practices are not educational psychology research as per usual, rather they are an example of what life and research for Indigenous youth might look like after disturbance. It must also be remembered that education plays a role on both sides of (genocidal) disturbances. In the Canadian context, residential schools had a massive role in cultural genocides that helped create and maintain ongoing inequalities and health risks for Indigenous communities in Canada (see Miller 2017). Research that attends to neocolonialism also needs to attend to threads of possibility left after these disturbances.

Parks and the disturbance of the commons

Cities rest upon thick layers of disturbance. A recent meeting of the American Educational Research Association in New York City placed many privileged and problematic educational scholars like myself smack dab in the middle of multiple disturbances. A notable one being Central Park, a huge expanse of urban parkland that spans Midtown to Harlem.

After reading Laura Cameron's (1999) work on disturbances some months earlier, the small reserve enclosures in Central Park, such as the Hallett Nature Sanctuary, and not entirely unlike Wicken Fen, immediately caught my attention. These (not-so) urban spaces break down the nature/culture/social/ biological/more-than-human/human divides through the mutual disturbance to both city and forest life, as well as to historical memory (sanitized accounts of the parks development) and forgetting (of colonization and white supremacy that made park possible). Spaces like Hallet's Nature Reserve are a reminder that both the arrival of Europeans in North America and elitist city planning are part of an ever diverging assemblage of disturbed life. Seneca Village, one of these disturbed entities, was a community that existed before Central Park and was forcibly destroyed in the mid-nineteenth century for the park's construction thereby displacing hundreds, primarily people of colour (Viele, 1856). Seneca Village was built largely by a vibrant Black community that organized to oppose the targeting and destruction of their relatively affluent economy and civic institutions. While it is appropriate for educators to focus on large ecological and social disturbances in cities, it is often forgotten that under the 'naturalness' of current modes of urban life lay massive and varied disturbances.

Seneca Village has largely been forgotten (Manevitz 2014), and much like Freud's subconscious, has become naturalized and buried. This act of forgetting is in-step with the gutting of American civics and social studies education, a once rich field of pedagogy and research. It seems educational researchers have forgotten, through years of neoliberal policies that serve private interests ahead of the public, that historical research is also educational research. Enter Haraway's (2016) reminder for justice-oriented scholars:

> It matters what we use to think other matters with; it matters what stories we tell to tell other stories with; it matters what knots knot knots, what thoughts think thoughts, what descriptions describe descriptions, what ties tie ties. It matters what stories make worlds, what worlds make stories. (p. 12)

It is no coincidence that consumerism and colonial narratives lead to dangerously simplistic notions that human development happens in empty spaces, in a linear fashion; and that (white) elites can unproblematically constitute and represent the aesthetic composition of what our shared worlds feel, look and sound like. Even when the results are a beautiful microcosm like Central Park! Taking note of disturbances involves relations of past and present – it is an onto-temporal-methodological task.

Intensive methodologies and attention to disturbance

So far, I have introduced the idea of disturbance as a relational and intensive concept – a concept dependent on context, relationships and considerations of ethics and being. I would like to conclude by discussing what this might mean for transdisciplinary educational research. From both a Deleuzian and Baradian perspective methodologies are intensive forces because they draw together difference and make ontological ethico-political cuts in the world. Approaches to research and methodology, such as Meghan's work on skin, and concepts, such as disturbance, disrupt categories that continue to propel us forward to ecological and social crisis. Instead educators and scholars might look towards different relational methodologies, of which attention to disturbance as an ontological force might be a part. Researchers who value open-ended inquiry already understand that methodologies are intensive, which means that it is often impossible to really understand them substantially about them until the 'end' of research – which might even be a long time afterward. Disturbances alter what might have been thought to be stable ground, opening space for forgotten details to matter (Haraway 2016).

Life on a damaged planet means finding different ways to live and survive. While disturbances are irreversible, the opportunities for resurgence in common can still be realized. If disturbance is a force of life, Anna Tsing (2015) has us imagine the 'small eddies of interlocking lives' among these great rivers of disturbance (p. 190). These eddies, according to Tsing, will be polyphonic and gather ways of being together. This includes engagement with the historical, social and material flows of production that have created many of the disturbances in the Anthropocene. Educational research should not accept any limits in seeking this polyphony. Tsing asks us to seriously question the taken-for-grantedness of scalability in research; how a one-process fits all approach does not put humans into healthy and ethical relationships with the beings that surround us. Irreversible and ambiguous disturbances, through contingency, indeterminacy and time, demonstrate that much of the world is not scalable, and that it may be damaging to simplistically see our shared worlds this way. Large education systems, the ones researchers help support and build, need to be infused with multiplicitous spaces of inquiry (see Wallace 2017). This does not mean technical projects are not absolutely valuable; it simply means that these projects are completely situated. Theory and method in this space are always in the middle, or as Donna Haraway puts it, in the 'mud'. As far as a career in education goes, I have felt most alive when I am attentive to the vast majority of things that live largely outside of tiny academic bubbles.

A response from Meghan

When I emailed Meghan to send me an electronic copy of her thesis on skin I received an immediate response. Meghan's words, I think, relate the frustratingly ambivalent stakes of research in a nutshell: we are constantly trying to get our hands dirty and sometimes, maybe often, we need to leave some dirt behind. And whatever path we choose, fashionable or not, the possibility of creativity, connection and even love remains immanent.

Jesse!

I am visiting my sister in Peterborough right now. Don't have my laptop with me. Also, I wouldn't want to send it to you anyway. It's such bullshit and crappy work.

I am over academia. I'm all about the blood and fluids now. I just finished my first placement and saw 27 babies be born. I caught six of them with just my own hands!

What's new with you??

M

(Meghan Cheng, Personal Communication, 2 May 2018)

Acknowledgements

I would like to thank the editors of this collection, Matthew Thomas and Robin Bellingham, Noel Gough, as well as Meghan Cheng for making this chapter possible. I also want to recognize the persistence of the Indigenous Lac La Croix Ponies and those that worked intensively for their recognition and preservation. Lastly, I would like to thank Angela Snowshoe for thoughtfully taking the time to share her work in ways that honour our more-than-human kin and the continuing Indigenous struggle against neocolonialism.

Glossary

Anthropocene Our current, and somewhat controversial, geological epoch where the activities of one species (*Homo sapiens*) will come to mark our planet physically, biologically and geologically for millions of years.

Disturbance A sensed or perceived interruption to a settled or stable state of affairs. A disturbance may be ecological, psychological, social, philosophical, organizational and geological.

Assemblage Multiple entities, whether living/nonliving, actual/virtual, discursive/material, in relation with one another; where each entity (or part) has unique capacities and relations of exteriority depending on its position relative to other entities.

Intensive In this chapter intensive is used in the Deleuzian sense: a property or aspect of something that cannot be divided or quantified, but describes a state of being. Something intensive, or an intensity, exists only because of a relational difference with other states of being; and therefore potential transformation or becoming-different is inherent in intensive relationships.

Transdisciplinary The practice of crossing disciplines in such a way as to render the boundaries between them fluid and unclear.

References

Barad, K. (2007), *Meeting the Universe Halfway: Quantum Physics and the Entanglement of Matter and Meaning*, Durham, NC: Duke University Press.

Barad, K. (2011), 'Nature's queer performativity', *Qui Parle: Critical Humanities and Social Sciences*, 19 (2): 121–58.

Bazzul, J. and Kayumova, S. (2016), 'Toward a social ontology for science education: Introducing Deleuze and Guattari's assemblages', *Educational Philosophy and Theory*, 48 (3): 284–99.

Bazzul, J. (2018), 'Ethics, subjectivity, and sociomaterial assemblages: Two important directions and methodological tensions', *Studies in Philosophy and Education*, 37 (5): 467–80.

Bazzul, J. and Santavicca, N. (2017), 'Diagramming assemblages of sex/gender and sexuality as environmental education', *The Journal of Environmental Education*, 48 (1): 56–66.

Bazzul, J., Wallace, M. F. and Higgins, M. (2018), 'Dreaming and immanence: Rejecting the dogmatic image of thought in science education', *Cultural Studies of Science Education*, 13 (2): 1–13.

Bazzul, J. and Tolbert, S. (2017), 'Reassembling the natural and social commons', in A. J. Means, D. R. Ford and G. B. Slater (ed), *Educational Commons in Theory and Practice*, 55–73, New York: Palgrave Macmillan.

Cameron, L. (1999), 'Histories of disturbance', *Radical History Review*, 74: 5–24.

Cheng, M. (2 May 2018), Email communication to Jesse Bazzul.

DeLanda, M. (2006), *A New Philosophy of Society: Assemblage Theory and Social Complexity*, New York: A&C Black.

Deleuze, G. and Guattari, F. (1986), *Kafka: Toward a Minor Literature*, vol. 30. Minneapolis: University of Minnesota Press.

Deleuze, G. and Guattari, F. (1988), *A Thousand Plateaus: Capitalism and Schizophrenia*, New York: Bloomsbury Publishing.

Deleuze, G. (1994), *Difference and Repetition*. New York: Columbia University Press.

Deleuze, G. and Parnet, C. (2007), *Dialogues II*, trans. H. Tomlinson and B. Habberjam, New York: Columbia University Press.

Donald, D. (2012), 'Forts, curriculum, and ethical relationality', in N. Ng-A-Fook and J. Rotman (ed), *Reconsidering Canadian Curriculum Studies*, 39–46, New York: Palgrave Macmillan.

Gilbert, S. F. (2017), 'Holobiont by birth: Multilineage individuals as the concretion of cooperative processes', in A. L. Tsing, N. Bubandt, E. Gan and H. Swanson (eds), *Arts of Living on a Damaged Planet: Ghosts and Monsters of the Anthropocene*, 73–89, Minneapolis: University of Minnesota Press.

Gough, N. (2017), 'Specifying a curriculum for biopolitical critical literacy in science teacher education: Exploring roles for science fiction', *Cultural Studies of Science Education*, 12 (4): 769–94.

Haraway, D. J. (2016), *Staying with the Trouble: Making Kin in the Chthulucene*, Durham, NC: Duke University Press.

Kafka, F. (1998[1914]), *The Trial*, New York: Knopf Double Day Publishing Group.

Manevitz, A. (28 July 2014), 'Guest post: Seneca village memory: The problem of forgetting', *The Junto: A Group blog on Early American History*. Available at: https://

earlyamericanists.com/2014/07/28/seneca-village-memory-the-problem-of-forgett
ing/ (Accessed 25 April 2018).

Moore, J. W. (2015), *Capitalism in the Web of Life: Ecology and the Accumulation of
Capital*, New York: Verso Books.

Le Guin, U. K. (2017), *Dancing at the Edge of the World: Thoughts on Words, Women,
Places*, New York: Grove Press.

Miller, J. R. (2017), *Residential Schools and Reconciliation: Canada Confronts Its History.*
Toronto: University of Toronto Press.

Osborne, C. (2018), *The Moonspeaker: Where Some Ideas Are Stranger Than Others.*
Available at: http://www.moonspeaker.ca/TurtleIsland/TurtleIslandMap/turtleisla
ndmap.html (Accessed 2 May 2018).

Peters, J. D. (2015), *The Marvelous Clouds: Toward a Philosophy of Elemental Media*,
Chicago, IL: University of Chicago Press.

Rancière, J. (2015), *Dissensus: On Politics and Aesthetics*, New York: Continuum
Publishing.

Snowshoe, A. and Starblanket, N. V. (2016), 'Eyininiw mistatimwak: The role of the
Lac La Croix Indigenous Pony for First Nations youth mental wellness', *Journal of
Indigenous Wellbeing*, 2 (2): 60–76.

Sharma, A. (2012), 'Global climate change: What has science education got to do with
it?' *Science & Education*, 21 (1): 33–53.

Tsing, A. (2015), *The Mushroom at the End of the World*, Princeton, NJ: Princeton
University Press.

Viele, E. (1856), Topographical Survey for the Grounds of Central Park. *Collection of the
New-York Historical Society.*

Wallace, M. F. (2017), 'Subjects in the threshold opening-up ethnographic moments
that complicate the novice/veteran science teacher binary', *Issues in Teacher
Education*, 26 (3): 96–110.

9

Transversalities in education research: Using heterotopias to theorize spaces of crises and deviation

Marguerite Jones and Jennifer Charteris

Introduction

A concept used by geographers, architects and literary critics alike (Knight 2017), heterotopias are liminal spaces, portable territories or places that can be conceived of as 'other'. As the earlier quotation illustrates, heterotopias (the mobile space of a boat in this instance) can be imbued with a political function when juxtaposed with other spaces. Research practices, when seen as heterotopic, help us to think otherwise about the world. Foucault (1984) outlines dimensions of heterotopias that can be used as a conceptual framework to support research practice – a particularly helpful heuristic for early career researchers. In this chapter, we offer an application of Foucault's (1986) six heterotopic principles to Education. The extraterritoriality of heterotopias is disruptive in their capacity to unsettle normativity.

Drawing from the Foucauldian concept of 'heterotopology', we provide a spatio-temporal approach to be used in both theoretical and conceptual research frameworks. The conceptual dimensions of 'heterotopology' provide a rich scaffold for systematic description and thus enable a mapping, critique and potential disruption of social spaces. We present two heuristics to support early career research. The first lists authors who have written about heterotopias and outlines their fields of Education research. The second details six different heterotopic principles. These can serve as points of departure to recognize and leverage non-normative research possibilities for disruptive readings of Education spaces. The chapter concludes with an account of the authors' experiences in using collective biography (Davies and Gannon 2006, 2013) as a research approach that creates heterotopic spaces.

How do heterotopias function?

Associated with the work of Jorge Luis Borges, an Argentinian philosopher, the word is a combination of the notions of place (*topos*) and (*heteros*) meaning different or another (Johnson 2006). Liminal places are conceptualized through this etymology. The use of heterotopias, as a means to theorize space, came to the fore through the work of Michel Foucault. Foucault first introduced heterotopias in the preface of his 1966 book *Les mots et les choses* (Foucault 1966) (later translated as *The Order of Things: An Archaeology of the Human Sciences* in 1970). Heterotopias serve to query and unravel the certitudes of spaces as constellations of experience. As such, heterotopias provide vantage points for critiques, commentaries and other vistas. They are zones 'where identities, maps of cultural meaning, relations of power and technical uses of the body are enforced in traditional and non-traditional ways' (Atkinson and Kehler 2010, p. 74).

In Greek mythology, Charon, the Egyptian god, rowed his boat, a heterotopic zone, to cross the river Styx and usher newly deceased souls to Hades. Like Charon's boat, heterotopias are spaces of alteriority that do not belong in the worlds that they traverse. The vessel is a heterotopic space-transversal in that it moves across other spaces and provides an 'outside position' from which to view relationships or the interplay of concepts in a context. Through mapping heterotopias, transversal readings can be generated that represent and simultaneously invert or distort spaces in social science research. Heterotopias enable us to explore the politics of extraterritoriality. They presuppose a system of opening and closing that can both isolate and make penetrable. Heterotopias disrupt continuity and normality (Rymarczuk and Derksen 2014), breaking down borders within and between places into spaces of 'otherness'.

Conceptualized by Foucault (1984), heterotopias include brothels, colonies, boarding schools, sites for military service, cemeteries, cinemas, saunas, gardens, libraries, festivals, resorts, motels, trains and boats. Foucault divides the notion into heterotopias of crisis and heterotopias of deviation. (See examples in Table 9.1, and further explanations in the six heterotopic principles later in the chapter.)

Table 9.1 Definition of Two Types of Heterotopia

Type of Heterotopia	Definition	Examples
Deviation	Heterotopias of deviation as places for those who deviate from the norms of their society	Psychiatric hospitals, rest homes, prisons
Crisis	Heterotopia of crisis as privileged, sacred or forbidden places where sacred activities take place 'elsewhere'	Boarding school, military service, temples where menstruation is not permitted, the honeymoon

Spaces are defined through particular sets of relations (Foucault 1984), for instance 'sites of transportation', 'streets' or 'trains'. As Foucault (1986, p. 3) points out: 'a train is an extraordinary bundle of relations because it is something through which one goes, it is the means by which one goes from one point to another and, it is also something that goes by.' Secondly, clusters of relations define spaces. Foucault (1986, p. 3) uses the 'sites of temporary relaxation – cafes, cinemas, beaches' as examples of places that are premised on human activity. Thirdly, spaces can also be described via the conceptualization of networks of relations, for instance, 'the closed or semi-closed sites of rest – the house, the bedroom [or] the bed' (Foucault 1984, p. 3). A defining feature of a heterotopia is that it has the 'curious property of being in relation with all the other sites, but in such a way as to suspect, neutralize or invent the set of relations that they happen to designate, mirror, or reflect' (Foucault 1984, p. 3). A ship is a heterotopia that is 'a place without a place, that exists by itself, that is closed in on itself and at the same time is given over to the infinity of the sea' (Foucault 1984, p. 9).

Foucault's conception of heterotopia has been critiqued over the years, considered 'banal' (Harvey 2000) and even 'flawed' (Saldanha 2008) in its structuralist provenance. Saldanha (2008) posits a significant critique of the structuralist origins of the term heterotopia.

> [T]he spatiality of Foucault's heterotopology repeats certain flaws of the structuralism in vogue in 1960s France. In order for heterotopias to be 'absolutely different' from 'all the rest' of space, Foucault needs to posit a totality to society and to perform a 'slice of time' … As both geography and postcolonial theory have shown, slicing time often conceals particularist suppositions and is therefore inadequate to account for the multiplicity and unevenness of geographical change. (Saldanha 2008, p. 2080)

Further, Saldanha observes that postcolonial theorists and critical geographers have launched compelling arguments against structuralist conceptions of space:

> [H]istory never simply happens to bounded places or identities. History is made out of many encounters between different populations, multiple 'societies' with multiple sets of habits and norms, as exemplified. (p. 2093)

Pugliese (2010) critiques Foucault for 'uncritically colonialist and gendered discourse' in his description of Foucault's celebration of maritime technology as a 'roving and unfettered entity' (p. 121):

> [F]rom port to port, from tack to tack, from brothel to brothel, it goes as far as the colonies in search of the most precious treasures they conceal in their gardens, you will understand why the boat has not only been for our civilization, from the sixteenth century until the present, the great instrument of economic development … but has been simultaneously the greatest reserve of the imagination. (Foucault 1984, p. 9)

Despite gender, postcolonial and poststructural critiques of Foucault's original conceptualization, the notion of heterotopia can serve as a useful one for writers and researchers. Heterotopias can be useful for exploring the liminality of space and their juxtaposition alongside other spaces can reveal grounded insights in data.

Theoretical use of heterotopias

Many writers have distanced themselves from heterotopias' structuralist foundation. Stanger (2016) considers how heterotopias offer a choreographic mode of thinking to 'examine the spacetime co-mingling by which utopias are made present as heterotopias' (p. 65). The notion of heterotopia synthesizes space and time:

> Running against notions of absolute time and space, this dialectics grasps a situation in which space is temporal and time is spatial or in which movement is the only constant. (Stanger 2016, p. 65)

The concept of heterotopia has been applied in diverse ways by a wide range of people including architects, historians, cultural geographers and literary critics. There are many examples from the literature (See Table 9.2.) that describe a discordant space that juxtaposes several sites that are 'in themselves incompatible' in a single real place (Foucault 1984, p, 6).

Table 9.2 Authors' Use of Heterotopias

Type of Heterotopia	Authors	Research Context
Deviation	Rankin & Collins 2017; Wilks & Quinn 2016; Villadsen 2016; Gannon 2017; Soja 1995; Harrison 2009; Jacobs 2004; Hope 2016	Cruise ship, folk festivals, settler movement; travel diary; spaces in Los Angeles; online communities; internet pornography; Facebook
Crisis	Schliehe 2016; Sandberg, et al. 2015	Female prisoners in Scotland, municipal adult education

Like Stanger (2016), Rankin and Collins (2017) also distance their work from structuralism. They draw from the work of Manuel DeLanda (2006) to apply a speculative realist approach in their exploration of the cruise ship as a heterotopic assemblage. Rather than adopting structuralist interpretations of heterotopias as fixed spaces, they analyse how the relationality of space offers a more constructive and nuanced way to consider cruise ship spaces.

Heterotopias have also been used to explain spatial practices of the nineteenth-century settler movement in England, which championed better conditions for the working poor (Villadsen 2016). Counter sites of folk festivals have been considered for the way that the experience transforms interconnections between people, space and culture (Wilks and Quinn 2016). Cultural capital (for instance knowledge of music) is needed to gain full entry to the folk festival heterotopia (Wilks and Quinn 2016).

Soja (1995) uses the concept to explore heterogeneous and contested socio-spatial areas of Los Angeles, such as the Bonaventure Hotel, Walt Disney Hall and El Pueblo de Nuestra Senora la Reina de Los Angeles. Chaplin (2000) employs heterotopias as a concept to consider spaces and architectural styles in Las Vegas. The city is described as a 'bizarre' world in the middle of the desert that functions according to different rules and yet is paradoxical as it is an 'achieved utopia' in an 'ultimate development of civilisation under capitalist society' (Chaplin 2000, p. 209). Evoking both space and time, Gannon (2017) uses the concept to theorize how her experimentation with a travel diary supports emerging intercorporeal subjectivations through the heterotopology of placetimes, subjectivities and corporealities.

Schliehe (2016) uses heterotopias to theorize spaces of detention, describing the experiences of young female detainees in Scotland. The constructions of heterotopias in the literature on historic houses are investigated by Oram (2012) who explores the complexities around sexuality and gendered spaces in these contexts. Sandberg, et al. (2016) constituted municipal adult education as a heterotopia of deviation that allows students to escape precarious employment. Arguing that adult education provides a place for displaced and abnormal citizens to gain temporary stability, these authors point out how these heterotopic spaces shape and mould 'desirable subjects'.

Technologically constituted spaces can be heterotopic. Social media websites have been examined for how the spaces conform to and transgress external legal requirements, social mores and economic incentives (Marlin-Bennett and Thornton 2012). Facebook is a heterotopia where students develop social relations, experience possibilities for creative deviations, participate in learning communities and also evade face-to-face seminars (Hope 2016). 'Heterotopian selfie practices' are embedded in networked arrangements of bodies, technologies and brands (Rokka and Canniford 2016, p. 1789). The proliferation of selfie images can 'destabilize the properties of brand assemblages', causing issues for ongoing brand management and marketing (Rokka and Canniford 2016, p. 1789). Heterotopias have also been used to apply to explain the otherness of cyberspace (Veel 2003), Second Life online communities (Harrison 2009) and internet pornography (Jacobs 2004).

There have been interesting examples of heterotopias in the arts. Film theorists have used the concept of heterotopia to describe how on-screen child protagonists construct and offer 'a combination of dislocation in time and space' to the adult spectator (Powrie 2005, p. 350). In Penny's (2016) article on 'Crossing the Line', she describes a theatrical shipboard ritual from the nineteenth century that performatively delivered the message to the crew, the wider naval community and the public, that the vessel had crossed the equator. In a 'floating heterotopia', the captain sanctioned a new heterotopia within it as a marginal space that allowed 'the real and imaginary worlds to coincide and a new aquatic order to prevail' (p. 35). In their performance the crew entered a 'betwixt and between space' and 'a moment in and out of time' (Penny 2016 p. 35). Radford, Radford and Lingel (2015) consider how fiction writers, playwrights and theorists convey heterotopias in their reflection on their experiences within libraries:

> Each of these narratives will be used to articulate the relationship between the library space and one's experience within that space, as well as the synthesis between heterotopia and serendipity, or the extent to which the library as place provokes experiences of surprise, adventure, and play. (Radford, Radford and Lingel 2015, p. 735)

There are conflicting views in the literature as to whether heterotopias are real or hypothetical. Knight (2017) posits that heterotopias are textual representations that can be described as semi-mythical and unimaginable spaces that are representable only in language. Alternatively, Veel (2003) writes that they are 'simultaneously real and unreal and their function is to represent, contest, and invert real places' (p. 152).

One of our favourite examples of a heterotopia is the 'Time and Relative Dimension in Space' (TARDIS) machine from the BBC television series *Doctor Who*. In the programme, a Time-Lord travels through space and time in a time machine (the TARDIS), which appears as a 1960s police telephone box. Radford, Radford and Lingel (2015) allude to Foucault's (1984) example of a library enclosure, its range of forms and literary genres and capacity to encompass and step outside of time (p. 26). As a space, the library is similar to the TARDIS with its heterotopic characteristics:

> From the outside, the telephone box/TARDIS looks as if it contains just enough space for a single person to step inside and make a telephone call. However, when the inside of the TARDIS is revealed, it becomes clear that the TARDIS is much bigger on the inside than it appears on the outside. The TARDIS is able to defy the constraints of physical space and contain a virtual space of potentially any size as well as transport its occupants to any point in time or space. (Radford, Radford and Lingel 2015, p. 739)

Although there is a time continuum, the assemblages inside and outside of the TARDIS comprise objects and organisms from multiple historical timeframes.

Heterotopias have been applied in a range of disciplines. The six principles identified by Foucault (1970) offer a heuristic for researchers to make non-hegemonic conditions possible, to think differently and to disrupt educational milieus.

Six heterotopic principles as a disruptive research method

As a methodological concept, heterotopias can support analyses aimed to disrupt normative social practices and conditions. As 'counter-sites' they simultaneously represent, contest and invert other spaces (Foucault 1984, p. 3). The following six principles (Foucault 1984) provide a taxonomy of heterotopias (Sudradjat 2012), and establish a 'heterotopology' with the potential to support analysis of relational contexts.

Spaces of crisis and deviation

Heterotopias exist across cultures and can take a range of forms. Although they vary in cultural groups, no universal form of heterotopia can be conceived (Foucault 1984). Crisis heterotopias are privileged, sacred or forbidden places where individuals and groups, identified as 'Other', reside. For example, menstruating women, pregnant women and the elderly may be allocated their particular places in societies (Foucault 1986). The TARDIS, mentioned earlier, is a crisis heterotopia. Deviation heterotopias, in contrast, are spaces for individuals who demonstrate behaviour aberrant to a cultural norm; for example, the female detainees in Scotland were incarcerated for their crimes (Schliehe 2016). Foucault (1986) includes rest homes, psychiatric hospitals, prisons and retirement homes in this category.

Changing purposes

Heterotopias function in different ways in history and serve particular purposes. They are guided by society, have particular purposes and function differently over time. For example, with the exponential change associated with technologically constituted spaces (Hope 2016; Marlin-Bennett and Thornton 2012; Rokka and Canniford 2016), there have been changing attitudes to libraries. Many texts are now accessible electronically, and one does not need to physically attend a library to issue a book.

Sites of juxtaposed differences

Within a heterotopic place, there can be several incompatible spaces juxtaposed. Foucault uses a range of examples. Theatres are places that can include multiple set changes that create different spaces. Gardens are places where there is an accumulation of diverse organic elements that create unique spaces. Libraries have books leveraging a range of ontologies. Zoos house incompatible animals from different parts of the planet within close proximity.

Heterochronisms – Links with other times

Heterotopias are linked with slices of time and therefore can be conceived as 'heterochronies' (Foucault 1984, p. 6). The term 'heterochrony' joins together *heteros* (other) and *chronos* (time) to signify a characteristic of some heterotopias. We can be separated by conventional time frames by the juxtaposition of different elements from different periods in one place. This can be seen in accumulations of collections across time, for instance museums, libraries and cemeteries. In these collections, like the TARDIS heterotopia, there is a simultaneous timefulness and timelessness.

Contrasting heterotopias that open out to a quasi-eternity are fleeting and transitory. Festivals, fairgrounds and holiday resorts are temporal spaces where alternative times are created as heterochronies. These spaces enable escapes from normal time. Heterotopias can therefore be ephemeral, appearing and disappearing from time to time.

Rites and rituals of gatekeeping

A fifth feature of heterotopias is that they are isolated from the spaces surrounding them. Heterotopic sites are not freely accessible like public spaces; they open and close in acts that require permission to enter or leave. If rites are ignored, they are not accessible. Permission to enter is granted through the performance of certain acts like 'purification, identification, registration, payment, demonstration or worship' (Rymarczuk and Derksen 2014, para 8). For instance, Disney World is only possible to enter through an entrance fee and therefore Mickey Mouse exists only through a fiscal offering (Bruchansky 2010). Facebook is free (although monetized through advertising). Access to the pages of participants functions through a system of opening and closing (Rymarczuk and Derksen 2014). For the prisoners in Scotland detention (Schliehe 2016) is contingent on sentences handed down by judges. Therefore, there are gatekeeping systems that maintain a singularity of purpose for a particular heterotopic space. In schools, entry can be mandatory, as in the case of the legal requirement to attend. Students may enter 'time out' spaces, a detention room or sickbay.

Individuals, when entering heterotopias, are required to yield to rites and purifications. In schools these may include behaviour modification practices, teacher professional learning communities or coaching and mentoring practices. There can be practices, on the contrary, that appear as transparent openings, yet are shrouded in mystery as strange exclusions, for instance staff promotion or specialist teaching appointments.

A function between poles

A final characteristic highlighted by Foucault (1986) is the dual function of heterotopias. Firstly, they operate in relation to all other spaces that exist outside of them. This implies that they relate to existing spaces through providing disturbances that surface and question normative and potentially hegemonic practices. The TARDIS heterotopia provides disturbances that intervene in the politics of the planets where it lands. In addition to providing contrast, they simultaneously demarcate a territory of the 'real', creating an 'other' space that is 'as perfect, as meticulous, as well arranged as ours is messy, ill constructed, and jumbled' (Foucault 1984, p. 6). This polarity can be seen in the juxtaposition of the pristine worlds of high street fashion, which is visible in shopping malls, and the mundane world of the shopper. In the former space, the glossy prints of super models and glamorous celebrities are highlighted in strategic places by shop lighting, coupled with evocative music and designer fragrances. In stark contrast, the flat shoes of the shopper, shopping trolleys, squirming children and queues in the car park juxtapose the banality of the mundane world.

The six heterotopic principles can be used by early career researchers as a framework with which to 'invert, juxtapose, transgress and combine spaces' – both 'mental and physical' (Schweiger 2013, p. 62). We provide an account of our conceptual work using collective biography as an application of a disruptive methodology (Davies and Gannon 2006, 2013).

Bringing theory and method together with heterotopias

Collective biography is a method developed by Davies and Gannon (2006), which draws from the earlier 'collective memory work' of Haug (1987) and associates. Collective biography inverts static approaches to research work, juxtaposing various stories, transgressing normative discourses and combining perspectives often to decentre humanist practice. As a poststructuralist research approach, collective biography brings 'theory into collision with everyday life … to rethink, collectively … the discursive contexts within which our lives make sense' (Davies and Gannon 2006, p. 4).

To provide an example of collective biography that illustrates heterotopias, we describe our theoretical application. We have used the heuristic of a heterotopic assemblage to mirror, distort, unsettle and invert other spaces. In this article by Charteris, et al. (2017a), we re-storied academic life experiences to conceptualize agency in the academy. In doing so, the collective biography accounts functioned as heterotopias (Davies and Gannon 2006, 2013). We initially penned memory stories as short-detailed, embodied moments. Meeting together, we drilled down into the memory work, to interrogate the stories for insights into ways to subvert hegemonic practices in higher education. This analysis of the re-storied accounts of the academy generated discordant meanings, models and further narratives (Bruchansky 2010). The collective biography process opened physical and discursive spaces for alternative stories to be told. Sharing memories 'felt dangerous and vulnerable, yet cathartic' (Charteris, et al. 2017a, p. 4). Whether collective biography is the particular process taken up or not, slow, shared scholarship of this kind can facilitate the creation of heterotopic spaces. We encourage early career researchers to think creatively with collective biography as a method where there can be mentoring and mutual support for research practice.

Collective biography and Foucault's six principles

In the following, we expand on our own experiences with collective biography scholarship and our engagement with the scholarly work of others who have written in the field. This exposition is intended to provide methodological examples for further research work. In the account of each of Foucault's six dimensions of heterotopias below, we propose that collective biography can be a generative heterotopic methodological approach. We hope that this can afford specific guidance for early career researchers who would like to use heterotopias as a disruptive methodology.

Spaces of crisis and deviation

In some instances, collective biography can be used as a space of crisis. For instance, there have been gatherings of women scholars who have created spaces as an 'elsewhere' for particular forms of scholarship, away from hegemonic norms of the academy (Davies and Gannon 2006). In such spaces, critiques are lodged that problematize gendered, racialized discourses and material practices. Collective biography projects, where there are collaborative spaces for feminist poststructural research work, can function as places of deviation. Through scholarship, academics can speak back to and rupture socio-material politics of the institutions that strive to govern their bodies. The Magnetic Island Group (Davies and Gannon 2006) worked with Bronwyn Davies to undertake collective biography as embodied research work. Creating a heterotopia on Magnetic Island, which is located off the far north coast of Queensland, Australia, the group took a week out from their regular work places to rework memories and generate a legacy for researchers who leverage their scholarly work (Davies, et al. 2005).

Changing purposes

Heterotopias can change in purpose and function. As an example, there has been a morphing in collective biography practice over the last few years. One key purpose of the academic application of collective biography is to critique hegemonic scholarship and norms (Charteris, et al. 2017a). Initially collective biography took the form of re-storied memory narratives (Davies and Gannon 2006), but in recent years academics have conducted deterritorializing practice in accordance with poststructural ideas (See Gannon, et al. 2014). Furthermore, there has been recognition in the field of embodied research practices that include a rhizo-textual choreography (See Jones, Nye and Charteris 2016).

Sites of juxtaposed differences

Just as Foucault (1986) mentions a theatre or a garden, the bodies of academics and their assemblages of ideas contribute to collective biography as a juxtaposition of differences. Therefore, the embodied process of writing together leverages a compilation of bodies and objects that are brought into connection through the collaborative scholarship. The stories emerge through the sharing that takes place and new conceptual work is forged. The overlaying of stories surfaced critiques of the particular politics that were inherently unique to that particular university research space (Charteris, et al. 2017a).

Heterochronisms – Links with other times

As memory work, collective biography produces linkages and relationality, through accounts of times past and aspiration for times future. It also forges an assemblage that links with storied accounts that are detailed in the present. In the storytelling moment, there is both timefulness and timelessness. The former in that the participants are physically present, and may vicariously 'live' the affective experiences recounted by a colleague, and timelessness in that the act of retelling experiences creates a heterochronism. The researchers sit apart from the day-to-day measures of the seconds, minutes and hours of academic work, engaging substantively with theoretical frameworks and/or critiquing the politics in storied memories.

Rites and rituals of gatekeeping

There are rituals associated with collective biography involving building knowledge of processes of writing for academic scholarship. There are protocols that may be negotiated in groups, including the establishment and ongoing maintenance of relational trust. This is particularly relevant when academics are sharing personal stories of hardship or adversity (See Charteris, et al. 2017a; Charteris, et al. 2017b). Gatekeeping systems focus on a singularity of purpose. One example being a collective biography that emerged from an 'Australian Association of Research in Education' (AARE) Early Career research Workshop. There was a rite in that members of AARE initially paid fees to be part of the association and the researchers made an additional payment to attend the weekend. In one of the workshops that members had elected to join (a further rite), the group were invited to proceed with a publication (ritual) and members of the group constructed a collective biography on their experiences of 'academicity' (Petersen 2007). This joint generative process involves the circulating of a manuscript, exchanges of email communications and the determination of author order – often through alphabetical arrangement. The process is indicative of the academic generosity associated with collective biography as a feminist research practice.

A function between poles

The opportunity for collective biography juxtaposes spaces and serves a dual function. Research writing groups create generative heterotopic spaces and operate in relation to all other spaces that exist outside of them. They can provide spaces with which to create disturbances that surface and question normative and potentially hegemonic practices in other spaces. For instance, a group at the University of New England created research space for memory work into the issue of casual teaching work (Charteris, et al. 2017a). A heterotopia of collective biography was created through the group re-storying memories from their experiences as casual relief teachers. Critiques associated with the circumstances of casual relief work were problematized as the condition associated with being part of a precariat workforce (Charteris, et al. 2017a). This research, which took place in the academy, was simultaneously demarcated as a territory of the 'real' that created 'other' spaces (Foucault 1984 p. 6) for problematizing work conditions in schools. Dimensions of these spaces illustrate polarities. There are schools and universities, casual and permanent workers, uncertain and certain employment, unstable and inconsistent work conditions, and the 'perfectly arranged' image of what schooling should be and the messy reality.

We have used collective biography as an example context for Foucault's six principles in this chapter. The dimensions outlined can be used as a theoretical and as a conceptual framework for a disruptive methodology. Early career researchers can take up the six dimensions to locate and interrogate the nature of specific spaces in research contexts.

Conclusion

The conceptual dimensions of 'heterotopology' enable a rich scaffold with which to generate a non-normative and disruptive methodology in education research. Within heterotopic locations, there are diverse histories, overlapping spaces and the associated positioning of bodies. As Foucault (1986) points out, '[t]he heterotopia is capable of juxtaposing in a single real place several spaces, several sites that are in themselves incompatible' (p. 6). Heterotopias can serve as transformative points of departure that enable the recognition of spaces of crises and deviation in Education. Through their identification and inhabitation, normative, bounded and taken-for-granted spaces can be 'othered' and inherent illusions exposed. Just as there is richness within heterotopias, they are mobile heuristics that provide counterpoints in normative terrains.

Glossary

Collective biography A poststructuralist research approach that inverts static approaches by juxtaposing various stories, rethinking collectively, transgressing normative discourses and combining perspectives often to decentre humanist practice.

Heterotopias Liminal spaces, portable territories and/or places that can be conceived of as 'other'.

Heterotopology A spatio-temporal approach used in theoretical and conceptual research frameworks as a rich scaffold for systematic description and mapping, critique and potential disruption of social spaces.

References

Atkinson, M. and Kehler, M. (2010), 'Boys, gyms, locker rooms and heterotopia', in M. Kehler and M. Atkinson (eds), *Boys' Bodies: Speaking the Unspoken*, 73–90, New York: Peter Lang.

Bruchansky, C. (2010), 'The heterotopia of Disney World', *Philosophy Now*, 77: 15–17.

Chaplin, S. (2000), 'Heterotopia deserta: Las Vegas and other spaces', in I. Borden and J. Rendell (eds), *Intersections: Architectural Histories and Critical Theories*, 2013–220, London: Routledge.

Charteris, J., Jenkins, K., Jones, M. and Bannister-Tyrrell, M. (2017a), 'Structural marginalisation, othering and casual relief teacher subjectivities', *Critical Studies in Education*, 5 (1): 104–19. doi:10.1080/17508487.2015.110820.

Charteris, J. Jones, M., Nye, A. and Reyes, V. (2017b), 'A heterotopology of the academy: Mapping alterior assemblages as possibilised heterotopias', *International Journal of Qualitative Studies in Education*, 30 (4): 340–53. doi10.1080/09518398.2016.1250178.

Jones, M., Nye, A. and Charteris, J. (2016), 'Choral refrains-Joussiance an ecstasy of escape', Australian Association for Research in Education (AARE), Melbourne, 28–31 Nov.

Davies, B., Browne, J., Gannon, S., Honan, E. and Somerville, M. (2005), 'Embodied women at work in neoliberal times and places', *Gender, Work & Organization*, 12 (4): 343–62.

Davies, B. and Gannon, S. (2006), 'The practices of collective biography', in B. Davies and S. Gannon (eds), Do*ing collective biography*: *Investigating the production of subjectivity*, 1–15, London: Open University Press.

Davies, B. and Gannon, S. (2013), 'Collective biography and the entangled enlivening of being', *International Review of Qualitative Research*, 5 (4): 357–76.

DeLanda, M. (2006), *A New Philosophy of Society, Assemblage Theory and Social Complexity*, London: Continuum.

Foucault, M. (1966), *Les Mots et les choses*, Paris: Editions Gallimard.

Foucault, M. (1970), *The Order of Things*, Andover Hants: Tavistock.

Foucault, M. (1984), 'Des espaces autres' [Of Other Spaces]. *Architecture, Mouvement, Continuité*, 5: 46–9. Retrieved from web.mit.edu/allanmc/www/foucault1.pdf

Gannon, S. (2017), '"After the humidity and stillness of yesterday..." Drifting, reading, writing self and others, traveling in otherwhens and otherwheres', *Qualitative Inquiry*, 23 (4): 252–6. doi:10.1177/1077800416686374.

Gannon, S., Walsh, S., Byers, M. and Rajiva, M. (2014), 'Deterritorializing collective biography', *International Journal of Qualitative Studies in Education*, 27 (2): 181–95. doi:10.1080/09518398.2012.737044.

Harrison, R. (2009), 'Excavating second life: Cyber-archaeologies, heritage and virtual communities', *Journal of Material Culture*, 14 (1): 75–106.

Harvey, D. (2000), 'Cosmopolitanism and the banality of geographical evils', *Public culture*, 12 (2): 529–64.

Haug, F. (1987), *Female Sexualization: A Collective Work of Memory*, London: Verso, 25.

Hope, A. (2016), 'Educational heterotopia and students' use of Facebook', *Australasian Journal of Educational Technology*, 32 (1): 47–58.

Jacobs, K. (2004), 'Pornography in small places and other spaces', *Cultural Studies*, 18 (1): 67–83. doi:10.1080/0950238042000181610.

Johnson, P. (2006), 'Unravelling Foucault's "different spaces"', *History of the Human Sciences*, 19 (4): 75–90. doi:10.1177/0952695106069669.

Knight, K. T. (2017), 'Placeless places: Resolving the paradox of Foucault's heterotopia', *Textual Practice*, 31 (1): 141–58. doi:10.1080/0950236X.2016.1156151.

Marlin-Bennett, R. and Thornton, E. N. (2012), 'Governance within social media websites: Ruling new frontiers', *Telecommunications Policy*, 36 (6): 493–501.

Oram, A. (2012), 'Sexuality in Heterotopia: Time, space and love between women in the historic house', *Women's History Review*, 21 (4): 533–51.

Penny, S. (2016), 'Crossing the line', *Performance Research*, 21 (2): 32–7. doi:10.1080/135 28165.2016.1162524.

Petersen, E. (2007), 'Negotiating academicity: Postgraduate research supervision as category boundary work', *Studies in Higher Education*, 32: 475–87. doi:10.1080/03075070701476167.

Powrie, P. (2005), 'Unfamiliar places: "Heterospection" and recent French films on children', *Screen*, 46 (3): 341–52.

Pugliese, J. (2010), *Transmediterranean: Diasporas, Histories, Geopolitical Spaces*, Brussels: Peter Lang.

Radford, G. P., Radford, M. L. and Lingel, J. (2015), 'The library as heterotopia: Michel Foucault and the experience of library space', *Journal of Documentation*, 71 (4): 733–51. doi:10.1108/JD-01-2014-0006.

Rankin, J. R. and Collins, F. L. (2017), 'Enclosing difference and disruption: Assemblage, heterotopia and the cruise ship', *Social & Cultural Geography*, 18 (2): 224–44. doi:10. 1080/14649365.2016.1171389.

Rokka, J. and Canniford, R. (2016), 'Heterotopian selfies: How social media destabilizes brand assemblages', *European Journal of Marketing*, 50 (9/10): 1789–813. doi:10.1108/EJM-08-2015-0517.

Rymarczuk, R. and Derksen, M. (2014), 'Different spaces: Exploring Facebook as heterotopia', *First Monday*, 19 (6). Retrieved from: https://firstmonday.org/article/vie w/5006/4091.

Sandberg, F., Fejes, A., Dahlstedt, M. and Olson, M. (2016), 'Adult education as a heterotopia of deviation: A dwelling for the abnormal citizen', *Adult Education Quarterly*, 66 (2): 103–19. doi:10.1177/0741713615618447.

Saldanha, A. (2008), 'Heterotopia and structuralism', *Environment and Planning A*, 40 (9): 2080–96.

Schliehe, A. K. (2016), 'Re-discovering Goffman: Contemporary carceral geography, the "total" institution and notes on heterotopia', *Geografiska Annaler: Series B, Human Geography*, 98 (1): 19–35.

Schweiger, F. (2013), '"*Mapping the Land of Nod*": The spatial imagination of John Steinbeck's *East of Eden*', in M. Meyer and H. Veggian (eds), *East of Eden: New and Recent Essays*, vol. 16, 59–86, New York: Rodopi.

Soja, E. (1995), 'Heterotopologies: A remembrance of other spaces in the citadel-LA', *Postmodern Cities and Spaces*, 13–34. Cambridge, MA: Blackwell.

Stanger, A. (2016), 'Heterotopia as choreography: Foucault's sailing vessel', *Performance Research*, 21 (3): 65–73. doi:10.1080/13528165.2016.1176739.

Sudradjat, I. (2012), 'Foucault, the other spaces, and human behaviour', *Procedia-Social and Behavioral Sciences*, 36: 28–34.

Veel, K. (2003), 'The irreducibility of space: Labyrinths, cities, cyberspace', *Diacritics*, 33 (3/4): 151–72.

Villadsen, K. (2016), 'The settlement utopia: Brotherly love, discipline, and social critique', *Journal of Civil Society*, 12 (2): 141–57. doi:10.1080/17448689.2016.1161279.

Wilks, L. and Quinn, B. (2016), 'Linking social capital, cultural capital and heterotopia at the folk festival', *Journal of Comparative Research in Anthropology and Sociology*, 7 (1): 23–39.

Part Three

Entanglements and innovations: Method and theory

10

Swarms and murmurations

Matthew Krehl Edward Thomas

Swarms and murmurations

Prologue

Researcher presses play on CVgRM example

Icebergs falling into the ocean, A Dalek pans across the room, glimpses of action blockbusters, Chinese democracy and global protests abound wherein small rebellious minorities vie for change.

'How do you see yourself'? Sprays across the screen … I as researcher cringe internally … wishing I'd spent longer editing before embarking on fieldwork. CCTV cameras pan a courtyard and signs of social media fade into sweat shops, YouTube clips and effortless consumption.

A young boy flicks another in the ear, a stiff teacher barks reprimands at his class. Ads for iPods, Coke equates to happiness, the golden arches of McDonalds.

A musical crescendo far outstrips the 13-inch monitor …

'So does any of that speak to you at all?' I say tentatively, hopefully, pointedly … the credits of the film finish and the participant looks up.

Blinks (a beat) …

'I guess I quite like Dr. Who™ … she said' Lucy (Teacher, 32)

The initial project

The data I draw on has been excised from a pilot study engaging teachers and students from secondary schools across Australia. The participants undertook four methods of data generation focusing on the connections between their professional lives, the consumption of popular culture and their recognition of organizational structures within education. They attended a forty-five-minute semi-structured interview during which a camera recorded their body and facial gestures engaging video as unedited documentary that culminated in the screening of a short film crafted by the researcher. This short film comprised images of schooling, surveillance footage and various iterations of culture and politics. An example of this is available here.[1] It was a form of Critical Videographic Research Methods (CVgRM). I illustrate how CVgRM presents packets of intermingled data via the swarm drawing on multiple theoretical networks.

CVgRM in construction

The critical videographic elicitation approach initiates a seventy-five-second film. It is a researcher-designed, purposefully crafted stimulus package melding politics, schooling and iconography, interspersing cultural icons and mass consumption to challenge the viewer to respond. The film combines fragments of political surveillance shaped through CCTV and iconographic resistance in the form of Tankman. It draws on cultural iconography including Daleks, Stormtroopers and The Simpsons. This particular CVgRM example invokes images of schooling through instruction, discipline and behaviour, whilst the entire film is interspersed with images of mass consumption in the form of Apple products, McDonalds signage and the promise of happiness elicited through Coca-Cola. Finally, the entire CVgRM example is set against the backdrop of environmental degradation, social media and 11 September 2001.

From method to swarm

The swarm, as I use it, entangles the demarcations of methodology and method intra-actively (Barad 2007, p. 206). From inception, the initial swarm draws on my own classroom experience (as a secondary teacher) and was framed with specific tropes. Notably, the commodification of schooling, popular culture and the ways in which power both implicitly and explicitly reframes learning. In this created swarm, my design intention aimed to elicit teachers and students' positionalities, by provoking theoretical dispositions of criticality, culture and pedagogy.

---

[1]   https://youtu.be/TCd55bVtFbc

The CVgRM method, a researcher-developed video experienced by the participants, comprises a pastiche of political and cultural representations tailored to the participant group (Thomas and Moss 2018). Through their acceptance, rejection or apathy, a murmuration is created. Binding video to teacher, culture to participant, their research murmuration can be understood relationally via an entanglement between human social dynamics in order to make sense of the landscape in which the larger swarm occurs – that is, when what is presented forms a bridge between a cultural world and a participant's perception of reality. However, it must be acknowledged that the video holds no absolute truths, only possibilities – it is a generative stepping off point. While reflexivity seemed initially fruitful it remains 'caught up in the geometries of sameness' (Barad 2007, p. 72). As Harraway says it only 'displaces the same elsewhere' (1997, p. 16) and if I'm not careful I won't be able to find it! Consequently, I turn to diffraction to make sense of the swarm. Diffraction has a long history in educational research (Barad 2007; Haraway 1997; Thomas and Moss 2018); at its heart it is a 'process of producing difference' (Bozalek and Zembylas 2017, p. 117) in which patterns of difference are created via the swarm as a kind of interference pattern. Diffraction offers the capacity to work ontologically 'from identifying bodies as separate entities with distinct borders to think in terms of processes of entanglements and interdependences in processes of ongoing co-constitutive co-existence' (Taguchi 2012, p. 271) – apt for the swarm which serves to make sense of how students and teachers understand classroom and cultural phenomenon.

Enter the swarm

The swarm 'comprises isolated individuals' (Han 2017, p. 23), whom through diffraction form a temporary union, a tangible way in which exploratory researchers may bear witness to the temporal and illusory nature of multiple theoretical dispositions actualized in the application and reception of method. To demonstrate this, I assemble my global methodology, the swarm. The swarm has been a useful concept in insect research, financial modelling and more recently artificial intelligence (Beni 2004) applications. Bonabeau notes that swarms are 'where many simple agents occupy one-or two-dimensional environments to generate patterns and self-organise through nearest-neighbour interactions' (Bonabeau, Dorigo and Théraulaz 1999, p. 7). It has been useful to poststructural and posthumanist theorizing, building from Deleuze & Guattarian configurations of multiplicity 'defined not by the elements that compose it in extension, not by the characteristics that compose it in comprehension, but by the lines and dimensions it encompasses in "intension'"(Deleuze and Guattari 2004, p. 270) where 'ideas swarm in the fracture[s]'(Deleuze and Guattari 1994, p. 169) and more recently with industrial, military and posthumanist interest, respectively, the 'swarm occupies an ambiguous categorization between the 'many' and the 'one' in terms of individual independence and collective coordination' (Wilcox 2017, p. 33). I am explicitly drawing out diffracted patterns in which a singular focus is artificially valorized and no longer legion. Conversely, the swarm helps us to understand how disparate ideas become consensus behaviours, forming what is understood as the collective starling flock, school of fish or predator drone fleet networks of organization (Cavagna et al. 2010, 2017). To examine the ways in which schools, culture and consumption practices or indeed fear-based actions coalesce to establish a kind of intricate, seemingly naturalized social engineering is to still the swarm. As researchers when we shift focus from the collective whole to a thematic or component part, we artificially privilege that articulation. While we must render the swarm in isolation, such an analysis can only be understood temporally.

The swarm is an evolution of critical scholarship in posthuman times. It allows the practical and abstract qualities of a methodological design constructed of 'alienated parts' (Ellis 1979, p. 126) to be networked highlighting complex collective behaviours. By flocking in and among the research data, the swarm encourages the capacity for transversality as diffractive patterns are made and remade. Following Lykke (2010, p. 27) the swarm 'is open toward new and emerging theoretical and methodological synergies'. To that end, splicing the machine to the starling, the starling to the teacher, the teacher to the industrial workplace model of exploitation provides opportunities to witness nuance and complexity, with the tools necessary to explore complex phenomena understood as 'differential patterns of mattering' (Barad 2007, p. 206) and when a murmuration occurs 'intra-actions iteratively reconfigure what is possible and what is impossible' (Barad 2007, p. 234)

Swarming theory into method

Swarming theory and method together privileges sociological complexity. The swarm produces a patterning that is supportive of symbolic representation, subjectivity and language in the formation of how we come to understand who we are in the world showcased through the CVgRM method. The CVgRM method itself was constituted by three theoretical dispositions: critical theory, cultural studies and critical pedagogy. While this specific swarm will be experienced differentially, the process remains generative and iterative. Through critical theory, I hoped for access to the uneven distribution of power and symbolic violence in Australian schools. Access to the political worlds of the participants was secured through a combination of Western iconography of the last half-century such as the unknown protester in Tiananmen Square, obstructing a column of tanks in the student led 1989 protests in Post Mao-China. Further, the iconic final images of the 11 September 2011 terrorist attacks on the World Trade Centre and the subsequent contagion of those same images which have worked to supplant hope with fear. Through this discourse it was anticipated that the interface between schooling and the personal lives of teachers could be problematized. My suspicions of neat lines and imperfect boundaries in a digital age when performance cultures run rampant was manifest (Done and Murphy 2016; Page 2017).

Through cultural studies, I desired access to the visual, the iconic and market forces undergirding the commodification of modern schooling. It was anticipated that access to the cultural worlds of the participants and as such the iconography of the white iPod headphones, the swirling pepper shape of a Dalek or the telephone TARDIS box was secured through this interdisciplinary field. The long running Simpsons™ cartoon provided a snippet that satirized sweat shops feeding the mass marketed consumable world. It was anticipated that this could draw participants towards discussing marketization, consumption practices and herd like mentalities sometimes experienced in schooling.

Through the application of critical pedagogy, I sought access to the intentions of the teacher, what incited them in their classrooms as the ontological confronted the epistemological. The CVgRM example drew out images of teacher discipline, student misbehaviour and the dehumanizing nature of education (Taylor 2013) triggering associations of surveillance, monitoring and compliance . Images of environmental degradation coupled with snippets of dystopian science fiction and social media forge a pastiche of popular culture which was anticipated might promote a consideration of subversion, resistance and their represented digital lives as schooling permeates boundaries (Biesta 2012) confusing perception and representation.

Making the cut: Diffraction becomes murmuration

The swarm is intertextual, moving beyond simple representations, displaying a complex 'emergence of global order' (Cavagna et al. 2010, p. 11865) allowing diffracted correlations and perturbations. Early career researchers in particular must attend to what Lee (2010, p. 75) terms 'boundary work' bleeding across theoretical frameworks, coagulating in transformative social practices eschewing superficiality. It is here that multimethodological innovation rises. Proponents of the swarm, who wish to trespass across traditional methodological lines, must be careful not to neglect foundations upon which they are built upon – all things have histories. The swarm becomes a space for conflict to be reappraised in its disparate fragmentary state since swarms are movements facilitating alternative representations. One such concern may be reflexivity. This has been accounted for in the current example through the active use of diffraction. When we consider the swarm, we appraise a multimethodological model as a means to understand complex systems through abstractions. Diffraction helps us to see more than we are through a 'dynamic, non-linear method of reading and writing in which stable epistemological categories are challenged, temporalities are disrupted and disciplines are complexified' (Hickey-Moody, Palmer and Sayers 2016, p. 217). In the next section of this chapter, I make a series of agential cuts for the purpose of illustrating the nature of the swarm. This allows us to 'peek inside the phenomenon' (Barad 2007, p. 314) to account for 'description in terms of the mixtures'(Barad 2007, p. 348) of multiplicity and through the patterns of diffraction that are created by the swarm, avoid and grasp the 'entangled nature of differences that matter'(Barad 2007, p. 381).

I take this further with a research murmuration, a 'self-organised' (Procaccini et al. 2011, p. 759) extracted flock of metaphoric starlings that are singular 'physical time-varying data points. As they participate in murmuration, they change direction, speed, and volume' (Campbell and Samsel 2015, p. 8) in which the 'flight paths become glyphs that naturally retain temporal and spatial information' (Campbell and Samsel 2015, p. 11). An excellent visual of a murmuration is available here (van IJken 2016).

Critically, a murmuration remains connected to a diffracted collective but witnessed as an '[a]utonomous collaboration … a means of massing, where each member of the group acts without a leader' (Campbell and Samsel 2015, p. 12). Murmuration is often understood implicitly in the actions of animals flocking together. What may we discover if we consider the effect of pack on the related smaller collective? From school students compliantly wearing their blazer home on hot days? To privacy conscious investors who invest in bitcoin and police with body cameras operating autonomously or a hacktivist group such as Anonymous understood as a 'thriving and constantly evolving online collective' (Phillips 2015, p. 63). Indeed, if we trace the patterns of the few, how

Figure 10.1 Starling mumuration. Courtesy of Andrea Cavagna – COBBS Lab, National Research Council, Rome, Italy (Cavagna 2018a).

might we better understand the implicit sociological forces that support hidden pedagogy as it comes to influence forms of social engineering.

In the following section of this chapter I assemble research murmurations to understand artificially stilled narratives. I do this by privileging particular diffracted patterns of school power, popular culture and consumption in a form of soft assembly.

Swarming method into data: Critical theory

Schools cease to be places of learning and can be appreciated as products of a wider system when tensions are amplified between the 'local and [the] global' (Rivzi and Lingard 2010, p. 51). Critical theory provides a means to see power imbalances through the swarm in the mediations of the participant, allowing the researcher to see a matrix of data points as they appear to the participant.

Teachers, through action, make transactional choices steeped in values, politics and power when the system they are engaging in is 'unequal by design' (Au 2009, p. 141). If we consider the swarm, this alerts us that teachers can be both critical and despondent. However, their capacity for resistance is minimal. This is understood in the actions of teachers who enforce the rules of the school in contradistinction to their own espoused values. When leading teachers reflect that they 'sell a product' to students, which mirrors what are ostensibly '"market values" on the one hand and they hold a neoconservative attachment to "traditional values" on the other' (Apple 1996, p. 6). By appreciating that a teacher's role is consumption driven, they implicitly understand that 'parents do not buy a system, they buy a school' (Bonnor and Caro 2007, p. 174).

Through the CVgRM method participants watched scenes of environmental degradation and many reflected candidly on the inertia surrounding social activism. Responses drew out disharmonies and contradictions as teachers gave examples of their values through the creation of home gardens and discussions of recycling believing the performativity of modern schools vis-à-vis kitchen gardens. Social practices can reveal ways to understand the practice of 'pedagogy [as something] that is more representational than the traditional pedagogy of representation' (Biesta 2009, p. 109). This occurs when the performance of presence is valued over substance. The stories of teachers from beyond the classroom help us to understand what is happening within it. Teacher and student agency expand and contract within educational institutions reinforcing and normalizing uneven distributions of power when a 'network of power' (Foucault 1980, p. 119) is realized.

The characterization of the teacher as an authoritarian figure is in the CVgRM example, disciplining his class. This is further seen in the tensions of teaching and learning practices, as they come to frame possibility in a teachers' classroom. Teaching understood in this way may be the most important political act. Criticality provides a language to forge understanding that schools exist in a neoliberal context, through understanding education as a politicized purchasable commodity. Several expressed that they need to adapt to the machinations of the school and encourage uniformity in their students, noting that this is best achieved by submission, to the values of their context. This for many teachers played out as enforcing disciplinary measures they didn't agree with. Adoptions such as these bind the teacher to the institution and involve the effect of local policy (such as classroom management) being enacted in practice.

The critical research murmuration exposes a composition of values driving action in schools, curtailing identity and making plain the power struggles that exist in small pedagogical choices.

Swarming method into data: Cultural studies

Through the CVgRM method the theoretical disposition of cultural studies affords a means to superimpose an image which holds an 'infectious, viral character'(Mitchell 2011, p. 2) onto the lived experiences of the participant exploring their immersion in visual culture through images which are 'difficult to contain or quarantine' (Mitchell 2011, p. 2). Engaging the swarm in this way invokes iconography as approaching transcendent when the CVgRM example of the twin-towers collapse becomes a 'postlinguistic, postsemiotic rediscovery of the picture as a complex interplay between visuality, apparatus, institutions, discourse, bodies and figurality' (Mitchell 1995, p. 16). I trace lines between the research subject and the stimulus of the image, the swarm provides avenues to see the symbolic and practical as values ridden. Storey (2014, p. 72) tells us that 'the everyday is composed of objects', where we learn, work and play become composite junkyards of 'powerful symbols … [that are] are manipulated and redefined to justify competing social arrangements' (Margulies 2013, p. x). The swarm, problematizes such symbols as representative entities with competing values and abstracted beliefs from which teachers and students deduce framed possibilities. Iconography consumed by the teacher, moves from perception of environmental values, to the realities of pedagogical practices when classroom teachers consume the iconography of their schools, adapt broadly to its ideals.

Evinced from the CVgRM example are the iconic golden arches that promise access to a shared history. So strong is the iconography of McDonalds that 'when one bites into a Big-Mac one is consuming the sign values of good times, communal experience, consumer value and efficiency, as well as the (dubious) pleasures of the product' (Kellner 2003, p. 39). This relationship is further elaborated upon by Ms. Honey and her country students, who see a trip to McDonalds as a rite of passage, where the 'signifiers of Americana, the legitimacy of free market economics, and the lure of modernity' (Kincheloe 2002, p. 134) are promised through its iconic golden glow. Ms. Honey explained (from her own student days):

> We'd be begging our teachers to take us because we hadn't had it in six months. But my students have it every week. Every second week. Every day, some of them. Some of them work there, yet they beg when we go on an excursion. Can we get McDonalds! (Honey).

In Ms. Honey's anecdote, the children beg not for the product, but what that product symbolizes. This echoes Kincheloe's experience when he 'took pride in knowing the Big Mac Jingle' (2002, p. 32) and walked in feeling an 'indescribable sense of awe and reverence' (Kincheloe 2002, p. 32). Both, Kincheloe's and Honey's reflections underscore a relationship to the idea of McDonalds. I draw it out here to emphasize that the power of the icon transcending culture, temporality and perhaps even good taste. The childhoods of Ms. Honey in outback Australia and Kincheloe in the United States could not be further apart and yet they share resonance.

Through the swarm, practices of consumption become grounds for understanding what research participants desire and value. Schools have adapted to this turning into commodities available for purchase, via customer satisfaction, performance and when 'parents … appropriate consumer vocabularies' (Wilkins 2012, p. 73). Schools attempt to manage this commodification through the iconography that students are exposed to in school branding, self-serving narratives and marketization.

The uniforms of schoolchildren in the CVgRM clip invoke a capacity for some teachers to create a cultural murmuration from the diffracted swarm. Drawing on the dispositions of critical theory and cultural studies, alterity occurs. This was highlighted starkly when questioned on the merits of uniform with contrasting opinions from an elite private schoolgirl who noted, 'I don't have to get up every morning early and be like what am I going to wear' (Girl). A boy from a state secondary school claimed his uniform was, by contrast 'restrictive and uncomfortable' (Boy). Uniforms comprise representations of values and beliefs, acceptance of and resistance to the reaches of school power. Effortless consumption is established, when it means something to be a student or a teacher at a particular institution. This is ably showcased in the expectations of daily dress in which being a member of a group means adopting the consensus practices of the collective professional, respectable, neat group. To that end, schooling doesn't simply prepare students to work; it prepares them to be part of a commodity exchange through the appropriation of sanctioned values in which many students develop strategies to get along unnoticed.

A cultural murmuration of students in uniform may be understood as a part of a wider exchange that acts to control and propagate particular behaviours and specific sanctioned values (Vinson and Ross 2003). The iconography of school culture pervades pedagogical practices beyond the literal. Insisting that a chair belongs on a classroom table at the end of a class, a shirt is tucked in or standing over a student in a disciplinary moment becomes universally understood through a cultural murmuration as compliance to a workplace.

A student raising their hand in a Australian classroom becomes a symbolic act implying a specific acquiescence to authority. To witness power play out through diffractions of the swarm stills the often-contradictory forces which maintain that 'images are a basic component of the social construction of [a] reality and operate fundamentally to control human behaviour and shape human thought within institutional contexts' (Vinson, Ross and Welsh 2010, p. 275). The figuration of the singular cultural murmuration affords insight into the relationship between imagery and the individual 'reveal[ing] very complex dialogues and transactions to do with identity status, aspirations, cultural capital, and position within a social group[s]' (Paterson 2006, p. 7). Donning a blazer or submitting to a teacher become moments of significance in which the swarm demonstrates culture as an educative force exacerbating positions of countenanced.

Swarming method into data: Critical pedagogy

Education has become time pressured by numerous measures in the enactment of policies leveraging high-stakes testing against performance and accountability (Thomas and Whitburn 2019). To achieve this teachers are operationalized and students put to the test. Parents come to commodify the process of schooling establishing a user pays mentality and a volatile mix of aspiration against a 'backdrop of moral panic' (Keddie 2016, p. 714) takes hold. Parents as the purchaser of the commodity expose their values as domestic concerns ape global pressures and a largely public system is pushed to achieve private efficiencies. Australian classrooms mimic international trends wherein standardized tests have narrowed the goals of a curriculum to serving the economy. Schools naturally seek efficiencies to deal with the additional pressures when time poor teachers are pushed to produce quantifiable results. Critical pedagogy through the CVgRM method provides a capacity to question the assumptions upon which society is built and in doing so explore inequality by design. Participants, upon seeing Facebook™ log in screens in the CVgRM, recoiled and explained a need to divide a clear line between who they understand themselves to be and their required role.

Negotiating the boundaries of professional identity and a semblance of a personal life is complicated for teachers whose professional persona is caught between serving the interests of their students and the mandates of policy imperatives. Teachers exist in challenging spaces as they come to expect, even valorize synchronicity and uniformity as part of a deliberate social and pedagogic project fuelled by agendas of competition, measurement and productivity establishing a state of conservative modernization.

Kincheloe (2007, p. 856) reminds us that 'people enter school with views, constructed by their experience and the social contexts'. The project of the school then is to conquer an ideological battleground in which school bells, the curriculum, ties and mottos determine official knowledge. When those with power shape the practice of pedagogy for the teacher and the experience of classroom life for the student established practices, icons and expectations are normalized (Thomas and Whitburn 2020).

After witnessing rows of constrained and orderly students from the CVgRM example, Ms. Abbey, a classroom teacher, creates a pedagogical murmuration noting that bringing in alternative practices into an established environment, challenges established and entrenched top-down teaching and learning approaches privileged in such places.

In her words:

> It's harder on the kids because it's so different to what everybody else is doing and that for kids can be really confronting. It's like, I knew the answer with Mr T, but you're saying that in your class, there is no answer, and that conflicts with my whole understanding of education. (Abbey)

In Abbey's experience students who are acculturated to the rituals of school feel threatened by exploratory ideas in the absence of certainty. In such situations, the students themselves push back – blaming the teacher for not providing them with the appropriate scaffolding to understand their learning. This idea was further elaborated upon by Abbey's students, trained in tradition to understand and interpret like classes. They underscore that school is no place to critically inquire into new knowledge and any teacher who tries will be relegated as 'experimental mind maps and stuff – instead of doing real work' (Milly). Despite training and desire, subversive teachers who attempt difference, come to internalize and adapt to their environment. As King (1997, p. 171) tells us, 'mechanisms such as the design of the curriculum, the supervision and evaluation of their work, and the models for reform of the profession itself, teachers are subjected to technologies of discipline that shape their identities, control their work, and induce them to conform'.

Similarly, the CVgRM snippet of classroom life led Lucy to impart what conforming looks like for teachers who adapt to the expected practices of their organizations. A recognition of the pull to become part of the pack was demonstrated in the creation of her own pedagogical research murmuration leading her to divulge that when she took on the role of a teacher, she 'plug[ed] into a system' (Lucy) and, despite her own misgivings of how her classes should be, she came to discover that the 'kids would behave if I put my hair up in a bun' (Lucy). Prior to this realization of her own teaching, she had attempted to shift the students' towards 'open projects and they would freak out' (Lucy). Conversely, when she shaped herself to the expected behaviours of her school environment, the students would willingly comply. The lesson being that when schooling, teaching and learning look a certain way, compliance is assured as actors within the system adopt to the codified forms of such lessons – even if it is at the cost of possibility, curiosity and persistence.

Continuing our reading of the ways in which school may limit rather than open possibility, Ms. Honey offered that prolonged exposure to environments that frame the limits of possibility remove the capacity to think beyond such limitations. In our diffracted patterning of the swarm, imbued by critical pedagogy, power-driven approaches coupled with a lack of creativity can

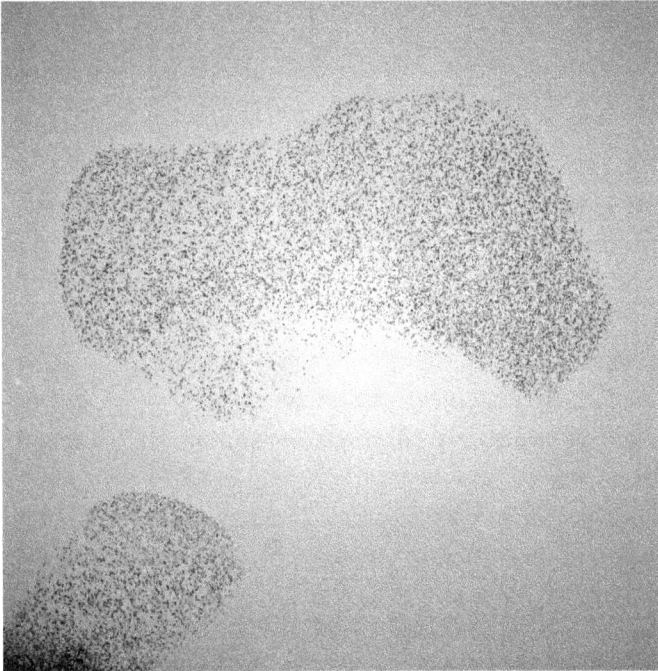

Figure 10.2 Always forever becoming. Courtesy of Andrea Cavagna – COBBS Lab, National Research Council, Rome, Italy (Cavagna 2018b).

only encourage a culture of sameness, in which schooling is a product to be consumed passively. As Denscombe (1982, p. 259) reminds us, 'classroom experience has a hegemonic influence by controlling the range of alternatives that can be considered.' Struck by the CVgRM snippet of logging into social media profile via a handheld mobile device, Honey creates a pedagogical murmuration as she divulges that students who have become accustomed to being told what their options are, where desensitized to possibility. Honey attributes this to the wholesale adoption of technology which set parameters for user experience.

She notes:

> I find globalisation or consumerism … particularly video games … desensitise kids. They don't allow them to be creative. They create a world for them, which has parameters. You get to design your house, [with] six options of the walls. You have to do it their way. If you are an army officer, you have to choose one team or the other. You can't just be a civilian. You know? (Honey)

Honey's pedagogical murmuration echoes earlier sentiments that schools strip teachers of their agency to enact pre-purchased and defined futures, constricting imagination through the valorization of established patterns and behaviours.

Between diffraction and murmuration

The swarm is always in process between diffraction and a murmuration. Throughout this chapter I have elected to make three agential cuts via the CVgRM example and appraised by the diffracted patterns enabled by the swarm. To do this effectively is to accept that we cannot ever fully know our subjects, as they are 'differentially constituted through specific intra-actions'(Barad 2007, p. 342). Further, by examining smaller applications of the swarm, through murmurations as 'temporary coalitions'(Richardson and Chemero 2014, p. 40) of a larger swarm, we can draw towards narrative lines which cut across participants, focus on individuals or privilege a specific theoretical disposition provided we understand that its strength lies in its interactions, relationships and networks.

Purposefully placing the focus and the foci between diffraction and murmuration, the research both reflects and represents onto itself. The research participants become an inter-imbricated node in a web of consequences both empowered by the collective and masked by it. Swarms, fish, birds or cockroaches notably appear to move with a collective conscious. The murmuration invokes multiplicity in a soft assembly. Working in this way is to encounter issues of representation, augmentation and interpretation.

Conclusion

Entering into the swarm and/or framing a murmuration is a critical posthuman research act which allows for complex configurations of design to interweave against analytical representational approaches. The swarm is at once a collectivized approach to conceiving of teachers' work and lives that refuses to view the social world as having a rigid ontology. The swarm is an intra-active process that resists the supposed neatness of values free research work. While the swarm and the murmurations encapsulated above sustain a mosaic of political, cultural and social possibilities, they simultaneously attempt to reject reductive readings of what teachers do. The swarm allows 'a series of discrete flows' (Haggerty and Ericson 2000, p. 605) while appreciateing as Deleuze & Guattari suggest that '[s]ometimes forces blend into one another in subtle transitions, decompose hardly glimpsed; and sometimes they alternate or conflict with one another' (1994, p. 186). If we are to make sense of what lurks beyond singular readings, an appreciation of the discordant is necessary and that is what the swarm provides: unity and difference together. Understanding our own research and the worlds of our participants in this way affords multiple ways of seeing, blending and engaging with the world.

Researchers who find themselves at the fringes of analysis and wish to mine the frontiers of lived potentiality must remember that all experience imbues multiple and varied possible readings. Since all readings are necessarily fragmentary, temporal and fluid, a singular 'objective reality can never be captured' (Denzin and Lincoln 2011, p. 5) as it is only ever emergent, multiple and contingent. To that end, this chapter highlights generative affordances which may be enacted through an articulation such as the swarm, foregrounding the centrality of complexity more aptly understood in temporary murmurations. Such amalgams enable ambiguity through the application of what is needed in order to make sense of experience. Through careful moderation the swarm together with research murmurations draw out a soft assembly and weave together difference. Relationships are interimbricated and a swarm of competing theoretical dispositions is understood as far more appropriate to make sense of the unstitched moments of everyday life.

Acknowledgements

I would like to extend my sincere gratitude to Dr Andrea Cavagna and Associate Professor Corcoran for their contributions to my thinking on swarming and collective behaviours.

Glossary

CVgRM A video-based elicitation method comprising researcher-generated material for generating data.

Diffraction An act of interference in the swarm, creating a temporal pattern of what the swarm may look like.

Murmuration A context dependant, temporary, fluid coalition of emergent patterns (theories, experiences, contexts) are momentarily energized to work together as a form of soft assembly

Swarm A dynamic synergy of interwoven multiple-methodologies, systems and structures that compete and coalesce for control.

References

Apple, M. W. (1996), *Cultural Politics and Education*, John Dewey Society Lecture Series, New York: Teachers College Press.

Au, W. (2009), *Unequal By Design: High-Stakes Testing and the Standardization of Inequality*, Critical Social Thought, New York: Routledge.

Barad, K. M. (2007), *Meeting the Universe Halfway: Quantum Physics and the Entanglement of Matter and Meaning*, Durham, NC: Duke University Press.

Beni, G. (2004), 'From swarm intelligence to swarm robotics', in E. Şahin and W. M. Spears (eds), *Swarm Robotics*, 1–9, Berlin, Heidelberg: Springer.

Biesta, G. (2009), 'Education after deconstruction: between event and invention', in M. A. Peters and G. Biesta (eds), *Derrida, Deconstruction, and the Politics of Pedagogy*, 97–114, New York: Peter Lang Publishing.

Biesta, G. (2012), 'Becoming public: Public pedagogy, citizenship and the public sphere', *Social & Cultural Geography*, 13 (7): 683–97.

Bonabeau, E., Dorigo, M. and Théraulaz, G. (1999), 'Swarm intelligence: From natural to artificial systems', *Proceedings Volume in the Santa Fe Institute Studies in the Sciences of Complexity*, Oxford University Press, New York.

Bonnor, C. and Caro, J. (2007), *The Stupid Country: How Australia Is Dismantling Its Public Education System*, A New South book, Sydney: University of New South Wales Press.

Bozalek, V. and Zembylas, M. (2017), 'Diffraction or reflection? Sketching the contours of two methodologies in educational research', *International Journal of Qualitative Studies in Education*, 30 (2): 111–27.

Campbell, B. D. and Samsel, F. (2015), 'Murmurations: drawing together art, visualization, and physical phenomena', *IEEE Computer Graphics and Applications*, 35 (4): 8–12.

Cavagna, A. (2018a), *Starflag_9*, National Research Council, National Research Council, COBBS Lab, Rome, Italy.

Cavagna, A. (2018b), *Starflag_10*, National Research Council, National Research Council, COBBS Lab, Rome, Italy.

Cavagna, A., Cimarelli, A., Giardina, I., Parisi, G., Santagati, R., Stefanini, F. and Viale, M. (2010), 'Scale-free correlations in starling flocks', *Proceedings of the National Academy of Sciences*, 107 (26): 11865.

Cavagna, A., Conti, D., Creato, C., Del Castello, L., Giardina, I., Grigera, Tomas S., Melillo, S., Parisi, L. and Viale, M. (2017), 'Dynamic scaling in natural swarms', *Nature Physics*, 13: 914.

Deleuze, G. and Guattari, F. (1994), *What Is Philosophy?* European Perspectives: A Series in Social Thought and Cultural Criticism, London: Verso.

Deleuze, G. and Guattari, F. (2004), *A Thousand Plateaus*, Continuum impacts, London: Bloomsbury Academic.

Denscombe, M. (1982), 'The "hidden pedagogy" and its implications for teacher training', *British Journal of Sociology of Education*, 3: 249–65.

Denzin, N. K. and Lincoln, Y. S. (2011), 'Disciplining the Practice of Qualitative Research', in N. K. Denzin and Y. S. Lincoln (eds), *The SAGE Handbook of Qualitative Research*, 4th edn, 1–20, Los Angeles, CA: SAGE Publications.

Done, E. J. and Murphy, M. (2016), 'The responsibilisation of teachers: A neoliberal solution to the problem of inclusion', *Discourse: Studies in the Cultural Politics of Education*, 39 (1): 142–55.

Ellis, K. (1979), 'Monsters in the garden: Mary Shelley and the Bourgeois family', in G. L. Levine and U. C. Knoepflmacher (eds), *The Endurance of Frankenstein: Essays on Mary Shelley's Novel*, 123–42, Berkeley: University of California Press.

Foucault, M. (1980), 'Two lectures', in C. Gordon (ed.), *Power/Knowledge: Selected Interviews and other Writings, 1972-1977*, 78–108, New York: Vintage.

Haggerty, K. D. and Ericson, R. V. (2000), 'The surveillant assemblage', *The British Journal of Sociology* 4: 605.

Han, B.-C. (2017), *In the Swarm: Digital Prospects*, Untimely Meditations, Cambridge, MA: MIT Press.

Haraway, D. J. (1997), *Modest– Witness@ Second– Millennium. FemaleMan– Meets– OncoMouse: Feminism and Technoscience*, Cultural Studies, London: Routledge.

Hickey-Moody, A., Palmer, H. and Sayers, E. (2016), 'Diffractive pedagogies: Dancing across new materialist imaginaries', *Gender & Education*, 28 (2): 213.

Keddie, A. (2016), 'School autonomy as "the way of the future": Issues of equity, public purpose and moral leadership', *Educational Management Administration & Leadership*, 44 (5): 713–27.

Kellner, D. (2003), *Media Spectacle*, London: Routledge.

Kincheloe, J. L. (2002), *The Sign of the Burger: McDonald's and the Culture of Power*, Philadelphia, PA: Temple University Press.

Kincheloe, J. L. (2007), 'Research in educational psychology: The bricolage and educational psychological research methods—part 2', in J. L. Kincheloe and R. A. Horn (eds), *The Praeger Handbook of Education and Psychology*, vol. 4, 950–9, Westport, CT: Praeger.

King, B. M. (1997), 'Disciplining teachers', in J. Zajda (ed), *Learning and Teaching*, 171–90, Albert Park: James Nicholas Publishers.

Lee, A. (2010), 'What counts as educational research? Spaces, boundaries and alliances', *Australian Educational Researcher*, 37 (4): 63–78.

Lykke, N. (2010), *Feminist Studies: A Guide to Intersectional Theory, Methodology and Writing*, Routledge Advances in Feminist Studies and Intersectionality, New York: Routledge.

Margulies, J. (2013), *What Changed When Everything Changed: 9/11 and the Making of National Identity*, New Haven: Yale University Press.

Mitchell, W. J. T. (1995), *Picture Theory: Essays on Verbal and Visual Representation*, Essays on verbal and visual representation, Chicago, IL: University of Chicago Press.

Mitchell, W. J. T. (2011), *Cloning Terror: The War of Images, 9/11 to the Present*, Chicago, IL: University of Chicago Press.

Page, D. (2017), 'The surveillance of teachers and the simulation of teaching', *Journal of Education Policy*, 32 (1): 1–13.

Paterson, M. (2006), *Consumption and Everyday Life*, London: Routledge.

Phillips, W. (2015), *This Is Why We Can't Have Nice Things: Mapping the Relationship Between Online Trolling and Mainstream Culture*, The information society series, Cambridge, MA: MIT Press.

Procaccini, A., Orlandi, A., Cavagna, A., Giardina, I., Zoratto, F., Santucci, D., Chiarotti, F., Hemelrijk, C. K., Alleva, E., Parisi, G. and Carere, C. (2011), 'Propagating waves in starling, Sturnus vulgaris, flocks under predation', *Animal Behaviour*, 82 (4): 759–65.

Richardson, M. J. and Chemero, A. (2014), 'Complex dynamical systems and embodiment', in L. Shapiro (ed), *The Routledge Hanbook of Embodied Cognition*, 39–50, New York: Routledge.

Rivzi, F. and Lingard, B. (2010), *Globalizing Education Policy*, London: Routledge.

Storey, J. (2014), *From Popular Culture to Everyday Life*, New York: Routledge.

Taguchi, H. L. (2012), 'A diffractive and Deleuzian approach to analysing interview data', *Feminist Theory*, 13 (3): 265–81.

Taylor, E. (2013), *Surveillance Schools: Security, Discipline and Control in Contemporary Education*, Palgrave pivot, Houndmills, Basingstoke, Hampshire; New York: Palgrave Macmillan.

Thomas, M. K. E. and Moss, J. (2018), 'Critical videographic research methods: Researching teacher's lives and work post "9/11"', in L. Xu, G. Aranda, W. Widjaja and D. Clarke (eds), Video-*based Research in Education: Cross-disciplinary Perspectives*, 83–102, London: Routledge.

Thomas, M. K. E. and Whitburn, B. (2019), 'Time for inclusion?' *British Journal of Sociology of Education*, 40 (2): 159–73.

Thomas, M. K. E. and Whitburn, B. (In press) 'Zeit Kraft und Bildung', in E. Schilling and M. O'Neill (eds), *Einführung in die interdisziplinäre Zeitforschung – Frontiers in Time Research*, Wiesbaden, Germany: Springer Fachmedien Wiesbaden GmbH.

van IJken, J. (2016), *The Art of Flying*, 30/12/2018, Short Film, https://youtu.be/V4f_1_r80RY.

Vinson, K. D. and Ross, E. W. (2003), *Image and Education: Teaching in the Face of the New Disciplinarity*, Extreme Teaching, Rigorous Texts for Troubled Times, New York: Peter Lang.

Vinson, K. D., Ross, E. W. and Welsh, J. F. (2010), 'Controlling images', in K. J. Saltman and D. Gabbard (eds), *Education As Enforcement: The Militarization and Corporatization of Schools*, 2nd edn, 274–90, New York: Routledge.

Wilcox, L. (2017), 'Drones, swarms and becoming-insect: Feminist utopias and posthuman politics', *Feminist Review*, 116 (1): 25.

Wilkins, A. (2012), 'School choice and the commodification of education: A visual approach to school brochures and websites', *Critical Social Policy*, 32: 69–86.

11

Post-Anthropocene imaginings: Speculative thought, diffractive play and *Women on the Edge of Time*

Chessa Adsit-Morris and Noel Gough

Introduction: *Women on the Edge of Time*

Woman on the Edge of Time, by Marge Piercy (1976), stormed into the traditionally male-dominated genre of dystopian fiction. Set in (then) present day New York City, the woman on the edge of time is Consuelo (Connie) Ramos, an impoverished Chicana street woman struggling to survive amidst political, institutional, economic, racialized and gendered inequality. As a hopeful college girl, loving mother, protective aunt, grieving widow, incarcerated pickpocket and angry certified insane woman, Connie embodies the complexities and contradictions of oppression. Piercy imagines that before being committed, Connie's empathy allows her to communicate with Luciente, an androgynous young woman time-travelling from a seemingly utopian future (2137) world – Mattapoisett – in which many of the political and social goals of the late 1960s and early 1970s have been achieved: humans are integrated back into nature, and social, political, racial and gendered power relations are eliminated.

Yet, as Piercy (2016, pp. vii–x) warns:

> The point of writing about the future is not to predict it … The point of creating futures is to get people to imagine what they want and don't want to happen down the road and maybe do something about it … what we imagine we are working toward does a lot to define what we will consider doable action aimed at producing the future we want and preventing the future we fear.

Echoing Ursula Le Guin (2016, p. 4), who argues that imagination is 'an essential tool of the mind', Piercy offers a speculative thought experiment countering the notion that it is impossible to imagine an anti-totalitarian future society. Like Connie, we (*Anthropos*) are at a pivotal time in history, standing on the precipice of the Anthropocene, at a political moment of uncertainty and mounting oppression. Drawing inspiration from feminist science/fiction scholars such as Piercy, Le Guin, Donna Haraway and Karen Barad who ask us to think otherwise and otherways, as well as Deleuzean practices aimed at disrupting and complexifying Kuhnian structures/strictures, progressive logics and deterministic models, we embrace thought experiments as critical and constructive educational tools to explore what these logics do and don't allow us to imagine and create.

We write essays as narrative experiments, viewing writing as a mode of inquiry: usually we don't know what the 'thesis' of a completed essay will be when we begin to write. We use 'essay' as a verb – to attempt, to try, to test – characterizing ourselves as essayists to emphasize the process of 'essaying' rather than the product designated by a noun. 'Essay' and 'assay' come to Anglophones via the French *essayer* from the Latin *exigere*, to weigh. We write essays to 'weigh' ideas and give us (and readers) a sense of their worth. In this essay, we begin by unpacking the 'Anthropocene narrative' – the 'narrative of an entire species ascending to biospheric supremacy' (Malm 2015) – which is already assumed to be a matter of fact by many education researchers. However, there are cogent reasons for contesting the proposed new epoch's name and the ways in which it is conceptualized, so we assess its worth and weight in relation to a number of alternative nomenclature suggestions and then imagine what *unnaming* the Anthropocene might produce.

In the second half of the essay, we develop and deploy the methodological practice of 'diffractive play' as we read selected fictional and theoretical texts diffractively through each other. We use these strategies to rethink and reconfigure current practices in creative and visionary ways with a reading of *Woman on the Edge of Time* that troubles causal notions of linear time and conventional naming practices and that explores the material affects and imaginative potentials of speculative thought experiments. Rather than reproducing methods/methodologies that name where we are based on where we have been (grounded in spatialized conceptions of time as linear and segmented) we advance generative and speculative methodologies for a *post-Anthropocene*. We move beyond a focus on creating 'new' concepts, towards co-creating situated re/configurations and intersectional assemblages, focusing not on what they are *named* but on what they *do*; exploring possibilities that contest, rework and intervene in 'the world's becoming' (Barad 2007, p. 175).

We conclude by exploring Margaret Atwood's concept of *Ustopia* as a superposition of what Marisol de la Cadena and Mario Blaser (2018, p. 4) describe as the *pluriverse* – 'heterogeneous worldings' – resulting in *worldly indeterminacy*. Viewing Piercy's speculative worldings as an attempt to make visible and make possible the pluriverse that currently exists outside of modern anthropocentric logics – beyond what John Law (2015) calls the 'one-world world' – requires unfixing the past, reconfiguring the present and transfiguring the future to open possibilities for producing the future we want. Through these thought experiments, our intention is not simply to 'imagine' a utopia, because as Piercy (1982, p. 100) explains, her worlding of Mattapoisett 'is very intentionally not a utopia because it is not strikingly new', but a reconfiguring of present possible worlds; it is not a utopia 'because it's accessible', imaginable and *creatable*.

Anthropocene nomenclature

Since the term 'Anthropocene' was put forward to name, define and describe a 'new' epoch of geological time in 2000, it has sparked heated debate within various academic fields resulting in a flurry of proposed alternative names. The names 'Capitalocene' (Moore 2015), 'Corporocene' and 'Econocene' (Norgaard 2013) have been put forward to emphasize the driving force the capitalist global economy has exerted on the planet. The 'Homogenocene' (Mann 2011) and the 'Plantationocene' (Haraway 2016) highlight the devastating transformation through colonialism of rich biodiverse landscapes (human and non-human) into extractive and labour-intensive monocultures, arguing that colonial expansion and the plantation system was the precursor to the 'carbon-greedy' industrial systems. Nils Bubandt (Haraway et al. 2016) proposes the 'Euclidocene' pointing to how Euclidian geometry made capitalism thinkable. The 'Gynocene' and the 'Manthropocene' (Raworth 2014; Demos 2015) call attention to the connections between environmental violence and patriarchal domination, drawing together both ecocide and gynocide. The 'Plasticene' highlights the lasting effects of plastic waste on the biosphere, and the 'Technocene' and the 'Anthroboscene' (Parikka 2015) respond to the impacts of technology and resulting toxic waste. Stefan Helmreich (2014) suggests the name 'Proteocene' after Proteus, the god of sea change, who can foretell the future yet continually changes shape to avoid doing so, drawing attention to the powerful, unpredictable and unstable qualities of the planetary systems in crisis.

Others argue strongly against it including T. J. Demos (2017) in his book *Against the Anthropocene*, and Joshua Clover and Juliana Spahr's (2015) satirical depictions in their poem '#MISANTHROPOCENE: 24 Theses'. Echoing Molière's (1666) *The Misanthrope*, the poem ironically points to the flaws of humanity in rageful prose, and also echoes Marx's 'Theses on Feuerbach' and Walter Benjamin's 'left melancholy' to draw lines of flight through issues of labour, class, gender, sexuality and politics that shape the context of the Anthropocene. Other scholars who provide alternative decolonial experiential worldings of the Anthropocene include Zoe Todd (2015), Gabrielle Hecht (2018) and Giovanna Di Chiro (2017). We are confident that more names and counter-narratives will be proposed as the debate continues. Haraway (in Haraway et al. 2016) argues that we need many names for our current epoch, including the Anthropocene, because it does 'good work' despite how problematic, inescapable and inefficient it is as a concept. Yet, following Cadena and Blaser (2018, p. 6) we question what 'work' these names are doing, because 'inasmuch as knowledges are world-making practices, they tend to make the worlds they know'.

Speculative thought experiment 1 – Unnaming the Anthropocene

Drawing on Le Guin's (1985) short story 'She Unnames Them' we wonder what *unnaming* the Anthropocene might do. Le Guin traces the history of the Euro-American contemporary politics of identifying, naming, capturing and defining the 'new' back to the garden of Eden where she 'mocks the biblical assertion that Adam determined the names of every living creature' (Gough 2009, p. 8). Instead, by unnaming all creatures, giving back 'all the Linnean qualifiers that had trailed along behind them for two hundred years like tin cans tied to a tail' (Le Guin 1985, p. 27) the geometries of difference held up by such naming practices were invariably altered allowing other previously impossible practices of relating and becoming-*with* to be realized, fostered and attended to. As Le Guin writes: 'None were left now to unname … They seemed far closer than when their names had stood between myself and them like a clear barrier; so close that my fear of them and their fear of me became one same fear' (Le Guin 1985, p. 27).

As we have argued previously (Gough 2009; Adsit-Morris 2017) language has functioned to support human exceptionalism and methodological individualism through the linguistic colonization of relations. Naming exemplifies, amplifies and solidifies relations of difference, causing us to lose sight of indifference, that which draws us together and connects us. This can clearly be seen within the academic debate around the nomenclature of the Anthropocene as we stumble and drag our disciplinary categories around, arguing about whether the Anthropocene is more of a scientific, cultural, political or economic all-too-human problem. As Barad (2008, p. 128) warns: 'If we follow disciplinary habits of tracing disciplinary-defined causes through to the corresponding disciplinary-defined effects, we will miss all the crucial intra-actions among these forces that fly in the face of any specific set of disciplinary concerns.' Since the emergence of the Anthropocene, there has been an urgent call for more critical and creative interdisciplinary work, we pose that unnaming our academic affiliations might be a way to do good work across the disciplinary divides and establish closer connections and continuities with one another and with the earth. Particularly because unnaming makes it harder to explain ourselves, as Eve concludes: 'I could not chatter away as I used to do, taking it all for granted' (Le Guin 1985, p. 196).

Imaginaries of the post-Anthropocene

The concept of the Anthropocene has prompted many academics to ask 'what next?' for environmental education and social science research, spurring a recent surge of interest in so-called 'new' theories or 'new movements of thought' (especially 'new materialisms') and calls for the production of new concepts and methodologies – perhaps owing to the suffix 'cene' which is Greek for 'recent' or 'new'. We prefer to exercise caution in adopting allegedly 'new' concepts and ideas, and instead explore ways in which we might rethink and reconfigure existing ideas/concepts using the discourses and cultural resources of popular media and non-Western knowings, which tend to be ignored or devalued in mainstream science and philosophy. We need an assemblage of diverse names, concepts and theories to address the complexity of the spatially and temporally dispersed problems of the Anthropocene. Our task is to collect the toxic trash of the Plasticene and Technocene, the CO_2 emissions of the Capitolocene and Corporocene, and the extermination of the Homogenocene and Plantationocene (see Haraway 2016, p. 57).

Nevertheless, Haraway and others accept the term 'Anthropocene' as a concept that is an inheritance we must grapple with, noting that it 'is now inescapable, and is doing good work', yet 'the term Anthropocene is not enough … the concept itself will not do the work. But a change in imagination is also part of the kind of new relationships that are evolving' (Haraway et al. 2016, pp. 539–54). As Haraway (2016, p. 100) explains: 'I think our job is to … cultivate with each other in every way imaginable epochs to come that can replenish refuge.' With this statement, Haraway calls for a focus on the 'post-Anthropocene', which requires speculative practices aimed at imagining a future beyond catastrophe and extinction. The most notable post-Anthropocene imaginaries put forth to-date include Haraway's conception of the Chthulucene as a speculative mythic, mortal and tentacular age of multispecies sympoietic assemblages able to address the varied and multiple challenges of making the post-Anthropocene livable. Jamie Lorimer (2015) proposes the 'Cosmoscene', drawing on Isabelle Stengers's (2010) work on cosmopolitics, and Joanna Boehnert (2016) who suggests the 'Ecocene' as an ontology, epistemology and ethic drawn from the good work already done around ecological thought and literacy.

We are still wary of Western naming practices, following Benjamin Bratton (2013, n.p.) who suggests that the post-Anthropocene should 'not name in advance, as some precondition for its mobilization today, all the terms with which it will eventually have at its disposal in the future'. The aporia of the post-Anthropocene, as he continues, 'is not answered by the provocation of its naming, and this is its strength over alternatives that identify too soon what exactly must be gained or lost by our passage off the ledge'. Instead we believe we need multiple naming practices – acknowledging that there are alternative naming practices outside of Western scientific naming practices – and multiple speculative narrative practices for imagining possible epochs to come. The next section of this chapter will explore and further extrapolate the role of speculative thought experiments – what we are calling 'diffractive play' – in the process of re/trans/configuring and re/imagining possible post-Anthropocene worldings.

Speculative thought and diffractive methods

James Burton (2015, p. 9) traces the intersecting genealogies of science fiction and philosophy, describing their overlapping territories as a non-historical philosophy of wonder. He asks: 'Might it not be argued that this [shared] sense of wonder … [which] gives rise to speculation and narration about what *may* be, is the source of a kind of science fiction as much as it is of philosophy?' Burton (2015, p. 8; italics in original) describes how the (post-)enlightenment development of modern science via rationalism and empiricism separated out what was considered unscientific, unnatural and unknowable from the knowable and measurable. That which became considered unscientific – knowledge disconcerted via speculation, imagination and wonder – got thrown towards, what he describes as 'the wrong side of the real', *fiction*. Emboldened by Deleuze's (1994, p. xx) assertion that a philosophical work should be 'in part a kind of science fiction', as well as Haraway's (1988, 1989, 2007, 2016) work at the intersection of the biological sciences and SF, we have both developed and utilized a methodological approach that troubles the boundaries between fact and fiction (Gough 2004, 2008, 2010; Adsit-Morris 2017). Our hope, through this chapter, is to explore the entanglements and differences within our methodological practices in order to put forth a practice of 'diffractive play' in which we read selected fictional and theoretical texts diffractively through each other, inspired and influenced by Gough's (2010) 'rhizosemiotic play' and a more recent interpretation of diffraction by Barad (2014, p. 168) as 'an iterative (re) configuring of patterns of differentiating-entangling'.

Gough's concept of 'rhizosemiotic play' developed from Haraway's (1994, p. 63) provocation of diffraction as 'the noninnocent, complexly erotic practice of making a difference in the world, rather than displacing the same elsewhere'. Since then Haraway's concept of diffraction as 'an invented category of semantics', has been reinvigorated by feminist and posthumanist scholars, notably Barad (2007, 2014) who, drawing on her training in quantum theory, develops it as theory and method. Barad (2018, p. 216) recently states:

> Diffraction as methodology is a matter of reading insights through rather than against each other in an effort to make evident the always already entanglement of specifics ideas in their materiality. The point will not be to make analogies, but rather to explore patterns of difference/différance – differentiating-entangling – that not only sprout from specific material conditions, but are enfolded in the patterning in ways that trouble binaries.

One of us (Gough 2016) has performed a version of diffractive play through playfully scripted conversations around science fiction and poststructuralist textual practices in educational inquiry including feminism, technologies of self and embodiment, and the inter-/intra-lacing of epistemology and ontology that Barad (2007, p. 409) refers to as 'ontoepistemology'. The other (Adsit-Morris 2017) has utilized diffraction as a way to disrupt conventional narrative forms, holding together 'entanglements of here and there, now and then' by presenting stories 'threaded through one another, knotted, spliced, fractured, each moment a hologram, but never whole' (Barad 2010, pp. 243–4), fostering an attentiveness to the non/linear, in/visible, non/human traces that get left behind.

We combine our methodical experiences and practices to create a new version of *diffractive play* which attempts to rethink and reconfigure current practices in suggestive, creative and visionary ways by drawing together theoretical, fictional and scientific texts. Following Haraway, we see diffractive play as a kind of 'extraordinary loquacious conversation rooted in the desire of touch', one that attempts to undo pervasive conceptions and foster collective imaginaries around what might yet still be possible (Adsit-Morris and Gough 2016).

Specifically, we offer a reading of *Woman on the Edge of Time* that troubles causal notions of linear time and explores the material affects and imaginative potentials of 'thought experiments' (similar to the previous unnaming experiment). Such speculative diffractive thought experiments will draw together, reconfigure and explore the patterns of differentiating-entangling within the work of Piercy, and Barad's work on dis/jointed time, by imagining the Anthropocene as a diffraction grating, an apparatus that diffracts and disperses academics to explore a multiplicity of issues and areas raised by *Anthropos's* (human's) impact on earth, shedding light on multiple aspects of our troubled times, instead of focusing on identifying a single determinate namable origin. We follow Rosi Braidotti (2000) who suggests that 'fabulations' can help to propel 'becomings' by bringing the unthinkable into representation.

Speculative thought experiment 2 – The shape of time

Barbarossa cleared his throat. 'We could put it: at certain cruxes of history … forces are in conflict. Technology is imbalanced. Too few have too much power. Alternate futures are equally or almost equally probable … and that affects the … shape of time.'

(Piercy 2016, p. 212)

In a little-known article published in *Women: A Journal of Liberation*, Haraway (1979) drew upon and reviewed Piercy's *Woman on the Edge of Time* (2016) in order to: (1) imagine (and thus begin to materially formulate) a 'feminist science'; (2) begin establishing her conception of responsibility (or what she would later term 'response-ability'); and (3) ponder alternative conceptions and configurations of time/history/power. As Haraway (1979, p. 22) writes: 'Piercy develops the idea of responsibility for technology beyond a Marxist or humanist vision, and tells a story of possible anarchist-feminist community.' However, despite claiming that she was 'proud of the review' Haraway (2011, p. 5) was advised to (and did in fact) remove it from her CV:

'The past is the contested zone' – the past that is our thick, not-yet-fixed, present, wherewhen what is yet-to-come is now at stake – is the meme that drew me into Piercy's story, and I was proud of the review. A senior colleague in History of Science, a supporter of my promotion, came to me with a too-friendly smile and that betraying bottle of white-out, asking me to blot out this publication from the scholarly record, 'for my own good.'

Yet the traces remained, as Haraway (2011, p. 5) notes: 'to my relief to this day, no one was fooled.' As Barad (2018, p. 226) reminds us: '*Erasure is a material practice that leaves its trace in the very worlding of the world.*' Despite the present-historical colonial, capitalistic and technoscientific attempts at erasure (of peoples, places, pasts and futures), there is no universal white-out, no (quantum-) eraser that can change the past or determine the future. *Woman on the Edge of Time* is a 'travel-hopping tale' – what Piercy (2016, p. 120) describes as 'abrupt discorporatings and hoppings to and fro in time' – markedly different from traditional time-travelling novels in which, as Barad (2018, p. 223) describes, the protagonist returns to 'a past that once was, a past that continues to exist and remains accessible to those with sufficient ingenuity and technical know-how, in an attempt to rework some crucial point in a chain of events that will then propagate forward in deterministic fashion in a rewriting of history'. Instead, the protagonist lives and experiences not simply a multiplicity of times and lives (Consuelo the Mexican servant who suffers, Connie the headstrong loving mother and aunt, and Conchita the depressed abused and abusive alcoholic) these pasts/presents are threaded through one another, rupturing and haunting each other, as they flash up refusing to be ignored or erased.

In her most recent work, Barad (2017a, b, 2018) uses quantum field theory to 'trouble time' through the notions of *superposition* and *entanglement*. Arguing against what Walter Benjamin calls 'homogenous empty time', now morphed into what Barad (2018, p. 208) describes as 'the globalized space time grid' – that is, the time of colonialism, the time of capitalism, the time of militarism, the time of the Anthropocene – Barad (2018, pp. 206–7) queries:

[I]f debates on marking the origins of the Anthropocene suggest anything beyond an exacting reading of the layering of sediments used to justify adding a new segment of time to earth's geological clock, it is perhaps that the structure of temporality that timelines (in their linearity) smuggle into the discussion is inadequate to this moment.

Challenging notions of the 'new' versus the 'old' as separate and different times, Barad (2018, p. 218) describes *temporal diffraction* – or the 'time-energy indeterminacy principle' – as the ontological indeterminacy of time in which 'a given entity can be in (a state of) *superposition of different times*'. Temporal diffraction requires considering '*all possible histories (configurings of spacetime)*, understanding that each such possibility coexists with all others' (Barad 2018, p. 218; italics in original). *Woman on the Edge of Time* is not a traditional time-travelling novel; it is a 'time-diffraction tale' as Consuelo/ Connie, clutching her plastic purse ready to put up a good fight, navigates the complexities and contradictions of troubling times that refuse to work as past-present-future.

> *Dawn stuck out her soft chin. 'I want to do something very important like fly into the past to make it come out right.'*
>
> *'Nobody can make things come out right,' Hawk said, her straight nose wrinkled in disgust.*
>
> *'Dawn, it isn't bad to want to help, to want to work, to seize history,' Luciente said … 'But to want to do it alone is less good. To hand history to someone like a cake you baked.'* (Piercy 2016, pp. 212–13)

Conclusion – The worldly indeterminacy of the pluriverse

Since the concept of the Anthropocene was set in motion, a plethora of dystopian climate disaster (cli-fi) films have emerged, harbouring narratives and representations of techno-salvation and escapism fantasies (see, for example, *The Day After Tomorrow* [2004], *Snowpiercer* [2009], *Geostorm* [2017] and *Interstellar* [2014] to name a few). Such hyper conceptualizations erase the complexities of worlds and lived experiences that don't sort into pure categories – good/ bad, cause/effect, forward/backwards, primitive/advanced, utopian/dystopian. Atwood (2011, n.p. para. 10) describes what she calls *Ustopia*, a combination of utopia and dystopia, 'the imagined perfect society and its opposite … in my view, each contains a latent version of the other'.

Atwood's conception of Ustopia resonates with Barad's (2007, p. 140) conception of agential separability, the condition of exteriority-within-phenomena, illustrated by diffraction: 'illuminating the indefinite nature of boundaries – displaying shadows in "light" regions and bright spots in "dark" regions.' Such diffraction patterns are, as Barad (2018, p. 218) illustrates, a result of the superposition of all possible paths/realities; '*they all coexist and mutually contribute to the overall pattern*'. It's not that there are many possible worlds, but rather worlds are intrinsically manifold, what Cadena and Blaser (2018, p. 4) call a pluriverse influenced by the Zapatista's declaration for Indigenous sovereignty, 'the practice of a world of many worlds'. Their interpretation is in line with Barad's (2007, p. 91) understanding that '*practices of knowing are specific material engagement that participate in (re)configuring the world*'. There exists *worldly indeterminacy* – that is, worlds do not exist prior to the material-discursive practices and relations that make them manifest – instead worlds emerge through specific entanglements.

The question for those of 'us' attempting to do ethical research in troubled times of crisis is: how do we hold open space for multiple realities, knowledges, pasts and futures – multiple worlds – to be present and accounted for? How do we teach others to think in multiple ways, on multiple scales and through multiple temporalities *at the same time*? The current uncritical squabbles around the Anthropocene attempt to establish what Deleuze (1994) calls the 'golden mean' by, first, accepting the concept of the Anthropocene and, second, by negotiating its terms and its limits (weighing its pros and cons and quantifying its violence).

As 'we' stand at the precipice of an undeterminable future, an unfinished past and the urgent times of the here-and-now, we need imaginaries capable of grappling with epistemological uncertainty (and the epistemological insecurity it fosters) and ontological (worldly) indeterminacy. We (the authors) turn to science fiction and speculative thought practices to create ruptures within formal educational curricula and open spaces for our students to think otherwise and otherways. These thought experiments are not fantasy. They are not simply theoretical (in)queries, they have material affects, they make a difference in the world. In her article, Atwood (2011) describes Le Guin's differentiation between science fiction (things that really could happen) versus fantasy (things that really could not happen) stating that 'everything that happens in her novels is possible and may even have already happened'.

We believe that fostering SF imaginaries will help 'us' get on with the work of creating a *post-Anthropocene*, because as Barad (2008, p. 144) urges: 'Particular possibilities for acting exist at every moment, and these changing possibilities entail a responsibility to intervene in the world's becoming, to contest and rework what matters and what is excluded from mattering.' It allows us to imagine a world – such as Mattapoisett (wherein children can choose their own names when they come of age) – in which Indigenous knowledges and practices shape concepts of time, influence communal processes, inform educational programs and depoliticalize naming practices. Imagining such a future doesn't ensure that it will come to dominate all other possible futures, but it opens possibilities for its partial presence, because all realities are imperfect and multiple. As Atwood (2011) concludes, 'We're stuck with us, imperfect as we are; but we should make the most of us. Which is about as far as I myself am prepared to go, in real life, along the road to Ustopia.'

> *'You of your time may fail to struggle together.' His voice was warm, almost teasing, yet his eyes told her he was speaking seriously. 'We must fight to come to exist, to remain in existence, to be the future that happens. That's why we reached you.'* (Piercy 2016, p. 213)

Glossary

Anthropocene A term proposed by a working group of the 2016 International Geological Congress to name a new epoch of geological time dominated by human impact on the Earth, succeeding the Holocene which began 11,650 years ago.

SF The signifier 'SF' abbreviates a multitude of science fiction and fantasy narrative practices including speculative fiction, science fiction, science fantasy, speculative futures and speculative fabulation. Haraway expands the term to include string figures, speculative feminism, science fact and so far; and we add 'serious fun'.

Ustopia A term coined by Margaret Atwood as a combination of the terms 'utopia' (the imagined perfect society) and 'dystopia' (the imagined society suffering from environmental and social destruction and injustice) in order to explore the entanglements between the two.

References

Adsit-Morris, C. A. (2017), *Restorying Environmental Education: Figurations, Fictions, and Feral Subjectivities*, New York, NY: Palgrave Macmillan.

Adsit-Morris, C. A. and Gough, N. (2016), 'It takes more than two to (Multispecies) tango: queering gender texts in environmental education', *The Journal of Environmental Education*, 48: 67–78.

Atwood, M. (2011), 'Margaret Atwood: The road to Ustopia', *The Guardian* [Online]. Available at: https://amp.theguardian.com/books/2011/oct/14/margaret-atwood-road-to-ustopia.

Barad, K. M. (2007), *Meeting the Universe Halfway: Quantum Physics and the Entanglement of Matter and Meaning*, Durham, NC: Duke University Press.

Barad, K. M. (2008), 'Posthuman performativity: Toward an understanding of how matter comes to matter', in S. Alaimo and S. Hekman (eds), *Material Feminisms*, Bloomington, IN: Indiana University Press.

Barad, K. M. (2010), 'Quantum entanglements and hauntological relations of inheritance: Dis/continuities, Spacetime enfoldings, and justice-to-come', *Derrida Today*, 3 (2): 240–68.

Barad, K. M. (2014), 'Diffracting diffraction: Cutting together-apart', *Parallax*, 20: 168–87.

Barad, K. M. (2017a), 'No small matter: Mushroom clouds, ecologies of nothingness, and strange topologies of spacetimemattering', in A. L. Tsing, H. A. Swanson, E. Gan and N. Bubandt (eds), *Arts of Living on a Damaged Planet: Ghosts and Monsters of the Anthropocene*, Minneapolis, MN: University of Minnesota Press.

Barad, K. M. (2017b), 'Troubling time/s and ecologies of nothingness: Re-turning, Re-membering, and facing the incalculable', *New Formations*, 92: 56–86.

Barad, K. M. (2018), 'Troubling time/s and ecologies of nothingness: Re-turning, Re-membering, and facing the incalculable', in F. Matthias, L. Philippe and D. Wood (eds), *Eco-Deconstruction: Derrida and Environmental Philosophy*, 206–48. New York, NY: Fordham University.

Boehnert, J. (2016), 'Naming the epoch: Anthropocene, Capitalocene, Ecocene', Climate Change: Spatial, Environmental and Cultural Politics [Online].

Braidotti, R. (2000), 'Teratologies', in I. Buchanan and C. Colebrook (eds), *Deleuze and Feminist Theory*, Edinburgh: Edinburgh University Press.

Bratton, B. H. (2013), 'Some trace effects of the post-anthropocene: On accelerationist geopolitical aesthetics', *e-flux Journal*, 46.

Burton, J. (2015), *The Philosophy of Science Fiction: Henri Bergson and the Fabulations of Philip K. Dick*, New York, NY and London: Bloomsbury Academic.

Cadena, M. D. L. and Blaser, M., eds (2018), *A World of Many Worlds*, Durham, NC: Duke University Press.

Clover, J. and Spahr, J. (2015), '#MISANTHROPOCENE: 24 Theses', in H. Davis and E. Turpin (eds), *Art in the Anthropocene: Encounters Among Aesthetics, Politics, Environments and Epistemologies*, London: Open Humanities Press.

Deleuze, G. (1994), *Difference and Repetition*, New York, NY: Columbia University Press.

Demos, T. J. (2015), 'T.J. Demos: Anthropocene, capitalocene, gynocene: The many names of resistance', Frontiers of Solitude [Online]. Available from: http://frontiers-of-solitude.org/blog/442.

Demos, T. J. (2017), *Against the Anthropocene: Visual Culture and Environment Today*, Sternberg Press: Berlin.

Di Chiro, G. (2017), 'Welcome to the white (m)Anthropocene? A feminist-environmentalist critique', in S. MacGregor (ed.), *Routledge Handbook of Gender and Environment*, New York, NY: Routledge.

Gough, N. (2004), 'RhizomANTically becoming-cyborg: Performing posthuman pedagogies', *Educational Philosophy and Theory*, 36 (3): 253–65. https://doi.org/10.1111/j.1469-5812.2004.00066.x.

Gough, N. (2008), 'Narrative experiments and imaginative inquiry', *South African Journal of Education*, 28 (3): 335–49.

Gough, N. (2009), 'How do places become "pedagogical"?' in M. Somerville, K. Power and P. D. Carteret (eds), *Landscapes and Learning: Place Studies in a Global World*, Rotterdam: Sense Publishers.

Gough, N. (2010), 'Performing imaginative inquiry: Narrative experiments and rhizosemiotic play', in T. Nielsen, R. Fitzgerald and M. Fettes (eds), *Imagination in Educational Theory and Practice: A Many-sided Vision*, Newcastle upon Tyne: Cambridge Scholars Publishing.

Gough, N. (2016), 'Postparadigmatic materialisms: A "new movement of thought" for outdoor environmental education research?' *Journal of Outdoor and Environmental Education*, 19 (2): 51–65. https://doi.org/10.1007/BF03400994.

Haraway, D. J. (1979), The Struggle for a Feminist Science: Reflections Based on *Woman on the Edge of Time* and *For Her Own Good. Women: A Journal of Liberation*, 6, 20–23.

Haraway, D. J. (1988), 'Situated knowledges: The science question in feminism and the privilege of partial perspective', *Feminist Studies*, 14: 575–99.

Haraway, D. J. (1989), *Primate Visions: Gender, Race, and Nature in the World of Modern Science*, New York: Routledge.

Haraway, D. J. (1994), 'A game of cat's cradle: Science studies, feminist theory, cultural studies', *Configurations: A Journal of Literature, Science, and Technology*, 2 (1): 59–71. https://muse.jhu.edu/article/8029.

Haraway, D. J. (2007), *When Species Meet*, Minneapolis, MN: University of Minnesota Press.

Haraway, D. J. (2011), 'SF: Science fiction, speculative fabulation, string figures, so far', SFRA Meetings (acceptance speech), Lublin, Poland.

Haraway, D. J. (2016), *Staying with the Trouble: Making Kin in the Chthulucene*, Durham, NC: Duke University Press.

Haraway, D. J., Ishikawa, N., Gilbert, S. F., Olwig, K., Tsing, A. L. and Bubandt, N. (2016), 'Anthropologists are talking - About the Anthropocene', *Ethnos*, 81: 535–64.

Hecht, G. (2018), 'The African Anthropocene', Aeon [Online]. Available at: https://aeon.co/essays/if-we-talk-about-hurting-our-planet-who-exactly-is-the-we (Accessed 06 February 2018).

Helmreich, S. (2014), 'The water next time: Changing wavescapes in the Anthropocene', Paper presented at the Center for 21st Century Studies, University of Wisconsin-Milwaukee, 4 April.

Law, J. (2015), 'What's wrong with a one-world world?' *Distinktion: Scandinavian Journal of Social Theory* 16 (1): 126–39.

Le Guin, U. K. (1985), 'She unnames them', *The New Yorker*, 21 January.

Le Guin, U. K. (2016), *Words Are My Matter: Writings About Life and Books, 2000–2016 with a Journal of a Writer's Week*, Northampton, MA: Small Beer Press.

Lorimer, J. (2015), *Wildlife in the Anthropocene: Conservation after Nature*, Minneapolis, MN: University of Minnesota Press.

Malm, A. (2015), 'The Anthropocene myth: Blaming all of humanity for climate change lets capitalism off the hook', *Jacobin* [Online]. Available at: https://www.jacobinm ag.com/2015/03/anthropocene-capitalism-climate-change/.

Mann, C. C. (2011), *1493: Uncovering the New World Columbus Created*, New York, NY: Alfred A. Knopf.

Moore, J. W. (2015), *Capitalism in the Web of Life: Ecology and the Accumulation of Capital*, New York, NY: Verso.

Norgaard, R. B. (2013), 'The econocene and the delta', *San Francisco Estuary and Watershed Science*, 11: 1–5.

Parikka, J. (2015), *The Anthrobscene*, Minneapolis, MN: University of Minnesota Press.

Piercy, M. (1982), Parti-*Colored Blocks for a Quilt*, Michigan: University of Michigan Press.

Piercy, M. (2016 [1976]), *Woman on the Edge of Time*, New York, NY: Ballantine Books.

Raworth, K. (2014), 'Must the Anthropocene be a Manthropocene?'; *The Guardian*, 20 October 2014.

Stengers, I. (2010), *Cosmopolitics, Posthumanities*, Minneapolis, MN: University of Minnesota Press.

Todd, Z. (2015), 'Indigenizing the Anthropocene', in H. Davis and E. Turpin (eds), *Art in the Anthropocene: Encounters among Aesthetics, Politics, Environments and Epistemologies*, London: Open Humanities Press.

12

Replete sensations of the refrain: Sound, action and materiality in agentic posthuman assemblages

Jennifer Charteris and Marguerite Jones

Introduction

The attraction of Deleuzian theory is in its evasiveness. Just when one has purchase on it, it mutates and becomes fluid, slipping through the fingers to become something else. The imagery of matter here reflects the importance of materialism in feminist imaginings of Deleuze's (1988) work and its scope for new readings when plugged into research assemblages (Jackson and Mazzei 2013). An assemblage is the generative entanglement 'of a form of content (actions, bodies and things) and a form of expression (affects, words and ideas)' (Buchanan 2015, p. 390). We explore innovative methodologies that enravel researchers in intra-active assemblages.

Deleuzian inspired methodologies transcend a deficit focus on lack, by seeking to explore what can be produced. These methodologies of becomings are unstable, partial, incomplete and replete with possibility. Theory is constituted through 'heterogeneous concepts, materials, sources, examples and illustrations' (Taylor, C 2013, p. 43). A pluralistic notion from the Deleuzoguattarian toolbox, the refrain, can be plugged into research assemblages to enable innovative methodologies.

Refrains as a concept, can run an 'interference' (Deleuze and Guattari 1987, p. 280), serving as an innovation that supports the posthuman challenge to think otherwise about human and non-human relationality. Refrains create spaces, emerging through the differential patterning of relationality between rhythm, milieu and territory (Springgay and Zaliwska 2017). Refrains are commonly recognized in aural contexts. As patterns that create a familiar sound, music, songs, chants and animal voices have salience in a range of cultural and historical traditions. However refrains are also associations that forge new kinds of relations (Buchanan 2015). Refrains are ritualized pathways creating territories that can be existential and digital (Mayes 2018) as well as aural, physical and cultural (Sorensen 2009). The emergence of the refrain in the context of education research is very new (Jackson 2016; Springgay and Zaliwska 2017), providing methodological terrains with which to map situated politics in education.

Decentring human songs (for instance, humanist research interviews and interpretivist ethnographies and narratives) in assemblages enables difference in the form of links between posthuman voice – where objects influence the patterning of refrains. In this chapter, questions are posed to encourage experimentation and celebration of research encounters that take licence with innovative methodologies as an engagement with posthuman ethics. Deleuze (1989) encouraged experimentation of this sort, arguing that philosophical theory is a practice as much as an object. Consideration is given to how a 'practice of concepts' can function as a research approach, in particular how the refrain can be used as a heuristic that brings theory and method together. In education settings refrains can illustrate interspecies articulation – an anti-anthropocentric move in schools and early childhood centres that challenge human and non-human binaries in the way we teach about the natural world. They can also illustrate social media flows across education settings and communities – for instance, how human and non-human intertwine with the application Snapchat. These considerations of refrains may enable researchers interested in the new frontiers of research method, to grapple with the overlaps and rhizomatic movements that bring together, interfere and flow into new becomings.

Deleuzian theory, materialist research assemblages and the posthuman refrain

For early career researchers, it can be daunting to use Deleuzian theory methodologically in fresh and intrepid ways. Yet to reach the unfamiliar, one must 'leave sight of shore'. Posthumanist thinking unravels interpretivist research practices and provokes innovation. An elaboration on the Deleuzoguattarian refrain provides an entanglement of geophilosophy, methodology and method, the confluence of which produces a posthumanist ontology in research contexts. By mapping refrains as fluid relationality, early career researchers, and researchers interested in the new frontiers of research methods, can examine territoriality as a means to destabilize binaries in education settings so that human subject is no longer the dominant object of analysis.

Materialist research into assemblages evokes thought and methods that are non- or post-representational and leverage new material theories (MacLure 2013). It can be a challenge to transcend humanist interpretations of the researcher 'to identify assemblages, relations, affects and territorialisations' (Fox and Alldred 2013, p. 779). In assemblages there are processes 'whereby individuals, groups and societies are constituted and re-constituted and heterogeneous human and non-human elements interrelate via unexpected and productive connections' (Mayes 2016, p. 107). Affects are enacted, 'proto political' intensities that traverse bodies and objects and exceed our emotions and conscious thoughts (Massumi 2015, p. ix).

Relations are transversal links between objects and between non-humans and humans. They are assemblages that mark transitory territories. In education research, for example, these could be the movements and routines of students in the materiality of classroom spaces. Relations are in continuous motion, and, through their oscillations, form difference. For instance, although the pattern of a morning routine may be the same in the classroom, the furniture configurations, people and relational affects in the space may configure different assessments. Difference is a key tenet in Deleuzoguattarian theory. Refrains create difference as there are always new configurations, new understandings and additional discourses that create flux and change. One can never return to paradise lost or to past imprisonments. No matter how much things may appear to be 'as usual', once new terrains have been traversed, the assemblage is always recast anew. The motion of refrains placates, yet echo, resistance. Like the child in the dark singing to alleviate fear (Deleuze and Guattari 1987), refrains create a light in the darkness as a boundary of safety. There is resistance to the darkness and yet the very darkness itself, as a new assemblage, takes form. The singing is an intra-action with the darkness that co-produces new forms of spatial relations. In decentring the humanist subject, the darkness sings back.

This methodological approach enables researchers to attune to the features beyond the human voice, the 'voices' of things that enter the research assemblage. In embodied spaces 'things' are seen as agentic, inserting themselves between humans and humans, and humans and non-humans (Bennett 2010). In the latter part of this chapter, we provide accounts of how the material vitalism of the refrain can serve as a research heuristic. Deleuze and Guattari challenge the opposition and bifurcation of active life and dead matter (Pyyhtinen 2016). Drawing from Deleuze and Guattari (1987), Bennett (2010), writes, '[m]aterial vitalism suggest a material reconfiguration of life, a way of thinking life in terms of "matter energy", "matter flow" and "matter in variation that enters assemblages and leaves them'" (Pyyhtinen 2016, p. 53). The motions of refrains are transversal and transcend human movement, operating across a range of matter.

Through material vitalist readings of songs sung by objects, research assemblages are territorialized and deterritorialized. Refrains enable us to think and see differently through a process of exploring how objects and humans are entangled in assemblages. As such, refrains can be powerful conceptual frameworks with which to engage in methodological innovations. In the fullness of posthuman education research assemblages, it is possible to transcend research tensions and make visible the binaries associated with identity politics. As we illustrate in this chapter with examples of social media and interspecies relationality, through destabilizing the primacy of the autonomous self-willed individual researcher, a posthuman engagement with refrains takes account of co-emergence and entanglements of humans and objects.

As education researchers, refrains can enable us to map relationalities in the territories of assemblages. For instance, we can look at how matter like thermometers, beakers, chemicals and animals (live and dead; human and non-human) interrelate in a science classroom to produce particular forms of knowledge and power. An analysis of refrains lays bare spatial practices and the agency of objects as an interplay of diverse components that flow through and between human and non-human bodies in assemblages. As arrangements that transversally connect lines of flight, assemblages escape dominant codifications of social order (Penfield 2014).

Refrains in research work

Refrains can be used as a heuristic to question the power enacted in agentic and relational assemblages of schooling settings. The fluid motions of power that form refrains are becomings (Deleuze and Guattari 1987). Becomings are unlimited and unending with no point of origin or destination (Young 2013). Ingold (2011) observes that, for Deleuze, life is not lived 'within a perimeter but along lines'. Lines of flight or lines of becoming 'prise an opening' and 'bind the animal with its world' (Ingold 2011, p. 83). All life has its own transversal bundle of lines and intraconnections with matter:

> A line of becoming is not defined by the points it connects, or by the points that compose it; on the contrary, it passes *between* points, it comes up through the

middle, it runs ... transversally to the localizable relation to distant or contiguous
points. (Deleuze and Guattari 1987, p. 323. Emphasis in original.)

Refrains can be mapped as movements of becoming. This mapping provides
insight into 'the ways that economy and politics, policy, organizational
arrangements, knowledge, subjectivity, pedagogy, everyday practices, and
feelings come together to form the education assemblage' (Youdell 2010,
p. 316). Turning from the ruins (St Pierre and Pillow 2000) of humanist
qualitative methodology, that has been critiqued for its 'monolithic' and 'stifling'
ontological presumptions (St Pierre 2014, p. 3), a post-qualitative research
approach (Lather 2013) reimagines research relations and possibilities for (early
career) researcher creativity. There has been increasing interest in schizoanalysis
(Ringrose 2011), rhizoanalysis (Masny 2016) and Deleuzoguattarian inspired
collective biography (Davies and Gannon 2006), as methodological adaptations
of Deleuze and Guattari's (1987) toolbox of philosophical concepts. There
is, however, little scholarship on methodological engagement with refrains
(Jackson 2016).

Refrains encompass three elements with unique significance-chaos, earth
and world that are phases that can be located in research assemblages (Deleuze
and Guattari 1987). Firstly, there is departure from disarray or chaos to establish
a milieu or home. Secondly, there is a stabilization of 'interiorizing forces as
earth' (Herzogenrath 2009, p. 18). Thirdly there is a deterritorializing crack,
which opens an engagement with the world. The three phases (chaos, earth,
world) encounter one another and converge in the refrain as concurrent
territorializations and deterritorializations (Herzogenrath 2009). Through
motion, they constantly shape and reshape researched spaces into multiple
experiences and power relations (Lacey 2013).

Refrains allow continuous motion in assemblages. Like birds, that sing to
establish territories and mark out new ones, researchers are immersed in the
material conditions of their co-constitution. Thus, while refrains are rhizomatic
and locate 'new spaces-in-between', and bring forth 'new opportunities
for jumping milieus' (Philippopoulos-Mihalopoulos 2016, p. 88), they are
simultaneously grounded in assemblages. For instance, in education spaces,
there are aspects of multiple refrains that include: clock chimes; bells ringing
that signal temporal and spatial shifts; sounds of children skipping and
chanting; teachers laughing; chairs scraping; windows and blinds opening; and,
photocopiers clicking and whirring.

Refrains encapsulate relationality and motion in posthuman assemblages. As
fissiparous entities, refrains break apart and form further connections. The songs

turn back on themselves in reterritorializing moves, yet never return to exactly the same spot. In research contexts, refrains serve as ontological frameworks that decentre a focus on the humanist subject to destabilize, trouble and reconceptualize taken-for-granted relational practices. Thus, refrains produce difference through repetition and, through analyses of their geophilosophical motions, it is possible to sketch these relational flows as a methodological approach.

Bringing theory and method together through the refrain

Although there is no recipe for developing an innovative methodology from the Deleuzian conceptual toolbox, we provide orientations that we have found helpful in innovating method through theory. Like McLeod (2014), who provides a set of principles to support researchers to destablize the human and notions of agency through assemblage theory, we describe how to engage with refrains as a set of research practices. These orientations are not a recipe, rather a way to embrace the spirit of Deleuzoguattarian theory.

There is a range of conceptions of affect (Gregg and Seigworth 2010). Here we consider Deleuze's engagement with the Spinozist ethology, as a bodily capacity to affect and be affected, useful theoretically and methodologically (Ringrose and Coleman 2013). Affects are both internal and external vectors that cannot be easily reconciled. They elicit a 'certain inside-out-outside-in difference in directionality' (Gregg and Seigworth 2010, p. 6). As Fox and Alldred explain, 'research epistemologies, designs, methods, techniques and tools may all be subjected to analysis of affective flows, to reveal the affect economies and micropolitics of social inquiry' (2015, p. 405). In suggesting a posthuman approach to affect, we wish to hold various registers in play. Affect is transpersonal, embodied and situated, in that it circulates among and between subjects.

To bring theory and method together through the refrain, we suggest 'starting in the middle' by choosing a plateau, not as bounded framework, indicated by case study (Yin 2009), but rather as a point of departure. This plateau can form a territorial refrain that has multiple entry and exit points, connecting rhizomatically with a proliferation of other clusters. You may start with noticing, some field notes, a conversation, or tracing the refrain spatiality of a non-human object or animal. Close scrutiny is required when you plug into a research assemblage, as there is a willingness to decentre the primacy of discursive and linguistic privilege for material vitalist readings.

An embodied actor in the research, you observe and report your own refrains, as partial aspects of an assemblage which transverse the refrains of objects, animals and things. Question what is particular to the affective flows of the research assemblage and what kind of 'knowledge' is being produced (Fox and Alldred 2015). In thinking differently, new materialist considerations challenge the taken-for-granted ascendance of things that privilege the human over the co-implication, or intra-activity, of humans and non-human matter (Davies 2018). Knowledge creation requires an engagement with flows of affect. The 'lines of force that flow between and among both human and nonhuman subjects' can be mapped in research assemblages (Davies 2018, p. 121). The approach can be scrutinized to consider how affective flows embedded within them become 'sedimented' and 'inscribed into bodies and everyday practices' (Gannon 2008, p. 44).

Elements of the research assemblage co-produce transversalities. When mapping the three elements of the refrain for transversal movements, one may consider: a departure from chaos; a stabilization of forces; and, a deterritorializing crack. Try to think otherwise about the connections between things, bodies, non-humans, discourses and texts.

Read, read, read. Bring together the onto-epistemological thrust of readings to create questions that will enable a consideration of the elements in an assemblage, not to reduce the complexity to readings of component parts but rather to see the assemblage differently and engage with its materiality.

To illustrate how refrains can constitute new imaginative possibilities and work as innovative methodologies, we examine two kinds of assemblages where the motions of refrains can be mapped. These comprise interspecies relationality and flows of social media. The following questions may be used by researchers, to furnish support for a methodological imaginary:

- Where is the disarray (chaos)?
- Where are moments of territorializations (earth)?
- Where are deterritorializations (world)?

These questions are used to map refrains as seen in the examples below in 'Refrains in interspecies becomings'.

Refrains in interspecies becomings

In recent years consideration has been given to the primacy of nature–human binary where the human is 'the only active animated subject' (Malone

2016, p. 394). The motions and flows of interspecies relationality can be mapped in and across refrains. 'Interspecies articulation' is a concept that disrupts the human and non-human binary being produced through intra-action where humans and non-human animals 'create conditions for each other's existence' (Rautio 2013, p. 445). Rautio writes, '[i]nterspecies articulation is about finding and composing connections to our surrounding non-human world, with a focus on ... meaningful connections between us and the not us' (Rautio 2014, p. 445). Further, Rautio explains a distinction between the notions of interaction and Baradian intra-action:

> In interaction independent entities are viewed as taking turns in affecting each other, which implies that these entities are taken to each have an a priori independent existence. In intra-action, on the contrary, interdependent entities are taken to co-emerge through simultaneous activity to come into being as certain kind because of their encounter. (Rautio 2014, p. 2)

Two examples, where interspecies becomings have been used to rupture binarized 'child in nature' debates, are Karen Malone's (2016) child–dog encounters in the slums of La Paz and Rautio's (2016) human–pigeon cohabitation. Malone observes that 'dogs, earth, houses, neighbourhoods, trees have agency just like humans', and she uses images taken by children to illustrate 'child-dog-place engagement in La Paz' as an example of 'a reciprocal animated exchange' (p. 405). Further the children's accounts of 'intra-species companionship and survival' provide a challenge to 'Western middle-class sensibilities of an idealized child-nature encounter' (p. 405). Likewise Rautio (2016), an early childhood education researcher, describes the interactivity of humans and pigeons, an abject bird, generally considered feral. She questions whom and what should take part in education in addition to humans, in which ways and why should we care? Interspecies becomings are important in light of implications of the Anthropocene epoch where, as Taylor (2016) points out, we are facing mass extinction. She writes how studies evoking child–animal relations are framed by wider ethical considerations. These pertain to the political implications of inheriting an anthropogenically damaged planetary environment. In particular she alludes to the need to foster genial multispecies cohabitations in an era of mass species extinctions (Taylor 2016).

Entanglements of 'human and more than human relations' (Taylor A 2013, p. 118), like those mentioned earlier, can be explored for refrains. Where refrains forge transversal chords of unity in assemblage multiplicities, intra-actions of humans and non-human animals can be mapped for the territoriality they co-produce. This territoriality can be researched for its motions, that both transcend what is known, and return to new positions in a constant flow.

By mapping the non-human species flows within an assemblage, it can be possible to see humans and the material relationality differently through circumventing the anthropocentric gaze. Photographs can support partial readings of refrains that may be used to decentre the primacy of linguistic readings (Malone 2016). McLeod (2014) writes, '[p]hotos can enable research participants to communicate dimensions of experience that might have remained unsaid in verbal interviews' (p. 383). Photographs are an example of materials that can be read as agentic objects within a research assemblage that can highlight a range of elements including interspecies relationality. Questions to consider for mapping refrains of interspecies becomings may include:

- Where are the scenes of disarray (chaos) where interspecies relationality manifest? (e.g. slums of La Paz in Malone (2016)).
- Where are moments of territorializing (earth) that decentre the primacy of humanism in these relationships? (e.g. locating moments of liminal relationality in the images of dogs, objects and humans, photographed by La Paz children (Malone 2016)).
- Where are possibilities for new deterritorializations (world) afforded through the research flows? (e.g. profiling posthuman approaches to disrupt universalisms in debates that binarize child and nature (Malone 2016)).

Through a reassembled research reading of refrains, intra-active humans and non-human animals can be recast anew. The following provides a contextualization of refrains as a research heuristic, where social media technologies can be cast as agentic objects that influence affective flows.

Refrains of social media flows

Social media flows can be characterized as unstable, variable, fluctuating, 'oscillatory', 'malleable', 'a matter of 'fluid signs' where there are 'signifiers in motion' (Golding 2006, p. 250). Barad (2012) observes, how '[m]ateriality itself is always already a desiring dynamism, a reiterative reconfiguring, energized and energizing, enlivened and enlivening' (p. 59). The dynamism of social media, for instance, in particular the intra-activity of the Snapchat application, can be mapped in dynamic refrains.

'Snapchat' is a mobile technology application, where images are recorded and timed to disappear. It is strategically marketed to those under thirty-five years of age. There are a range of filters that morph bodies with objects, animals and other bodies to produce weird and amusing hybrids. Together the application 'Snapchat' and the materiality of mobile technology constitute a mattering that creates the more-than-human when embedded in youth assemblages. Researchers who take up a posthuman ontology can examine how the merging of technologies in assemblages produce reconstituted humans. Hayles (1999) writes of this intra-action 'there are no essential differences or absolute demarcations between bodily existence and computer simulation, cybernetic mechanism and biological organism, robot teleology and human goals' (p. 42).

Snapchat produces embodied virtuality where the materiality of mobile technology constitutes matterings in assemblages of networked publics (boyd 2010, 2014). Through this intra-active process more-than-humans are created in youth assemblages. Purposeful cybernetic distortions of humanity are disseminated in affective flows between bodies and mobile technologies. It is these flows that can be mapped as cartography of refrains. Barad (2012) challenges us to consider intra-activity in social media flows. She points out that particles and waves are the only kinds of entities in the world:

> Particles are very different from waves. Particles are localized entities that occupy a particular place in space and in time, and you cannot have two particles in the same place at the same time. On the other hand, there are waves, and waves are not entities at all. Waves are disturbances in fields. If you think about ocean waves, you see that waves often overlap with one another. (Barad 2012, p. 60)

The movements of social media images and texts can be understood as a wave pattern. The hardware of the devices is the particles. The waves are the flows of communication that transversally create embodied affect through the intra-action of the human and non-human machine–body becoming. These movements produce sexualized and racialized flows (Renold and Ringrose 2011) that can be mapped as an assemblage of co-produced transversalities.

There are different points of entry in assemblages, and the elements of the refrain (chaos, stabilization and deterritorialization) may be read differently. A sent message (i.e. a posted comment, image or video) may create a departure from chaos, with flows of discourses and bodily affect channelled within a new assemblage. Concurrent territorializations and deterritorializations can take place in such ongoing flows. There can be the creation of stabilized forces with the (possibly multiple) reading(s) of the one text. Deterritorializing cracks manifest with the production of sexualized and racialized meanings. An explicit image, recorded in an act of teen courtship, may be sent by a recipient to multiple peers, as a deterritorialized flow. The message is reterritorialized when there are responses to it. In some instances this may involve 'slut shaming' and/ or cyberharassment (Ringrose and Renold 2014, p. 774).

The technological object is entangled in flows of affect that produce an intra-active relationality. Therefore, the refrain can be used to investigate normative understandings of 'sexualized, racialized and naturalized interactions', which challenge the unquestionable through pure 'dislocations of identities' (Braidotti 2013, p. 99). In the earlier Snapchat example, the refrain as concept runs an 'interference' (Deleuze 1989) to the privileging of human-centred qualitative research. Questions to consider for mapping refrains of interference for social media flows may include the following:

- Where is the disarray surfaced, embodied and enacted through assemblages of social media (chaos)? (e.g. Digital communications are rhizomatic with flows injecting affect into socio-material relations.)
- When are there moments of territorialization that forge relationalities through social media interceptions (earth)? (e.g. Ephemeral technologies, like Snapchat, enable young people to 'develop recognisable subjectivities' (Charteris, Gregory and Masters 2018).)
- Where are relations deterritorialized (world)? (e.g. Transversalities can be identified and followed as flows of affect and emergences of affective intensities such as cyberharassment, cyberbullying practices or a media sexting scandal.)

The refrain when applied to social media contexts can enable the mapping of human and non-human elements as intertwined entities that, when read together, produce something new.

Refrains in the research assemblage

As illustrated earlier, refrains reflect elements of chaos, earth and world. Firstly, there is departure from disarray or chaos to establish a milieu or home (Deleuze and Guattari 1987). Secondly, there is a stabilization of 'interiorizing forces as earth' (Herzogenrath 2009, p. 18) Thirdly there is a deterritorializing crack, which opens an engagement with the world. These three phases encompass the three elements (chaos, earth, world) that encounter one another and converge in refrains. These elements can be used to pry apart research assemblages to identify how these elements function.

In his introduction to *A Thousand Plateaus* (Deleuze and Guattari 1987), Brian Massumi writes, '[a] concept is a brick. It can be used to build the courthouse of reason. Or it can be thrown through the window' (p. xiii). We hope that this chapter can spur 'brick throwing', to create new vistas from shattered fragments. Considering the materiality of refrains, through engagement with 'thingness' (Bennett 2010, p. 55) and relationality (Ceder 2016), emergent assemblages can be entanglements ripe for analysis. The following broader questions may be useful, in addition to the specific analytical questions above, to assist in conceptualizing research that embodies a posthuman framework:

- How do you locate posthuman ontologies in research contexts?
- What humans and non-human elements are intra-actively in play?
- What is brought together in assemblages when humanist interpretations are problematized?
- What is co-produced in posthuman research assemblages?

It can be easy to slip into a default humanist position, when undertaking innovative methodology through posthumanist research practices. However, a posthumanist research approach ensures that 'research cannot ever simply be about humans and their subjectivities' because we are not separate from other living beings and the matter that makes up our world (Davies 2018, p. 117). Through our consideration of existing work (Malone 2016; Rautio 2013), we have developed the notion of refrains as a research heuristic. Although Malone's (2016) article utilizes a diffractive methodology (Barad 2007), to surface new ways of thinking and theorizing, the fluidity of territorial refrains presented here can offer a landscape of territoriality that lends itself to mapping relationalities in the assemblage. The 'refrain as concept' is a theoretical lens that can surface the intra-active politics of milieu. Central is the impetus to resist the capture of an interpretivist research that imposes meaning and truth through interrogating realities (Denzin 1997).

Conclusion

Refrains simultaneously create territories and transversalities, crossing into other territories. The research approach provided in this chapter highlights affective flows between bodies and the materiality of objects. It is valuable to contemplate how these elements are co-produced in refrains. Unlike 'spontaneous' assemblages in daily life, research assemblages are machines that are designed to do specific tasks, comprising relatively few relations and affects (Jackson and Mazzei 2013). This attempt at containment is an oversimplification that is addressed in posthumanist research. When we conduct research through a 'practice of concepts' (Deleuze 1989), entanglements are produced as a co-emergence of method. This chapter has illustrated how early career researchers, and those who want to break new terrain in experimental work, can map refrains with questions used as a heuristic. Our questions are a point of departure for engagement with the richness of Deleuzoguattarian theory, to inform methodologies that offer innovation and run an interference.

Glossary

Affect An intensive force that bodies exert upon one another that increases or decreases their capacity to act.

Deterritorialization and Reterritorialization 'Deterritorialization' and 'reterritorialization' are terms coined by Deleuze and Guattari (1987) in their attempt to theorize the constitution of territories. Deterritorialization is the movement out of a territory, object or phenomenon into a new composition. Reterritorialization re-establishes a territory.

Posthuman A posthuman frame rejects binaries – for example, the dichotomized thinking underpinning artificial polarities of nature and culture, subject and object and the material and discursive modes of being in the world.

Refrain A refrain is an emergence from chaos. A rhythmic action, it both facilitates stability as a temporary configuration and deterritorializes the stability – continuously reconfiguring the relations of elements.

References

Barad, K. (2007), *Meeting the Universe Halfway: Quantum Physics and the Entanglement of Matter and Meaning*, London: Duke University Press.

Barad, K. (2012), 'Interview with Karen Barad', in R. Dolphijn and I. van der Tuin (eds), *New Materialism: Interviews & Cartographies*, 48–70, Ann Arbor, MI: Open Humanities Press.

Bennett, J. (2010), *Vibrant Matter: A Political Economy of Things*, London: Duke University Press.

Braidotti, R. (2013), *The Posthuman*, Cambridge: Polity Press.

boyd, d. (2010), 'Social network sites as networked publics: Affordances, dynamics, and implications', in Z. Papacharissi (ed.), *A Networked Self: Identity, Community, and Culture on Social Network Sites*, 39–58, New York: Routledge.

boyd, d. (2014), *It's Complicated: The Social Lives of Networked Teens*.New Haven, CT: Yale University Press.

Buchanan, I. (2015), 'Assemblage theory and its discontents', *Deleuze Studies*, 9 (3): 382–92. doi: 10.3366/dls.2015.0193.

Ceder, S. (2016), 'Through water: Towards a posthuman theory of educational relationality', Lund University, viewed 8 October 2017, https://lup.lub.lu.se/search/publication/d5e67517-146c-45b1-b622-b2dbeb0a0f75

Charteris, J. Gregory, S. and Masters, Y. (2018), 'Snapchat, youth subjectivities and sexuality: Disappearing media and the discourse of youth innocence', *Gender and Education*, 30 (2): 205–21. http://dx.doi.org/10.1080/09540253.2016.1188198.

Davies, B. (2018), 'Ethics and the new materialism: A brief genealogy of the "post" philosophies in the social sciences', *Discourse: Studies in the Cultural Politics of Education*, 39 (1): 113–27. doi:10.1080/01596306.2016.1234682.

Davies, B. and Gannon, S. (2006), 'The practices of collective biography', in B. Davies and S. Gannon (eds), Doing Collective Biography, 1–15, London: Open University Press.

Deleuze, G. (1988), *Spinoza: Practical Philosophy*, trans. Robert Hurley, San Francisco: City Lights Books.

Deleuze, G. (1989), *Cinema 2: The Time-Image* , trans. Hugh Tomlinson and Robert Galeta, Minneapolis, MN: University of Minnesota Press

Deleuze, G. and Guattari, F. (1987), *A Thousand Plateaus: Capitalism and Schizophrenia*, trans. Brian Massumi, Minneapolis, MN: University of Minnesota Press.

Denzin, N. K. (1997), *Interpretative Ethnography: Ethnographic Practices for the 21st Century*, Thousand Oaks, CA: Sage.

Fox, N. and Alldred, P. (2013), 'The sexuality-assemblage: Desire, affect, anti-humanism', *The Sociological Review*, 61 (4): 769–89.

Fox, N. and Alldred, P. (2015), 'New materialist social inquiry: Designs, methods and the research-assemblage', *International Journal of Social Research Methodology*, 18 (4): 399–414. doi: 10.1080/13645579.2014.921458.

Gannon, S. (2008), 'Messing with memories: Feminist poststructuralism and memory work', in A. E. Hyle (ed.), *Dissecting the Mundane: International Perspectives on Memory-Work*, 44–57, Lanham, MD: University Press of America.

Golding, A. (2006), 'Language writing, digital poetics, and transitional materialities', in A. Morris and T. Swiss (eds), *New Media Poetics Contexts, Technotexts, and Theories*, 249–84, Cambridge, MA: Massachusetts Institute of Technology.

Gregg, M. and Seigworth, G. (2010), *The Affect Theory Reader*, Durham: Duke University Press.

Hayles, N. (1999), *How We Became Posthuman: Virtual Bodies in Cybernetics, Literature, and Informatics.* London: The University of Chicago Press.

Herzogenrath, B. (2009), *Nature Geophilosophy Machinics Ecosophy*, Basingstoke: Palgrave McMillan.

Ingold, T. (2011), *Being Alive: Essays on Movement, Knowledge and Description*, Abingdon: Routledge.

Jackson, A. Y. (2016), 'An ontology of a backflip', *Cultural Studies ↔ Critical Methodologies*, 16 (2): 183–92. doi: 10.1177/1532708616634735.

Jackson, A. Y. and Mazzei, L. A. (2013), 'Plugging one text into another: Thinking with theory in qualitative research', *Qualitative Inquiry*, 19 (4): 261–71. doi:10.1177/1077800412471510.

Lacey, J. (2013), 'Conceptual overlays for urban soundscape', *Sound Effects*, 3 (3): 74–5.

Lather, P. (2013), 'Methodology-21: What do we do in the afterward?' *International Journal of Qualitative Studies in Education*, 26 (6): 634–45. doi:10.1080/09518398.2013.788753.

MacLure, M. (2013), 'Researching without representation? Language and materiality in post-qualitative methodology', *International Journal of Qualitative Studies in Education*, 26: 658–67. doi:10.1080/09518398.2013.788755.

Malone, K. (2016), 'Theorizing a child–dog encounter in the slums of La Paz using post-humanistic approaches in order to disrupt universalisms in current "child in nature" debates', *Children's Geographies*, 14 (4): 390–407. doi:10.1080/14733285.2015.1077369.

Masny, D. (2016), 'Problematizing qualitative research: Reading a data assemblage with rhizoanalysis', *Qualitative Inquiry*, 1–10. doi:10.1177/1532708616636744.

Massumi, B. (2015), *Politics of Affect*, Cambridge: Polity Press.

Mayes, E. (2016), 'Shifting research methods with a becoming-child ontology: Co-theorising puppet production with high school students', *Childhood*, 23 (1): 105–22. doi: 10.1177/0907568215576526.

Mayes, E. (2018), 'The ontological plurality of digital voice: A schizoanalysis of rate my professors and rate my teachers', in D. Cole and J. Bradley (eds), *Principles of Transversality in Globalization and Education*, 195–210, Singapore: Springer.

McLeod, K. (2014), 'Orientating to assembling: Qualitative inquiry for more-than-human worlds', *International Journal of Qualitative Methods*, 13 (1): 377–94.

Penfield, C. (2014), 'Toward a theory of transversal politics: Deleuze and Foucault's block of becoming', *Foucault Studies*, 17: 134–72. doi:10.22439/fs.v0i17.4257.

Philippopoulos-Mihalopoulos, A. (2016), 'Milieu territory atmosphere: New spaces of knowledge', in A. Cusinato and A. Philippopoulos-Mihalopoulos (eds), *Knowledge-Creating Milieus in Europe: Firms, Cities, Territories*, 79–95, London: Springer.

Pyyhtinen, O. (2016), *The Gift and Its Paradoxes: Beyond Mauss*, New York, NY: Routledge.

Rautio, P. (2013), 'Being nature: Interspecies articulation as a species specific practice of relating to environment', *Environmental Education Research*, 19 (4): 445–57. doi: 10.1080/13504622.2012.700698.

Rautio, P. (2014), 'Mingling and imitating in producing spaces for knowing and being: Insights from a Finnish study of child-matter intra-action', *Childhood*, 21 (4): 461–74. doi:10.1177/0907568213496653.

Rautio, P. (2016), 'Serendipitous human-pigeon cohabituation', Presentation at the Summer Institute of the Antipodes. Western Sydney University, Richmond. 21 November–25 November.

Renold, E. and Ringrose, J. (2011), 'Schizoid subjectivities? Re-theorizing teen girls' sexual cultures in an era of 'sexualization', *Journal of Sociology*, 47 (4): 389–409. doi:10.1177/1440783311420792.

Ringrose, J. (2011), 'Beyond discourse? Using Deleuze and Guattari's schizoanalysis to explore affective assemblages, heterosexually striated space, and lines of flight online and at school', *Educational Philosophy and Theory*, 43 (6): 598–618. doi: 10.1111/j.1469-5812.2009.00601.x.

Ringrose, J. and Coleman, B. (2013), 'Looking and desiring machines: A feminist Deleuzian mapping of affect and bodies', in B. Coleman and J. Ringrose (eds), *Deleuze and Research* Methodologies, 125–44, Edinburgh: Edinburgh University Press.

Ringrose, J. and Renold, E. (2014), '"F**k rape!": Exploring affective intensities in a feminist research assemblage', *Qualitative Inquiry*, 20 (6): 772–80. doi:10.1177/1077800414530261.

Sorensen, B. (2009), 'How to surf: Technologies at work in the societies of control', in M. Poster and D. Savat (eds), *Deleuze and New Technology*, 63–81, Edinburgh: Edinburgh University Press.

Springgay, S. and Zaliwska, Z. (2017), 'Learning to be affected: Matters of pedagogy in the artists' soup kitchen', *Educational Philosophy and Theory*, 49 (3): 273–83. doi:10.1 080/00131857.2016.1216385.

St Pierre, E. (2014), 'A brief and personal history of post qualitative research toward post inquiry', *Journal of Curriculum Theorizing*, 30 (2): 2–19.

St Pierre, E. and Pillow, W. (2000), *Working the Ruins: Feminist Poststructural Theory and Methods in Education*, New York, NY: Psychology Press.

Taylor, A. (2013), *Reconfiguring the Natures of Childhood*, London: Routledge.

Taylor, A. (2016), 'Child-animal relations', in M. A. Peters (ed.), *Encyclopedia of Educational Philosophy and Theory*. Amsterdam: Springer. doi:10.1007/978-981-287-532-7_265-1.

Taylor, C. (2013), 'Mobile sections and flowing matter in participant-generated video: Exploring a Deleuzian approach to visual sociology', in R. Coleman and J. Ringrose (eds), *Deleuze and Research Methodologies*, 42–60, Edinburgh: Edinburgh University Press.

Yin, R. K. (2009), *Case Study Research: Design and Methods*, 4th edn, Applied social research methods series; vol. 5, Thousand Oaks, CA: Sage Publications.

Youdell, D. (2010), 'Pedagogies of becoming in an end-of-the-line "special" school", *Critical Studies in Education*, 51 (3): 313–24. doi:10.1080/17508487.2010.508810.

Young, E. B. (2013), 'Becoming', in E. B. Young, G. Genosko and J. Watson (eds), *The Deleuze & Guattari Dictionary*, 40–2. New York, NY: Bloomsbury.

Index

www.ingramcontent.com/pod-product-compliance
Lightning Source LLC
Chambersburg PA
CBHW050433280326
41932CB00013BA/2103